NOTES FROM AN
ODD COUNTRY

NOTES FROM AN ODD COUNTRY

GEOFFREY GRIGSON

ALAN SUTTON
1984

Alan Sutton Publishing Limited
17a Brunswick Road
Gloucester GL1 1HG

Copyright © 1970 Geoffrey Grigson

First published 1970 by Macmillan
This edition published 1984

British Library Cataloguing in Publication Data

Grigson, Geoffrey
  Notes From an Odd Country.
  1. Villages—France   2. France—social
  life customs—twentieth century
  I. Title
  944.083′8′0924   DC415

  ISBN 0-86299-122-6

Cover picture: Field of Daisies.
The Image Bank: Nicholas Foster

Printed and bound in Great Britain

Contents

For J. and S.

Heureuses sont tes Nymphes vagabondes,
Gastine saincte, et heureuses tes ondes,
O petit Loir, honneur du Vendômois.
du Bellay

Voluptati et Gratiis

Spring and Summer

W E are on the edge of Touraine. Up here on the southern hill at Les Hayes I look back across the river Loir – the Loir and not the Loire – and see Trôo church, a blue circumflex on the parallel hill to the north, towards England.

Past a curly cast-iron wind pump the road goes on quietly southward into Touraine, to the grand Loire, and to the cathedral city of Tours. To the north, beyond Trôo church, dedicated to St Martin, the patron of Tours, are the rather muddy farmlands of the Perche. Not a long way to the west, down the Loir, Anjou begins.

~~~

I have stopped exactly where we stopped on this minor departmental road fifteen years ago, on our way from Wiltshire to Venice. Now we have it fixed in our minds – why? because I think there can be no genuine evidence – that the ridge to the east and the west was the favourite walk of Pierre de Ronsard, or gave Pierre de Ronsard his favourite view of the Loir valley. Fifteen years ago we didn't know we were looking at the Bas-Vendômois, the downstream country of Vendôme, bordering the Loir and enclosed by these northern and southern hills. We didn't know Ronsard was born a few miles away. We looked down on to the buildings of a farm half tucked into the chalk in a side valley, under the woods, and decided how pleasant a farmstead it would be to own – without an idea that it was called Vaubusson, *val buisson*, Valley of the Thicket; without an idea that we would come to know the soft-eyed eighty-year-old farmer whose property it has been for fifty years.

I am up here now to draw a distant view of Trôo church beyond a telegraph pole which is very evidently French. The fields are open and hedgeless. We have picked a large bunch of cornflowers, of genuine, deep blue, open-eyed, exceedingly French cornflowers, not to be confused with the pallid scabious of cornfields at home. Or is this at home?

～～

I must explain Trôo: it is the hub of the odd country of these notes, which is a country of the mind and a portion of France. First, it is about 220 miles south of England, south of Hastings or Eastbourne. It exists partly on, partly inside a hill of hard chalk, which was mined for building houses. On top are remains – enceinte wall and turrets and gateways, and a bare motte – of a castle which belonged once to the Plantagenets. Also that strong, prominent church, associated with the castle. Along the foot of the hill, dividing Trôo from a smaller village, St-Jacques, flows the Loir. Vendôme is fifteen miles upstream, making this river country the Bas-Vendômois, as I say; the lower country of Vendôme. The river continues through the widest meadows to the Ile verte, at Couture, on which Ronsard wanted to be buried. Couture is much visited for this island and for Ronsard's first home, La Possonnière, which Ronsard's father covered with Renaissance trickings and such inscriptions as *Voluptati et Gratiis*, to Pleasure and the Graces.

At Trôo vineyards begin, on slopes which wall the river plain. The climate is warm and dry. The Bas-Vendômois contains neolithic dolmens, neolithic polishing-stones, Gaulish camps, Roman camps, Gallo-Roman place-names, Romanesque wall-paintings, abbeys, priories, commanderies, pest-houses, ruins, drinking tables, wine caves, good restaurants, few factories, and riverside holiday huts on high legs.

～～

On that Venetian journey we had spent the night at Trôo, we had seen the cliff in sunshine, had seen that the cliff contained stone mines and houses. We had walked over the Loir

to the black-roofed church of St-Jacques-des-Guerets, and
looked for a passing five minutes at Christ in twelfth century
majesty and at the hand of God in a curve of a window. That
was all.

It was years later that we came to stay, in a rented cave house.
The pleasant thing this time which happened on the way, when
we were already in the Perche, with about thirty miles to go,
was seeing Deptford Pinks in the rain. The hedge of an ochre
lane was starred with them. Runnels of orange water poured
down the lane, under an oak tree, past a gateway where we
made a picnic pause. The hundreds of sparks of magenta spelt
a newness, a new actuality.

The rain stopped. The sun was fierce when we reached Trôo
and drove with timidity down one of the cliff lanes. The ground
was hard and dry.

༺༻

Inevitably an Englishman who comes here is soon told that
Trôo was an English town – as it was, a long time ago, in a
way. As a Plantagenet castle-town it was about as English as
Henry II, King of England, Duke of Normandy, Duke of
Aquitaine, about as English as his Queen Eleanor of Aquitaine,
about as English as their son Richard Coeur-de-Lion; which is
to say hardly English at all. On its cliff, it was a border town
round a border castle of the Angevin empire of the English
kings. Across the river was the land of the kings of France,
and their stronger castle – which was floodlit on the night of
our arrival – of Lavardin. I have no historical treatise in mind –
or topographical one, either. Trôo is French. Trôo was a new
culture to this Englishman. Trôo became a light in which
certain thoughts, certain conclusions became more clear. So
I think.

༺༻

The houses, the farmsteads, the villages – almost all of them,
sign of an ancient uninterrupted settlement – are related in this
valley to weather and landscape; to the direction of the commonest wind, to the sun when required, to shade when the sun
is too hot. When men build from plans to sell or rent this

13

power or sense of suiting house to terrain disappears – witness the United States. Dickens as long ago as 1842, in his *American Notes*, observed that in America houses seem to have been dropped from the sky.

ᴄ᷐ᴊᴇᷓᴄᴏ

When we came to Trôo nothing was more fortunate than getting to know Maurice Beaubrun, and Fernande. Maurice long ago established himself as the man who held many of the summer keys of Trôo, looking after the gardens of weekend and summer cave-houses. He is everything, he can do everything. He can build a wall, put in a window, design and make a verandah, fit up a kitchen, hack a room out of the chalk, dress the salad, find mushrooms, provide carp and eels. He knows everything, a smallish stooping man, with amused eyes, whose one peculiar contact with headline events was to have been the waiter (after their marriage at Tours) of the newly abdicated Edward VIII and Mrs Simpson. He knows everybody – more about many people in Trôo and in St-Jacques across the water (where he lives alone, now that Fernande has died) than they would like him to know. He makes good wine from his own vineyard, he grows good asparagus and strawberries. Having known the neighbourhood all his life, he is a human directory to present and past, to the means of satisfying all locally satisfiable wants or requirements. An extraordinary friend, an extraordinary example of the waste, if that is the word, or the under use, in the French social system, of quite exceptional intelligence and power of sympathy. He knows and is fond of three words of English, *Tank yiew verrimuch*, acquired from Fernande, who once made hats in London back premises somewhere near Carnaby Street.

ᴄ᷐ᴊᴇᷓᴄᴏ

Maurice has lived from the abject poverty era into today's more or less prosperity; from the *sabot* era into the gumboot era (though older men, like himself, will still wear *sabots* for gardening). Mention of something like *sabots* will at once release information from Maurice – that one of the last two *sabotiers* of Trôo had his shop in a cave behind the old Hôtel

Bellevue on the Rue Haute; that the wood used was alder, walnut or ash; that *sabots* can still be bought from a *sabotier* in Montoire (which is our shopping town three miles away); that when he first went out to work on a farm, guarding the cows, goats, etc., he was paid sixty francs a year, and a pair of *sabots*: he never sat at table, but ate his bread – bread with cabbage – in the corner of the fireplace.

Maurice hated the cabbage, and one day found a hen's nest in some straw, sneaked an egg, cut off the top as he had seen his father do, and dipped bread into the yolk. He didn't like it much at first, but was so hungry he ate two eggs, liked it better, and made a habit of sneaking eggs. He still eats them like that at midday outside his wine cave.

соڑ

Having his own vineyard has bent Maurice – hooked him up below the neck; bending over the rows, staking, wiring, digging, hoeing, cutting, looking after this tender and yet tough exotic from the Caucasus as if it were a child, and a child very difficult to rear and keep in health even with antibiotics.

I think of Maurice out in the rain among his vines, sacks tied round him with binder twine, out in the cold, out in the fog, out in the sun. I think of his seasonal anxieties. The vines are in flower at the beginning of May, or the end of April. Then the fruit begins to form, and Maurice to worry. The weather can be suddenly too cold, there can be thunderstorms, pelting rain, hail. It is difficult to get Maurice to come and help with any other work in May. We give up, we drive along the main road towards Poncé and La Chartre, look up at the slopes, and say 'Maurice is up at his cave, or he's up in his vineyard: there's his blue van.' Since this is our road when we are arriving from Cherbourg or leaving for Cherbourg, the blue van is often our first and last sign of Trôo – and Maurice – in April or May, October or November.

соڑ

Up at the cave this morning, the entrance slippery with rain, Maurice remarked of the vineyard – which will help with all

15

the single-handed drudgery to shorten his life – *C'est ma vie.*
That is true. And he is thinking of selling it, the work is too
hard.

He had been sniffing at the flower of the vine, and making
me bend down and sniff, too. I find this special scent which
Colette likened to the smell of pinks, this *nectareuse odeur*, a
little exaggerated in its charm. But I am not a *vigneron*, and I
wasn't the son of a poor peasant brought up among vineyards,
and at last owning one himself, and making some of the better
wine of the valley. Maurice agrees with Colette that the perfume
of the flowers of the vine resembles that of pinks, the kind
called *mignonettes* or *mignardises*: he says it can rise from a
vineyard strongly enough to be upsetting, to give one a
headache.

He is getting less energetic. I nearly told him, but it mightn't
have been tactful, of Ronsard wanting to be changed at death
into vine blossom. All his life I think he has been a labouring
version of a Ronsardian-cum-Anacreontic character, with his
pleasure in women – *J'ayme à faire l'amour, j'ayme à parler aux
femmes*, in France, in wine, in vines, in fishing.

❧

C'est ma vie, I would like to think that *vitis, vigne, vigneron,
vignoble, vin, vendange*, had something to do with *vita*, life,
etymologically. But a vine is only a crawler, something that
winds, something that creeps and covers.

❧

We drank at the cave of Père Auguste, which is cut into a sheer
face under trees, down a slope from the lane. He is nearly
ninety, a little feeble on his legs, very benign and humorous in
expression and voice, has buried his wives, and lives with a
housekeeper a few hundred yards away from Maurice's cave,
to which he often comes for a talk and a drink. A finely preserved and nurtured piece of this Bas-Vendômois, with bright
eyes among the wrinkles. Once a week he drives an extremely
old Renault into market at Montoire. He bought it in the

twenties, and the enamel is hardly scratched. I reckon that in forty years the mileage of this car (it is about ten miles from Père Auguste's house to Montoire and back) has amounted to less than twenty-five thousand.

There were half a dozen women in the party, two English-women, one American, the others French. Maurice picked flowers – including honeysuckle – and made wreaths for the women, plain and pretty. There we sat in the shade, and drank Père Auguste's white wine. He enjoyed himself. It was very hot. He mopped his humorous old face.

ᴄᴿᴖᴿᴎ

It's not easy for a stranger to a French *commune* to get the exact feeling of local divisions. But certainly Trôo divides into a church party, and the rest, who are non-church, and, when occasion calls for it, decidedly anti-church – though most of the rest send their children to the catechism classes. It is the 'good' against the 'bad', to look at it in the church way; or respectability against raffishness. To look at the division another way, it is the unimaginative against the imaginative or the free – either way the temperamental dualism of any society, complicated by possession and lack of money, position and being 'nobody', Gaullist (at present) and favouring any of the parties of the Left. In contrast with England (or the East Cornwall in which I grew up), a peculiarity is having no sectarian alternative; you are church or nothing in particular (a rationalist, perhaps), i.e. you are or you are not in cahoots with *M. le Curé*, more or less. I seldom hear a story against village parsons in England, where they are a poorish lot with little spiritual and no temporal authority. So far as I can see the parish clergy are a poorish lot, educationally and so on, in France. But spiritual authority they retain, and even with my short ears I pick up a story or two which seems to indicate, inside its fun, the resentment one would expect against such power, even if it is accepted. I suspect they are now the stories of the middle-aged and elderly.

One concerns a local priest of many years ago. Joseph, his new factotum, had the duty of waking him up every morning at eight o'clock and telling him the weather. Knock, knock on *M. le Curé*'s door.

'*Bonjour, M. le Curé, il est huit heures et il fait beau*' (as it does hereabouts more often than not).

'*Merci, Joseph, Dieu et moi nous le savons.*'

The formula of announcement and answer did not vary a great deal. A week went by. Joseph (and the *curé*) overslept. Joseph knocked on the bedroom door three hours late, at eleven o'clock. Before he could mention time or weather, the voice came from inside, unvarying, '*Merci, Joseph, Dieu et moi nous le savons: il est huit heures, et il fait beau.*' To which a now exasperated Joseph replied: '*Dieu et vous sont deux vieux cons, il est onze heures, et il tombe de l'eau comme vache qui pisse.*'

⚜

And I like a story – more amiable than resentful, this time – which Maurice Beaubrun tells about his father and the priest at Bessé-sur-Braye, the dull little town over the hill. He was a well-to-do cleric (who rebuilt the church at Bessé with remarkable hideousness and grandeur), and could afford to have Lucien – Maurice's father – as coachman. He was very fond of Lucien, who was as intelligent and delightful as his son, and often they had their meals together in the presbytery. One such time the lunch included two fine pears which Lucien had brought in, by way of the stables, from the *curé*'s garden. The *curé* took one of the two pears from the fruit stand and bit into it with great enjoyment, without peeling it. When he had finished, Lucien took the other pear and started to peel it with some attention. The *curé* suddenly realized what he was doing.

'*O, Lucien, qu'est-ce que tu fais là? Pour déguster un bon fruit, il faut manger avec le peau.*'

'*Mais oui, M. le Curé, je le sais bien, mais il y a une de ces poires qui a tombée dans la merde, et je ne sais plus laquelle.*'

⚜

Placard in Montoire, our shopping town:

Maison Recommandée
par le Syndicat d'Initiative
du Pays du Poète
Pierre de Ronsard

Baker's shop recommended by the Information Service of the Countryside of the Poet William Wordsworth, or the Countryside of the Poet A. E. Housman. Well, why not? At least hereabouts they remember their poet.

Visitez le pays du poète Ronsard: la douceur de vivre – that's another effort of the Syndicat d'Initiative, a notice up on the main roads which conduct Parisians into Montoire – usually nonstop for the motor racing at Le Mans. So he is remembered partly for tourism, partly for commerce (he also gives his name to a not very remarkable melange of local wine sold in the local groceries), partly for touching up the neighbourhood; even in part for his poems.

I once tried to explain that Yeats – at any rate that a poet in English – had translated or made a version of that famous sonnet for Hélène beginning *Quand vous serez bien vieille, au soir à la chandelle.* I didn't get far without misquoting – and without being corrected, and without a pretty accurate recitation of the opening lines, and my corrector was that Maurice Beaubrun, who began his working life at sixty francs and one pair of *sabots* per year.

Montoire has a fête on 15 August (the Assumption of the Virgin). In the procession there is usually a float on which local girls strike attitudes of beauty below a streamer which says *Mignonne, allons voir si la rose.* Then come the Giants fifteen feet tall, the Giants Piron, Ratepilate, Galimas and his wife Gali, and Amédée des Noyers de Lorme – and Pierre de Ronsard looking every yard the wan poet. The procession stops, the skirts of Pierre de Ronsard open, and an arm, two arms, two hands, come out at knee level. Beer is placed in the hands, they are withdrawn, the skirts close, and Ronsard and his comrade giants are off again, his pallid face inclined, on a level with bedroom windows. I suppose all of this local celebration of Ronsard came late after the very late revival of regard for him in France. He had fallen more or less into ruin – or neglect – like so many medieval or renaissance buildings round Trôo.

Respect otherwise seems as thin as might be imagined. In the church at Couture Ronsard's father and mother are none too undustily cared for. Time has bitten off *père* Ronsard at the knees. Couture church is hardly Stratford church. On the Ile verte, in the Loir, where Ronsard wished (rhetorically) to be buried, a scholar's notice talks about him. This is just outside his village, an excellent spot certainly, the river slow and black near its junction with the Braye, a place excellent especially in October when the yellow poplar leaves dwindle to the water. Up a side valley from Ternay to Montrouveau there isn't much left from Ronsard's time in the half old, half modern buildings of the farm which was the priory of Croixval, to which Ronsard retired more or less. Ronsard was for sure in his early, and some of his late, poems a faithful man of this Bas-Vendômois: poems, stanzas, lines by him, if general, are yet local, exactly.

⤜⟡⤛

Beards of ivy swing across the black mouths of the wine caves: *Lierre* (see Ronsard's Sonnets for Hélène) *le tapis d'un bel antre sauvage.*

⤜⟡⤛

They sway if there is a little wind. Birds nest in them. Greenfinches, sometimes, or Garden Warblers. But the beards touch the ground, bindweed climbs into the beards, they are anchored and cease to sway. The ivy begins to root, the beard is more firmly anchored. I have cut away the bindweed, pulled up the rooting tips, trimmed the end of the beard. It swings again, as for Ronsard (who could hardly be expected to have written 'beard' in place of 'tapestry').

One of my cave neighbours – Parisian neighbours – has such an ivy beard, which gives him pleasure. He adds to the pleasure by hanging some Burmese or Japanese wind-bells in it. (Reading that again, I see it is as if my neighbour's ivy hung from his chin, together with the wind-bells: as if he were an Arcimboldi figure. But let it remain.)

⤜⟡⤛

Nearly everything provided by soil, growth and water – and the penal labour of farm work – is still used here in the Bas-Vendômois, which makes it agreeable, if you don't do the work. The population has declined, you do come across

20

abandoned houses in the side-valleys and the folds of the plateau, north or south of the Loir. Less wine is made and there are vineyards overgrown with weeds or turning to scrub, with the vines shooting wild among brambles and branches. But otherwise you don't feel dereliction or waste, though you encounter plenty of shabbiness and make-do. Woods are cut and grown again for firewood (standing coppice in lots is auctioned every October). Poplars are planted as a twenty year crop in the river meadows; and every good piece of land is well looked after – corn, mangolds, pumpkins, maize.

≪✿≫

As for the agreeability of a used countryside, when I see men, and women, bent over the crops, I realize it isn't so agreeable for them. 'C'est dur l'agriculture' (read Zola in La Terre). I like seeing machines which keep the human back from bending, as in the last five thousand years – machines which pull, machines which plant sweet corn, and machines which harvest sweet corn and toss the cobs in the air in a peculiar cob fountain, or machines which transfer cobs into the long narrow séchoirs or drying frames, built of poplar stems and wire-netting.

Or do the machines, more and more of them every year, sufficiently guarantee that the land will remain used and agreeable-looking, let's say, for another hundred years? Will everyone go away into future cities immense in neglected wildernesses?

The intervening wildernesses in France at any rate will be enjoyed by the *chasseurs*. I cannot see the hard-drinking *chasseurs* giving up and disappearing in France.

≪✿≫

Symbol of perfect equilibrium, visual equilibrium. The mills visible from the cliff or the Rue Haute. One grinds, one no longer grinds, one houses a small factory. Each has a long low roof ridged with zinc, each has a squat tower at one end, with a roof like a decapitated pyramid (in England, say along the Shropshire border or the Herefordshire border, these mills could be churches). The walls are local stone, off-white. Each might have grown out of its river meadow. Each catches the light with gentleness, sitting firmly among willows and poplars. They are something between a stone house in a Nepalese village and a *château* or a cathedral; between unconscious, or semi-aware, fitness and architecture.

ᡃᠵᢟᡃᠵ

The mill which still grinds is the Moulin Papillon, half a mile upstream. When the wind allows, we can hear the clacking rhythmical noise made by the sifting gear. The mill which doesn't grind is immediately across the river in St-Jacques, next to the church which has the Romanesque paintings, and which marks a ford over the Loir on a pilgrim route to Santiago de Compostela.

Last summer when the river was low, and not much water was coming into the old ford below the mill-wheel, I saw (thinking of the School of Paris and the Musée d'Art Moderne) an old-fashioned sight, two easels set up in the water, with two canvases, and two stools, and two landscape painters wearing waders, one more or less behind the other. It was like Daumier's cartoon of *Les Paysagistes* of 1865 – *Le premier copie la nature, le second le premier.*

The two landscape painters had bandanas hanging from their hats against the sun.

ᡃᠵᢟᡃᠵ

Quite wonderful dahlias grow with abandon, and as if drunk, along the lane to the mill and the church. In this light of summer, even more in the sunlight of October, they are a sharp all-colour illustration on glossy paper of the difference in sheer light between England and Touraine (this side of the Loir actually is in Touraine).

ᡃᠵᢟᡃᠵ

Cave homes, people inside them, chimneys smoking through the rock or the ground, rabbit hutches in separate holes in the rock on one side of the courtyard, these all surprised me years ago in exploring the Vendômois, Touraine and Anjou. I knew they existed, having read *Cliff Castles and Cave Dwellings of*

Europe, by inquisitive old Baring-Gould; but I didn't suppose they existed by the thousand, even now, in France of the 1960s. There are locally printed books about cave houses and troglodytes in Anjou, next door; but that families should still live in man-made holes in the rock, that the paterfamilias should go off to work in a factory from such a burrow, does not agree with that universality of *la culture française* which Malraux talks about to international Francophone conferences in Paris. It is an interesting cultural and civilizational fact but not of the right kind; not part of *la gloire*, to be proclaimed.

～❀～

Let me tie up France and this fact. In another twenty or thirty years cave-living may have come to an end, though I rather doubt it. Meanwhile to say it is now over and done with, is like saying that thatch in England (try driving through Somerset, Dorset and South Devon in the thatching season) is 'a dying craft'. Habits of life and dwelling persist. This habit of life and dwelling goes back to Caesar's Gaul – at least Caesar had to smoke Gauls out of souterrains – and beyond Caesar, in Anjou at any rate into remote antiquity. M. and Mme Fraysse in *Les Troglodytes en Anjou*, published a few years ago, talk of palaeolithic evidence for cave-dwelling or shelter-dwelling in the Angevine chalk.

Les Troglodytes en Anjou confirms what anyone moving around the chalk villages can see – that many, many excavated homes have been abandoned in the last sixty years, and that many others, hidden behind ordinary houses of any date from French Renaissance to modern, are still in use as storerooms, hen-houses and the like. One does not willingly abandon a home – a property, a possession – which continues in good order; and I think that many of the cave-homes now deserted even as storerooms were left because they were cracking or falling, either because the bed of the rusty *tuffeau* or Turonien chalk they had been excavated in, was a weak one, or because they had not been excavated in the safe or correct way.

The most curious cave-villages are the ones in which these little peasant homes are cut into quite low faces of chalk, so that each has its own kitchen garden on top around the chimney. That book on the Anjou troglodytes says that above-grounders talk of the under-grounders in such villages or hamlets as *mousseaux*, which seems to mean people who are hidden away. It is not a word understood in Trôo, though rows of such homes exist in the side-valleys on either flank of our river.

⌁✻⌁

These *mousseaux* of the last century – even if they farmed in a small way – were strictly poor, their home a single main room, with two, or three smaller rooms cut into the sides: they had no horses, no cows, no carts. A family would have owned a pack-donkey, or a pack-mule, goats, poultry, a pig, and rabbits. In Anjou north and south of the other Loire they grew a little oats and wheat, and some flax or hemp, and a few vines. They lived by weaving, catching larks, drying prunes (in the plum district a cave-dwelling would have a large prune oven cut into the rock, as well as a bread oven), making baskets, or quarrying the *tuffeau*; and old quarry tunnels or quarry entrances would often be barricaded a room's depth inside and turned into a cave home.

I suspect Trôo (*Troo* already in the eleventh century, the etymology given usually as *trou*, a hole) was in original essence a quarryman's town where the stone-extractors and stone-cutters lived in such adapted tunnel mouths; and with its castle and collegiate church on top, its town walls, its hospital and its cave chapels, its wide sunny fields and vineyards, and its position above a ford across the Loir (along which stone could have been floated) Trôo would have been, Trôo certainly was, much superior to a sunken hamlet of obscure *mousseaux*.

The quarry passages twist and intersect inside the cliff in many miles of network. One or two great openings show behind the Rue Haute, the old main street of Trôo along the best beds of stone, the street by which thousands of tons of building stone have been removed since the Middle Ages.

⌁✻⌁

Another thing, a quarry hill, a scarp facing south, was splendid for vines, also for turning grapes into wine, since the worked out stone mines could so amply contain the equipment, the wine-presses in particular. In many caves at Trôo in which wine is still bottled and stored, and drunk, but no longer made, the *pressoirs* remain, jobs of the Iron and Steel Age of the nineteenth century. *Pressoirs* of the kind have a steel screw fixed vertically between the roof and the floor of the stone pit or trough in which the mash of grapes is built up. With long iron levers an iron collar, cogged and ratcheted to hold the pressure, is made to turn round the steel screw, forcing the wooden beam (the *cochon*) of the press, the large pieces of wood (the *cochonneaux*) which lie under the beam, and the thick planks, or *madriers*, which lie under the *cochonneaux*, down on to the mash.

Some caves retain a portion of an older, more primitive type of *pressoir*, a very large oak beam wedged into the walls of rock over the pit, with a screw-hole in the middle. The planks, cross-pieces and beam of the press were forced down on to the grapes by a wooden screw made to turn inside that enormous piece of oak, sometimes by a rope going round the grooved rim of a wheel fixed to the screw, and then round a vertical capstan. I have put my fingers up into the screw-hole in the heart timber of one of these roughly shaped trunks of oak and found the timber threads – after goodness knows how many years – still sharp and fine. These wooden screws are now common in French antique shops, and in restaurants as well.

People adapt rather than abandon. Wooden boxes and horse manure piled outside old stone-mines or caves indicate today's adaptation, which is growing mushrooms.

✧

Twenty thousand, twenty-five thousand years of burrowing for use and shelter. And I should say that this caving habit characterized localities rather than a class. Earlier on, it wasn't something to which only the *mousseaux* were driven, only the very poor who couldn't afford to build: their *seigneurs* lived the troglodyte life as well: see their manor-houses in the chalk along the larger Loire, along the noble river drive on the south bank, from the junction of the Vienne and the Loire to the bridges near Angers.

The Palaeolithic – with renaissance or classical façades.

All the same what distinguishes Trôo is not stone-mines, caves, cave houses and troglodytism, and the past, but sunshine, warming or heating soil, flowers, flesh, and everything which belongs to this headland of white and brown chalk. Including turtle-doves.

⟪✻⟫

Why is the small half destroyed mound just outside Trôo, on the Bessé road, still called Mercadier's mound? It looks as if it had been raised for a siege or for a recovery of Trôo. Perhaps the mound was raised, and then a wooden tower was raised higher still on top of the mound – a tactic used in other sieges – for assaulting the gate, the Porte de Bessé, or keeping activities at the gate under control. But by Mercadier? At any rate Mercadier held Trôo for Richard Coeur-de-Lion. He was one of those commanders of mercenary troops, recorded Matthew Paris, 'who thought nothing of bloodshed, pillage and arson'. He and Richard Coeur-de-Lion were always together, and always fought side by side.

⟪✻⟫

'*Moi, Mercadier, serviteur de Richard illustre et glorieux roi d' Angleterre . . .*' he says in a deed of gift to an abbey in the Dordogne, '. . . *ayant servi dans les châteaux du même seigneur roi avec autant de fidélité que de vaillance, m'étant toujours conformé à sa volonté, empressé d'exécuter ses ordres, je suis par là devenu agréable et cher à un si grand roi, et j'ai été mis à la tête de son armée . . .*'

⟪✻⟫

Mercadier's best known act of savagery was flaying and hanging the bowman, Bertrand de Gourdon, who had shot his master when Richard and Mercadier were besieging the castle of Chalus, near Limoges, in 1199. It was impossible to remove the head of the bolt, the wound turned to gangrene. Richard on his deathbed summoned the cross-bowman and asked him if the shot had been due to some grievance. The bowman said that with his own hand Richard had killed his father and his two brothers: he didn't care what tortures

Richard's cruelty would invent for him, now that Richard was going to die, after doing so much harm to the world.

Not the way to talk to a dying king. But Richard forgave him for the shot and ordered him to be set free.

Too proud to accept his life, Bertrand de Gourdon asked to be killed. Richard told him that whether he liked it or not, he was to be a living witness to the king's mercy and a source of hope to the defeated. He was released and given money – then skinned alive by Mercadier's order, as soon as Richard was dead.

Mercadier was murdered at Bordeaux, by another mercenary captain, in 1200.

Today (see *Who's Who*): Mercadier, Major-General Sir Henry, K.B.E., C.B., D.S.O., J.P. Educ. Eton, R.M.C. Sandhurst. Chairman, County Education Committee, Vicar's Warden. *Address*: The Old Gibbet.

ᏬᎾᏖᏋᏬ

The medieval walls and the outer walls surrounding the *château* were built with a centre of rubble, faced below with flints, and faced above with blocks of chalk stone, or *pierre tendre*. Often the flints have broken away (or been stripped away, for building?) leaving a bald tawny, or ochre coloured rubble, below the greyish white chalk. One bastion – but it was a long while before I found it at the back of one of the farms near the church – is still perfect with its flint and stone, above a moat deep on the western side, full of farm rubbish – old carts, waggons, instruments, tractor tyres.

ᏬᎾᏖᏋᏬ

I have learnt some more about Mercadier, or at least about the siege of Chalus and Richard Coeur-de-Lion. Richard was annoyed by the way his vassal, the Viscount of Limoges, refused to give up a hoard of Roman gold, which Richard claimed: he considered it his property as overlord. So he pilled the Limousin and set about reducing its castles, beginning with Chalus, which was held only by two score men. A small job, in a campaign of medieval bloody-mindedness and savage triviality: all Richard's men had to do was sit around while his miners grubbed under the castle walls, till they fell and were breached. So he strolled around, and was hit by de Gourdon's bolt.

❧

How extraordinarily thick God establishments were in this neighbourhood – let alone Great Man establishments, or castles. Up the valley the Benedictines had their grand house of La Trinité at Vendôme, and Bernadine nuns had their abbey of La Virginité outside Les Roches (nothing left but bumps in the ground). At Montoire there were Austin Canons and a Benedictine priory. Across the valley Geoffroy Martel housed Austin Canons in an abbey at St Martin-des-Bois, and gave them rights of one kind and another in the Forest of Gastines, which grew to their portal. Here at Trôo: the college of canons who served the big church, the monks of the priory of Les Marchais, and another priory across the river at St-Jacques. Over the hills, the Benedictines of the abbey at St-Calais – once important in the learning of Charlemagne's time – where William of St-Calais, Bishop of Durham, and builder of Durham Cathedral and Durham Castle, was a novice.

All these – and I could have mentioned other priories and commanderies – within twenty miles of each other. A Holy Land (I hope). All that medieval skill and learning in this small area. I wonder how many of my neighbours are threaded, so to say, on monastic genes.

❧

Indeed I have the sense, not so much around our village, up and down the river, but on the Beauce and in the Perche, of a lively medieval culture which was gradually reduced to local devices, and which is now, if slowly, becoming delocalized again in some ways.

Nothing roughly local about Romanesque or later wall paintings. Everything rough and local – including rough and local clergy – about the refitting of parish churches in the later centuries: rough hedge carpenter's work straddles a church roof with beams which are recognizably tree as much as timber. Slapped whitewash fills up and smooths out the precise carving of Romanesque or thirteenth century capitals. Clumsy saints in niches carved in the eighteenth century have neither the energy of a remote, self-energizing culture nor more than a trace of their urban originals.

These very crude interiors have an attractiveness of intricacy and colours, also a charm of casualness – religion when wanted, not very often – and of neglect.

This crudity in church fabrics and furnishing suggests the meanness of the top levels of French society: no sharing or caring.

♥

When we were first at Trôo, I was taken into something vaguely called the Hospital – a series of artificial caves opening off a mosquito dell of fallen earth, ivy, nettles, and damp shadow from an overhang of elms and elders. In this chaos of decay a white arch of the twelfth century defined the entrance.

The Hospital was inside the walls of Trôo, but in a quarter – the Clos des Forges, the quarter of the smiths – in which most of the buildings have disappeared. To reach it, you passed a well and two small locked wine caves, you pushed through nettled and dead elder branches and clambered over an old and fairly settled humpback of fallen earth. At which point we made torches from pages of a *Figaro* which I was carrying. Not that there was much to see; enough only to make one fairly certain that these underground chambers had never been a hospital or anything more than a set of store-caves opening at the back of a twelfth century building which long ago disappeared, and which occupied most of the dell.

The point. I have just gone to see the 'Hospital' seven years later to find that more earth – much more earth – has fallen, and that one can now see only the sharply defined tip of the white arch, through elder branches. A few more falls, and the arch will be covered. And then forgotten. All the time Trôo is burying itself in this way, hiding its past, with the Trojans of the present acquiescing.

♥

A holiday neighbour who prefers Touraine – or Trôo more exactly – to Provence or anywhere round the Mediterranean, maintains that one should select for a holiday home or for a second home, or for retirement (that debilitating concept), somewhere which isn't too different, but only a little better – in climate, fruit, flowers, and so on. He says that for rest and comfort the constituents of the second home mustn't be too unfamiliar: northerners – he is from Paris – should come only to the southern border of the north, or the northern border of the south; which he says is Trôo, where the vines begin, replacing the cider orchards of sour lands a few miles north. But if one thing slightly disappoints me at Trôo, it is that birds, for example, and flowers, are not more different here, 250 miles south of Wiltshire.

Black redstarts, a larger different owl, quails, orioles in a good year, yes. More jays, fewer magpies. Cornflowers, pheasant's eye, more poppies, one or two unfamiliar weeds (particularly a little scrubby marigold, on waste land, with a pungent smell, halfway between scent and stink), and several other flowers abundant or common here, instead of uncommon or very rare as in England. But in the daily encounter the vegetation remains much the same as it would be round chalk hills in Hampshire or Wiltshire.

If I go south again to the Dordogne, every day I see half a dozen flowers I don't recognize and cannot name. On a limestone glade between thin oaks behind the cliffs of Rocamadour – a 'lawn' in the sense that Milton or English landscape gardeners understood – where we stopped for a picnic in early May, we encountered four or five 'new' butterflies, one with black and white stripes moving about like a glider; and eight plants in flower whose genera I couldn't guess at. Refreshing. And comforting.

と※〜

Here orchids are the speciality. Most of the orchids – chalkland orchids rare with us in England – are exquisitely commonplace in Loir-et-Cher, or the Bas-Vendômois. On the Beauce in particular. By June they have dried up and gone. Round the village the *garde-champêtre* and his men have sliced them away earlier still.

Waste land is their preserve. There is one glade on a chalky platform of thin soil and thin grass on the Beauce, out towards Blois, starred every season with neat orchids, Burnt Orchid, the Spider Orchids, Bee Orchids and other kinds, in such quantity that first time seen is never forgotten, second time seen, or thereafter, is neglected.

The noblest orchids I have encountered were growing in lush shaded grass near the Roman camp down our valley. We descended the lane from this Camp de César with our arms full of orchid blooms each as fat and large as a head of lilac – and nearly trod on a very young hedgehog in the middle of the lane whose quills were still soft.

❦

Among our Trôo neighbours, the working ones, who have known field work, women or men, since they were children, flowers divide into garden flowers and rubbish, the admired and the wild. They look at our wild flowers filling a jug against a white wall – orchids, blue columbines, or purple loosestrife dropping petals and making an undoubted mess – and think 'Poor people, that's all they can do, they haven't a garden'; and they come with roses, or pink daisies, or sunflowers, or half a dozen dahlias of enormous splendour.

A Frenchman grows flowers round his house or along his walls or inside the painted circle of an old car tyre, or round a tyre well, to make colour. He grows taller flowers to cut, because his family must have flowers to put on the family graves.

❦

The north – we are not conscious of the north at Trôo. It is somewhere behind the cliff and its selvage of elm and lilac. At night, if we go out, we can only just see the Pole Star, over the edge. The whole vista of constellations lies to the south. The moon orbs itself above a blackness which is really the flank of the Beauce at its southern end; then it hangs over the Loir, on which it creates a narrow moonglade, where the Loir turns head on to our terrace.

England and problems extremely remote.

❦

Book reviews, England. *M. le facteur* arrives up the cliff with the post, which boils down to three air-mail copies of *The Times*, all at once; and one of the weeklies. There has never been a period in my life when *The Times* did not seem to me ridiculous, by and large, if read abroad; in the right kind of abroad, let's say on a headland in the Adriatic, where there is a strong sun-exposed odour of cypresses. Didn't Henry Adams say that he had read the London *Times* all his life, and had found that it never told the truth except on matters of the least importance? But it is not that – the remark goes for all journalism, all newspapers. It is the marrow inside the bone inside the ham, as well as the frills and the crumbs outside. 'H.M.W. writes . . .' There you have the frills or the crumbs. 'H.M.W. writes' a little extra, a little more of the asinine about some enormous ass, or some minuscule ass who has died. The leader-writer is the pro, the supplementary obituarist is the amateur, in the same pursuit; and I cannot see any advance in *The Times* vis-a-vis the rest of English life: both have changed, but the relation between *Times* and times, or the distance between *Times* and times, or the lag between *Times* and times, is much the same, or so I think when I sit down and unfold the air-mail flimsiness of the Rees-Moggian *Times* on a terrace above the Loir, under a lime-tree.

One only envisages the possibility of the perfect, philosophically illuminated, truth-telling newspaper when one is a young socialist in Fleet Street on the staff of an opportunist or a Tory newspaper.

↜↬↝

And that weekly left behind by the postman. I had written one of the reviews. I had written that in his book of critical articles the author had 'kissed every backside that he kicked'. This wouldn't do. It had been changed, to read the author 'mixes praise and blame'. Discovering this put me in a bad humour – stupidly, as if I did not know literary editors – with an excellent morning, in which everything else, including the temperature and the absence of clouds and the amount of breeze, and the movement of leaves, the movement of pliable acacia tops and the swing of the white acacia flowers, was exactly right.

One shouldn't review books.

✎

Not unless they are books one ardently wishes to promote. I should like to check in myself an ardent wish to demote, now and then.

Why does one criticize? When I was young, my mother (who had a tart turn of speech) used to be irritated by criticism of the way she arranged her drawing-room; also by criticism of her father's copies of works by Crome. 'Wait till you have a house of your own, wait till you have a wife – if you ever have one.' (She was my father's third wife, so she might have guessed that a plurality of wives went in the family.) Well, that was where book-reviewing began. I used to justify it – or justify cuts with the billhook – by a favourite quotation from Coleridge's *Biographia Literaria* – that 'praises of the unworthy are felt by ardent minds as robberies of the deserving'.

No doubt I should have read on, and remembered other sentences – that 'in promiscuous company no prudent man will oppugn the merits of a contemporary in his own supposed department', and that 'the eulogies of critics without taste or judgement are the natural reward of critics without feeling or genius. *Sint unicuique sua praemia.*'

✎

One starts reviewing books when young for the vanity of being asked to review them and of seeing one's name on the review, one continues it for money, one persists in it as a way of acquiring books one wants very much which are too expensive to buy. I grow older in reviewing and I like very expensive books which I can judge honestly and quickly because I know the kernel of the subject as well as the author does. But reviewing is a disease – or a compulsive habit.

✎

Another review, for a weekly. The book was about the Sitwells. This was how the copy reached the literary editor:

The flattest twaddle to be found in this book – that when we compare the collected poems of Dame Edith Sitwell with those of Yeats or Mr Eliot or Professor Auden it will be found that hers have the purest poetical content of them all' – is not, I must concede, Mr Lehmann's, it was quoted by him from Mr Cyril Connolly.

The reviewer was in France, the French were on strike, there were no posts: no consultation was possible. So 'the flattest twaddle' became – what do you think? – 'The most surprising judgement . . . '.

༼ৡৡ༽

And, by the way, who is *Professor* Auden? If a poet holds a chair for a while, does he have to be called *Professor*?

༼ৡৡ༽

We took one of our Paris neighbours blindfolded to a promised surprise up in the low hills of Montoire; or rather we blindfolded him within a hundred yards of the still invisible objective. Had a slight difficulty in getting him out of the car, without his eyes to aid him (he's a large man); walked him down the lane, and then said 'bend your knees', pressing his head down to the right level. He was very patient, and trustful. (Suppose we had then shot him, had pushed him over, and left?) When we took J's headscarf off his eyes, he found himself, knees bent, looking at what, do you imagine, nose nearly to nose?

A face in concrete, two green eyes made of glass marbles from the neck of old-fashioned lemonade bottles. The face, the eyes on either side of the sharp nose, looked out enigmatically, under the shabby overhang of the branches of a tent-like conifer. I don't know which was the more startled of the two heads.

I should add that the other head also wore a hat, an old homburg, gone hard and green. Also that it was mounted on a concrete neck on concrete shoulders, mounted in turn on an upright stone, on a small menhir, I suppose I should say.

This herm is miles away from self-consciousness or ideas; in pure country, in the unadulterate land of mangolds, wheat, barley, oats, vines, sweet corn, and prices, at a point where a second lane branches into a rough farmstead.

⋅⟜⁂⟞⋅

Of course the stone may have been there for centuries: but it is as if the man who completed it into Green Eyes had been possessed by the sense of a nameless god, a god that didn't even say he was a god.

That alga-tinted hat: I thought of a favourite god-king of mine, Idri-mi, King of Alalakh, near Antioch, who sits in one of the upstairs galleries of the British Museum, three and a half thousand years old, his eyes, of black stone inlaid in limestone, staring slightly upwards, with the intense indifference of Green Eyes here in the lane under the conifer.

'I am Idri-mi, son of Ilim-ilimma, servant of the weather god and his consort who is the mistress of Alalakh, my mistress.'

Idri-mi in a green homburg. But why not? Perhaps Idri-mi wore a hat.

⋅⟜⁂⟞⋅

The vitality of Green Eyes, that's the extraordinary thing. He dares you (as Idri-mi in fact does in his inscription) to lay a hand on him, even in respect. Figures by Henry Moore have rather an awkwardly self-conscious role between resemblance and notion. They are compacts of relationship, certainly; but they *weigh*, they don't have personality or energy – the energy or electricity of beings – in repose.

⋅⟜⁂⟞⋅

I knew a parson at Talland in Cornwall who made sculpture of the Green Eyes kind or the Green Eyes force. He cut down a number of trees in his overgrown vicarage garden, cutting them rather high because he did not like bending. Then he found he couldn't get the roots out, so he left the tall stumps and carved them into faces. As you walked up his drive, primitive faces peered at you out of shrubs, out of nettles, out of the white flowers and up-wreathing stems of bindweed. I

35

remember them among the leaves as bald-headed and foetal (the sap continued to rise and then dribbled greyly down these elm and sycamore stumps) in something of the way of a design by Beardsley.

✧

He told curious stories, that vicar, who was more or less unaware of any artist or style of art. Earlier, when he had a cure of souls in Dorset, he had chosen or inherited – since it seems to have been an odd choice – a retired sergeant-major as Vicar's Warden, a hard man, who had quarrelled with his only son and driven him out of the parish; to Canada, so they thought.

This warden was particularly hard on girls who found themselves pregnant, harder still on those who impregnated them. 'If I had my way, vicar,' he said of the impregnators, 'I'd shoot 'em, I'd shoot 'em.'

The warden's wife died, the warden died, his cottage was sold, and the new owner removed a large stack of rotting faggots piled against a pigsty at the end of the garden. Under the faggots lay a skeleton. The skeleton was all that was left of the sergeant-major's only son. A girl had been in trouble by him, he hadn't gone to Canada, and his father had shot him. There was a bullet hole through the forehead of the skull.

'If I had my way, vicar, I'd shoot 'em.'

Not, I think an attitude which could have directed the hand of a retired sergeant-major around Trôo.

✧

A Trôo spider, which ought to have a French name – pulling an abdomen of the clearest yellow, like an unwrinkled lemon.

✧

In the ditch outside the garden wall of Ronsard's La Possonnière I found for the first time an odd plant, Berry-bearing Catchfly, *Cucubalus baccifer*. 'Central and Southern Europe, and across Asia to Japan.' In England 'naturalized in a few places, e.g. on the Isle of Dogs, Kent'. It is like an elongated, softened weakened bladder-campion, proceeding by knots and angles, crawling, climbing, or at least clambering, a touch of green in its white petals, berries shiny, at first shiny green, then shiny black, swelling, as if from a collar, out of a yellowy green calyx.

Not exactly a Ronsardian object. Noise of doves came from the foliage above the Ronsardian wine cave. That was better:

> *Que dis-tu, que fais-tu, pensive Tourterelle,*
> *Dessus cest arbre sec? Viateur, je lamente,* etc.

ᴄ᙮ᴧᴈᴖᴧᴈᴖ

La Possonière is private (isn't it rather French that the home of the first or second grand master of French poetry should still be privately owned?). *On ne visite pas*, as guidebooks say smugly and so often. But I stand on the bank outside from time to time and regard those words *Voluptati et Gratiis*, over the wall.

ᴄ᙮ᴧᴈᴖᴧᴈᴖ

My feet are bleeding, Betty, say the English words which interpret the cooing of wood-pigeons, or *Take two swathes, Jesse.* A variant in these parts:

> *Cache ton cul, Claudine,*
> *Cache ton cul, Claudine,*
> *Cache ton cul, Claudine,*
> *Je l'ai vue . . .*

Hide your arse, Claudine . . .

But the pigeon is not always so polite.

> *T'es foutu, bonhomme,*
> *T'es foutu, bonhomme,*
> *Tu bonde plus, bonhomme.*

You can't manage it, good man; you can't manage it, good man. It's gone slack, good man.

ᴄ᙮ᴧᴈᴖᴧᴈᴖ

Saloperie, said Maurice, about a bush of Jerusalem Sage, just beginning to flower against the house. He hadn't planted it, it isn't grown in any garden round here, it is unusual, *saloperie*, rubbish, however 'beautiful'.

I notice that one or other of my family, or all of them, pick up a favourite French word or phrase each summer. *En principe* served one year, and proved very useful. *Saloperie* seems to be this year's word. It is surprising how often this indelicate word can be used, and how satisfyingly.

༷

I do not find it an unpleasant fact – though it is hardly convenient for moralists? – that certain substances which stink in concentration, smell sweet in dilution. The classic example is the olfactory substance common to dog shit and Madonna Lilies. Today – 19 May – on the dry hills above Trôo a puzzling sweetness or pleasantness blowing in a sunny north wind along a lane (it was rather like the scent from Jerusalem artichokes boiling for soup): it came actually from Wild Service trees – *alisiers* – in full blossom overhead. I had picked some Service flowers the other day without catching the sweetness, and had put them in a vase with wild columbines. In the small room the concentrated stink of the Service flowers was disgusting. It was like the smell of a large rotting boletus.

And Wild Columbine; yes, the supreme agreeability (as in Dürer's watercolour) of the blue of the flowers, each of which starts as a cluster of doves, tail down, which then slowly raise their wings and their posteriors. Columbines come into flower hereabouts when the doves from Africa start crooling inside hedges. I like this old linking of phenomena. Why not? It is the kind of linkage which helps to make our world less alien as the seasons come round. At any rate it means looking and listening.

༷

There is a critic of poetry whose taste and writing I find – well, the purest or impurest *saloperie*. He neither sees, hears, nor uses his nose. Smart *saloperie*, too. If he writes – he does – 'in this field', the last thing he means is a field, and the last thing he would hear or see in a corner of one of his fields would be invisible doves or blue columbines. His 'field' is poems exclusively, poems of anguish in particular. He eats under-cooked barbed wire (though probably I should have to explain to him the nature of so rural and palpable a thing as barbed wire).

If he came to Trôo, could I persuade this test-tube baby, born, so I suppose, in the vertical of an extra-long test tube in an urban laboratory, that it might – in the interest of explication and appreciation of Ronsard – be worth looking over the wall which surrounds Ronsard's renaissance manor house down the valley – or looking into the ochre wine caves in the chalk, which are Ronsard's ivy-bearded caverns, liable to shelter a nymph, if not exactly *in esse?*

Remember Ben Nicholson aggravated by an art official and exhibition promoter who came to visit him in the Ticino and was interested only in art: the blue picnic places the Nicholsons took him to he did not care for at all.

ᘓᣚᣲ

The transliteration, or should I say literation, of the call of birds again. On an evening walk through the open fields westward of Trôo, on the westward slopes, beyond the district curiously called Rome, the very pleasant sound of quails invisible inside the running corn. Maurice tells me that quails – are they the voice of farmers speaking through the corn, perhaps speaking to themselves? – say *Paie tes dettes, paie tes dettes.* A moral injunction, anyhow.

I prefer the English transliteration which I hear quails – now very occasional quails – saying out of Wiltshire and Gloucestershire or Cotswold corn: 'Wet my lips, wet my lips.' And it is more accurate. English folklore of this kind does seem to have a little more 'poetry' or pleasantness in it – perhaps, though, because it has been recorded through a more genteel sieve?

ᘓᣚᣲ

At the Château de Talcy, to see again the very large old wine-press rather than the execrable furniture and fittings (though Talcy does surpass many of the more pretentious *châteaux* of the Loire in character and in charm of oldness, if not of architecture).

But what I shall remember of this visit was a staggering fecundity, staggering prodigality of life. Everywhere in the shabby gardens, on the raked paths, on the steps, in the court-yard, in all the corners, there were *gendarmes* – not the police guarding the General at a *château* conference, but the small beetle-like insects striped black on a brilliance of scarlet which are called *gendarmes* (the usual name at Trôo) or *cherche-midis*. On this moderately warm day in early June, we could not walk without crunching *gendarmes* at each step (which might be the dream of a chronic agitator? The police down to the size of the beetles).

In my daughter's French insect book the *gendarme*, *Pyrro-chorio aptera*, has for immediate companion among the illus-trations its hemipterous relative, the Bed Bug. Down the page comes the Head Louse, on a later page appears the Human Flea – ultimate insect, larva, and nymph. *Tous les trois*. Let the young be instructed.

⌇⚜⌇

Also at the very end of the book comes that exquisite creature the Doryphore, the Colorado Beetle, which reached France in 1922. To see this beauty of ten golden stripes, *decemlineata* – *Leptinotarsa decemlineata* – nibbling at our neighbour's potato tops is rather a treat. At home we seldom get the chance; and I cannot say that my neighbour seems put out by these Colorado Beetles every summer. He is a heavy-handed workman em-ployed by the commune to work on the roads and paths under the *garde champêtre*, and he is one of the last souterrain dwellers of the village, an ancient Gaul. His hearth smoke comes up through the rock and the lilacs fifty yards away.

⌇⚜⌇

I cannot think that the art patrimony of France would be much injured if the heavy rubbish inside Talcy (and other *châteaux* rated as *monuments historiques*) were taken out into the court-yard and burnt – or sold to wealthy Americans from Dallas. Then Talcy might be refurbished in a way which would suggest the youth and looks of Cassandre Salviati, Ronsard's Cassandra (*Mignonne, allons voir si la rose*) who grew up in this country house.

One might start with the gardens –

> *Voici le bois, que ma sainte Angelette*
> *Sur le printemps anime de son chant;*
> *Voici les fleurs que son pied va marchant,*
> *Lors que pensive elle s'ébat seulette,* etc.

– and then take the sense of flowers and spring and lightness inside. I daresay it wouldn't do historically. Cassandra no doubt walked among heavy hangings and dull monstrosities of oak when she was a girl here in the 1540s, in spite of her father being half-Florentine and a relation of the Medici, and a court banker. All the furniture, or they say so, belongs to the house, some of it could have been made in Cassandra's lifetime. I suspect that the whole châteauful reflects the provinciality of seigneurs here on the Beauce at any time between 1570 and 1870.

The rich plain of the Beauce surrounds Talcy and extends flattishly to the north for mile after mile, as full of corn as ever. That would explain Talcy as a banker's demesne, a banker's investment.

❧

Avoir fermes en Beauce – to put your money in land. A book on ways and sayings of the Beauce explains that this isn't really contradicted by another old saying which indicated the character of Beauceron gentry – they stayed in bed while their breeches were darned. A mean backward lot, living their own life. Cassandra married the seigneur of Pray, out on the south-western end of Beauce, between Vendôme and Blois; and settled to a life of darning breeches?

❧

Last autumn in the thick bramble and thorn wood around the Dolmen de la Pommeraie in the next-door *commune* of St Martin-des-Bois I broke off a specimen of the fungus called *Ganoderma lucidum*; stem and cap are hard and dry, and are lacquered: they glisten in scarlet brown. The hardness, the lacquered durability is an illusion. This morning, eight months later, the specimen collapsed, shedding spores round the white shelf.

తికిరివ

Guidebooks are a kind of vacuum filler. Local guidebooks mention that dolmen: they don't say where it is, precisely: they don't describe it. The mention has been copied out of the guidebook before. And no one goes to see it, although the dolmen, or rather its cap, a large lump of puddingstone nearly level with the ground, is rather a beautiful object, bumpy with the green velvet of moss. There is no path into the wood. The farmer who came with us from his farmstead of La Petite Pommeraie, 'the little apple orchard', carried a hook and cut a path to the dolmen through blackthorn and thorny acacia. Other things difficult to see, or impossible to see because they have vanished, are mentioned piously in the guidebooks; so the vacuum is filled, so 'facts' are dotted round the emptiness, comfortably.

తికిరివ

The Trôo guidebook, excellently written, and full of good scraps, is very much about the Trôo-which-isn't, or that Trôo *qu'on ne visite pas*. It describes the Romanesque *maladrerie* or lazar-house – of which one can only see the exterior. It describes the Cafforts, the ancient underground quarries, but one cannot get into them. It gives details of an underground hall with a vaulted roof, in which people took refuge from the Germans in 1870. But it is not open. It describes the fortifications, they are mostly behind barbed wire or in private gardens. Also the ruins of Notre Dame des Marchais, but they are in private hands (and now restored as a house); and the Château de la Voute, which again is not to be visited.

There is hardly ever a would-if-we-could in describing these inaccessible pleasures. This is very French. But then so is Corot, or Daumier, or *bisque de homard*.

తికిరివ

Exceptionally small, squat children down the road at the Château de Poncé, playing, running under the stupendous girth of smooth-forking plane trees. The proprietor, over ninety, shrunken to his sinews, feebly clipping at a hedge of bay bushes. An elderly Judas Tree by the white pigeon tower has a scarlet fever of blossom, scarlet on the trunk, the branches, the twigs.

The *château* and the gardens today in sunshine are like Korf's Clock, in Christian Morgenstern's poem, which has two pairs of hands, one pair advancing, one pair moving backwards, so that Time is robbed of its terrors.

⌇⌘⌇

Year by year – certainly for the last three years – I have taken the poems of Wallace Stevens with me to Trôo. I have looked up, seen them, and felt guilty. I have started to read them, and have stopped, and they have come home again to England. Now I have been severe, and have done the job, and feel – as I expected to feel – unmoved and unpossessed.

Chancing a professorial snigger, I shall say that his poems don't go at all well with this equable and long humanized landscape. I sat and read them, I looked down at their contradiction (all right, a humanized landscape can be a form of art, even if half or three-quarters accidental). Years ago, years before *Notes Toward a Supreme Fiction*, the words I put above a notice of one of Stevens's books were 'The Stuffed Goldfinch'. His letters and references to the review suggest that Stevens did not altogether disagree. I would qualify 'The Stuffed Goldfinch' now: I would say the Stuffed Goldfinch – or some rarer bird – inhabits a gilded cage: you insert sixpence, and tinkling seems to come (the mandibles move), in fact does come from this dry creature of elegance; tinkling about poems, tinkling about what is and the worth or worthlessness of what is. I like the intelligence, I like the elegance; but want more of the quality which matures or detrivializes the elegance of Watteau or the elegance of Ben Nicholson; or of Louis MacNeice. Here is Wallace Stevens finicking round and round 'poetry', 'reality', 'imagination', in non-poems verbally fastidious.

The houses are haunted
By white night-gowns.

43

> None are green,
> Or purple with green rings . . .

He doesn't approve that only white night-gowns should haunt the night: he wants – and he knows it would be beside the human point – the purple ones with the green rings. He is on the clavier always; whereas, let us say Hugo or Ronsard, two poets, two incompatible poets I am always conscious of here at Trôo, are the clavier – the instrument, the composer, the player, the composition, and the sound of the composition.

> Perhaps
> The truth depends on a walk around a lake,
>
> A composing as the body tires, a stop
> To see hepatica.

But let's have the (imagined) hepatica, in five words, or five stanzas.

> The poem is the cry of its occasion,
> Part of the res itself and not about it.

Yes, and so on, and so on, a circumlocutory form of – I would say – a very American Musing or worrying; American literature about or out of literature, written by the everlasting exile surrounded by a *res* he does not care to look at, the external tourist of the mind.

❧

'We're wrong: Venice is a two-day city.'

❧

Stevens is a *pâtissier* of Anglo-American verse. At Montoire in the cake-shop, the *pâtissier*'s wife was inquiring about English wedding-cakes (she was a little horrified by the thought of keeping a piece of cake till the birth of a child) and showing us coloured pictures of the *pièces montées* her husband makes for weddings and the like.

    Pièces montées about the nature of the *pièce montée*, very light and colourful: that is Wallace Stevens.

    Then I thought of Erik Satie, who drops slow simple drops of music into music.

Yet how much I like the faintly ironic delights, the particular delights and sheens which Stevens was always trying to investigate.

ᑲᑐᑕᑐᑲ

A pleasure of France – that the better cornfield flowers have still to be extinguished.

Scarlet of poppies, searing blue of cornflowers, sharp red of pheasant's eye, and purple-pink of corncockles continue to exist, though not everywhere. It depends on the soil; and partly – another way of saying the same thing – on whether the farmers are poor and lax, or well-to-do and energetic.

Round Trôo I think there is a soil difference on the two sides of the Loir.

North of the river, where you are quickly in the Perche or the Dunois, in cider country, and less and less in wine country, you can drive miles without seeing more than the occasional group of poppies by the road or along the verge – only the verge – of a cornfield. The corn stands up in a boring purity.

South of the Loir, on the tail-end of the Beauce, that old dried-up lake, the soil has its thin patches, full of flints and very desiccated. Many poppies, many cornflowers –

Allez, allez, ô jeunes filles
Cueillir des bleuets dans les blés, etc.,

– and pheasant's eye here and there. But not many corncockles.

I regret the last in particular, rising high up to ear-of-corn level, and then opening their flowers flat to the hottest bite of the sun. In the south of Touraine, near Le Grand Pressigny, where the museum in the castle is full of gigantic axes of fudge-coloured flint, we searched some fields for flints, picking up only a few flakes and scrapers; but on the opposite side of the track through these fields, in a patch of untidy oats, thousands and thousands of corncockles eyed an unclouded sky without blinking. Further south, across the Creuse, in Vienne, very poor country where fields and gardens seem about ninety per cent small stones, we knew where to turn right to a friend's house, by a huge splash of red – a cornfield of poppies.

I see the eclogue image of farming is being destroyed. Logical absolutes can be unbeautiful. Pure green fields. Pure battery biological beasts. A Monet, Renoir or Pissarro or Sisley of 1968 would have to travel rather further for a corn-field mostly of red, or red and blue.

᷒ᖘ᷒

Until a few years ago it used to be possible to stop on the great corn-plain of the Beauce outside Chartres and see the gorgeous scarlet of poppies and the super-blue of cornflowers, mixed. Then one drove on towards the two spires of Chartres, which was the capital of the Beauce, and saw the two flower colours repeated, sublimated, and mixed again in the stained glass. Clean seed and selective weedkillers have put an end to that exercise.

Palaeolithic painting and Romanesque painting, or early Romanesque painting: earth colours.

Stained glass of the thirteenth century: a transcendency of flower colours.

Our painting, the danger – but only the danger – of too sterile, too chemical a brilliance.

᷒ᖘ᷒

French children are now beginning to walk about in socks coloured with new luminescent dyes. Pea-green turned mineral, mineral-orange. You see only the socks, not the girls.

᷒ᖘ᷒

Early in our days at Trôo I set myself to make a version of *Le voyage de Tours*, by Ronsard, written in his thirties.

I never finished it, never revised as much as I had written (only the first thirty lines). The notebook vanished, and I did not find it again for years.

By that time how well I had come to know the road Ronsard and 'Thoinet', his friend Jean-Antoine de Baïf, had taken. It is our own way to Tours, thirty miles to the south. We feel offended if we meet, let us say, ten cars in the thirty miles.

The road begins by going up the valley of the Cendrine, past the remains of Ste-Madeleine-de-Croixval, where Ronsard became prior in 1566, six years after publishing *Le Voyage*; past the green brows of the last fragments of Ronsard's forest. It climbs to Montrouveau, which is no more than a few houses and a church. A garden in front of one of the houses at Montrouveau is always, in summer and autumn, particularly happy with flowers, in tins, tyres, buckets, *sabots*, everything, large pansies invading the gravel and standing up face to face with the sun. Ronsard, in retreat at Croixval, was to write another poem, a hymn, a litany to St Blaise, who is the patron saint of Montrouveau, asking him to show favour to every paterfamilias of the village, every farmer, every family, their animals, their bees, their chickens, their crops, their vines, their orchards, their gardens. The garden near the church suggests that the saint is still on their wavelength.

う楽

From Montrouveau the road follows an old Roman road more or less up and down across farms and through woods. The verges are orchidaceous in May, on either side the fields dry to a strong ochre. Then the road drops into Beaumont-la-Ronce (which has a street of cave houses in a low bank of chalk, one or two still inhabited) and makes a right angle round the domain and the *château* which belonged to Ronsard's cousin, Philippe de Ronsart. Through the gateway one has a clear sight of the tall tower in freestone and faded red brick which Ronsard mentions in his poem.

Before it comes to a new factory suburb of Tours this road descends to a last village, Langennerie, where Ronsard and de Baïf slept out of door by the ford, under willow trees. The ford has been replaced with a bridge, and the two poets now could have slept at a small hotel by the stream, where poplars have replaced the willows. A lovable undramatic thirty miles. If it is a day full of light, if the flowers are out, I remember Ronsard, and his description of the journey, each time we go to Tours, each time we come to Montrouveau, Beaumont, and the stream at Langennerie.

So here goes with those still uncorrected, unrevised thirty, or thirty-one lines out of *Le voyage de Tours*:

It was the season when the amorous Flora
Was opening all the small flowers for her lover
Along the meadows as enamelled with their dyes
As with its colours the great rainbow in the skies;
When butterflies and golden bees along the gardens

47

Sip honey or else load it on their thighs
And small birds flutter through the woods
From bough to bough, gather
Their beakfuls, and among the verdure
Worry, like us, about their family's future.
   Thoinet, this April passing Vendômois,
Took me to see at Tours my Marion
(Who there was at a cousin's marrying),
His own Francine as well this Thoinet went to see,
A girl, whom Venus, planting her strict dart,
Had written deeply in his wounded heart.
   We two together started from the hamlet of Coutures;
We passed Gastine, and its high greenery,
Marré we passed, and came at noon to where
The shepherd Phillipot had raised that tower
Which honours Beaumont-la-Ronce's cottages
As a pine tree does honour to a thicket's trees:
This shepherd we name Phillipot is always gay –
With him we ate and drank till dark of day,
Went on, and slept at Lengerie ford
Beneath the willows planted on a meadow's length.
From break of day, redoubling speed,
We caught the sight at last of St-Côme's spire,
Uplifting in a wood not far from Tours,
Where in the sweet meadow-centre of an isle
The pleasant rites were under way . . .

It was at St-Cosme that sixty-one-year-old Ronsard was to die,
in 1585, twenty-five years after *Le Voyage* was first printed,
St-Cosme on the island as it then was, having been the first
of three priories Ronsard acquired – after St-Cosme, Croix-Val,
then St-Gilles on the edge of the river at Montoire.
   Once when we made the journey, to buy a collected Ronsard
and a book on the archaeology of Touraine fat with information
about Beaumont, Langennerie, St-Cosme and so on, we picked
some very perfumed butterfly orchids, some marsh orchids
and pink campion – no, it was Ragged Robin – by the road
near Beaumont, and we put this small bunch – to the devil,
to their own hells, for the moment with Orwell, Ken Tynan
and others – on Ronsard's tomb at St-Cosme.

∽✲∾

He thinks Ronsard a great poet, he has no sympathy for the pictures of Francis Bacon, and not much for the poems of Robert Lowell, or the plays of Beckett; he thinks he likes 'good writing', he thinks 'good writing' is enough. In fact he doesn't think it is enough. But it is something, so is grace. Ronsard for part of me; or Issa, making water in Japanese snow:

> Straight snow-hole
> Outside my gate
> Cut by my piddling.

But I was pleased to discover that Matisse had drawn on the stone for *Les Amours* of Ronsard. Old, his beard white, his head bald, the Germans in France, Matisse began his 126 lithographs after an illness – lithographs to go with the Ronsard poems he liked best. For years he had thought of making them. *Luxe, calme, et volupté.*

୶ஃତ

Stopped for once at Montrouveau, to look at St Blaise's church – nothing in it now which Ronsard would have known – and ask if they continue a patronal feast, and if they still sing Ronsard's hymn in procession. But there is no longer a resident *curé*, there is a labourer's family in the shabby parsonage. Only the children were at home and they didn't know.

If I had found the *curé* he might have said it was no good singing Ronsard's invocation – in 1967 – against plague, ague, St Anthony's fire, spells, and wolves from Gastines. But –

> May our heifers all the spring
> Feel no bites of cleg or fly,
> May their milky udders swell,
> And may cheeses, soft or dry,
> Our strainers fill.

There's much else in the hymn; which invokes St Blaise – and they all continue – against foxes, mad dogs, thieves, soldiers (the Germans were there not so long ago), lawyers, moneylenders, fevers, boils, psychosis, and slipping axes. St Blaise was asked by Ronsard to find good husbands for daughters.

That would be understood. But mightn't the *curé* have to leave out the stanza which couples labourers and oxen, and asks that the labourers – there are communist election posters up on the wall – should be content to labour?

Nos Bouviers sans murmurer
Puissent la peine endurer.

Nine o'clock evening light, the heat dying away, a smell of honeysuckle everywhere from the green garden of someone's still shuttered and locked *maison de plaisance.*

༄

I used to imagine that primitive English England – the first Saxon and Anglian England – had been something like a series of communist tribal settlements, share and share alike, in freedom and dignity, no serfs, no bondmen, without chiefs, or absolute lords at any rate. Approved, and even recent, historians say or suggest as much, as well as that medievalizing communist, William Morris, in his poems, and I would have imagined it for France as well. Once there was Paradise (if that would have been Paradise).

But there wasn't.

On the convincing say-so of an American medievalist[1] I discover this to be a nice wrong thought, deriving from historical suppositions made romantically in Germany in the last century.

I discover that it is only now, for the first time in history, that the *bouviers* have become free, more or less, and separated from the hay-munching *boeufs* – two sets of beasts of burden; that only now for the first time have they acquired some chance of dignity, in what is after all the great developing revolution of the modern rights of man.

I like to be told as much by an American from Berkeley, from capitalist, truncheon-wielding, robber-baron America, where police-cars are fronted with barbed wire. It cheers me up when I see labourers emerging – in 1967 – from their cave houses in the chalk, the yellowing *tuffeau* of Touraine, Anjou and the Bas-Vendômois; or when I see posters in every village as well as town for France's rather dismal communist party –

[1] Carl Stephenson, in *Mediæval Institutions*, 1954.

as well as for the Gaullists: they check each other: between the
two the rights can perhaps grow, or not be whittled; or merely
cower in continued existence.

A century ago my grandmother, the Vicar's wife if you
please, in a Norfolk parish, would get down from her horse
and box the ears of a girl for not 'making obedience' to her.

૮ᎮᏃ

No, from *M. le curé* at Montoire – who looks after Montrouveau and several other parishes, as well as his own – I discover
now that the Montrouveau people don't sing Ronsard's hymn
to Monsieur St Blaise, don't have processions, and don't have
a patronal fête. More prosperity, better health, less religion.

૮ᎮᏃ

If it is a poor game detecting or commenting on the differences
between England and France, I think I see quite an illumin-
ating difference in this expected discovery. If an English poet
of Ronsard's stature had written a hymn for a village, the
village would know about it. Someone would see to that, even
in this day of uneducated parsons. It would be sung: it would
be mentioned or quoted in every guidebook. In France people
make their necessary gesture to the past more in abstract, less
in particulars: if – they might say – we put up notices along the
road indicating that this is the country of the poet Ronsard,
the Parisians will stop and leave some of their money behind.
But we are not going to preserve anything ourselves, with our
money or theirs. We are not going to bother to wipe the dust
and dirt off the effigies of Ronsard's father and mother in
Couture church, or remove a dirty sheet of plaster board
which has been leaning up against the tomb for the last six
months.

But then the people who know, the local ones who should
care, are away in Paris. They are not the farmers, working and
drinking and safeguarding their francs; and the shutters are
closed for most of the year across the façade of their *château*
or their *maison de plaisance*. So it is that everything not very
great and grand and celebrated, and an evident part of the
glory and dignity of France, decays; a woeful amount of

excellent things have been lost around here in the last hundred years: dolmens, standing stones, *polissoirs*, Gallic souterrains, rock graves, wall-paintings, priories, chapels, castles. More will be lost in the next hundred years. Local francs are for local savings – of a different kind.

❧

Walking down the grass-centred track to the wine caves and the abandoned or ruined farmhouses of L'Abbaye, I was unexpectedly pushed into the brambles by a battered lorry. Found the lorry outside a cave lower down, the cave door open.

Three little humans were about – the first humans we had ever seen here: a little old man whose upper teeth came outwards in a narrow U, a little thin grey woman, and a little rubicund peasant, of any age from twenty-five to thirty-five.

The rubicund peasant invited us to a drink (with an old white horse the three of them had been trenching their vines on top of the hill). We went first into an abandoned steep-tiled house for glasses. The one living room was packed with broken furniture, including – why? – a dusty stuffed hen. Leaves on the floor. Then into the cave, which sloped up into the hill, cut out of the firmest rock, not a crack, not a fall, a cave surprisingly welcoming, and tidy.

❧

The father – with the teeth – had inherited the house, two steep meadows in front, and the vines. No living was to be gained there any more. He moved into Montoire as a labourer. His son – the rubicund one, who did all the explaining, as if his parents (and they looked it) were past the trouble of all except the most necessary talk – worked as a labourer making concrete poles and posts. But on Sunday – this was Sunday – they were peasants again, tending the vines, asserting property, having a drink of their own wine (red, a little flat and rough, yet agreeable). Their presence made the abandoned settlement, the dying overgrown bay trees, all the more sad.

❧

L'Abbaye again. An unsuccessful search for morels – three or four weeks (30 May) too late. But discovered fossils instead, in a chunk of ochre rock fallen from the farmstead built or cut into the hill where the lorry had passed us on Sunday. A wall of the house had tumbled from under a cantilever of sandy chalk. Our chunk of it was full of large fossil oysters, and more oysters were visible in the rock face thirty feet up. The oyster shells were often perched on top of each other – as in life. I read today of living oysters on island rocks off Western Australia – 'small but sweet oysters which, clustered upon themselves, make rocks of their own groupings'. Here was another Australian sea.

❦

Among the branches of a cherry tree, outside the one squalid farm place of the Abbaye group where a family continues to live and work, a rose, healthy, climbing, spreading, emerging, with shiny new leaves, a few carmine-hearted white roses already open. A good scent.

❦

Less cheerful note from outside a *château*, somewhere between Trôo and Vendôme. We were taken there on a dampish Sunday morning, along an avenue, across a bridge, under a little gatehouse with renaissance motifs, and into a shabby courtyard. There were hens' pointed footprints everywhere on the thin mud of the courtyard. Grey dogs bristled from outhouses and barked.

We had come to see the private chapel on the far side of the moat. Our friend told us to wait there while he tried to get the key. 'Watch the windows,' he said, and went up the steps to the front door of the *château*, where he pulled the long metal rod of a bell.

We waited, relieved that the dogs had gone away in boredom. We looked at the long windows, behind which there seemed to be nothing at all, and were then aware that the windows were watching us, or rather a face was watching us from one window; vacant, large-eyed, open-mouthed.

The door opened. No one came out at first, some words

were spoken, the door closed again for five minutes; and the invisible speaker, the Marquis of this *château*, now appeared on top of the steps in the drizzle, with a large key hanging from his left hand. His other hand drooped from a sling. The vacant face continued to stare from the window.

The Marquis came down – I saw he was wearing old gym shoes – joined us in the courtyard, and began a voluble, rhetorical monologue, enforced by a wave now and then of the free hand and a swing of the key.

We were an audience. He was lecturing us about his ancestors, their relation to this or that monarch, their arms on the renaissance panelling of the gatehouse.

His features – he had not shaved – were as white and dirty as the once white shirt he was wearing, without a tie. But they were good features, under the scrub and dirt. The sling was dirty, the hand which drooped out of the sling, and occasionally took the large key, was white and dirty, and soft with disuse. White and dirty ankles came out below black trousers which were frayed, he was wearing his gym shoes without socks. He turned to indicate beyond the *château* a mound which he said had been built by the Phoenicians (by now he had gone back past Charles IX and François Premier and Saint Louis and Charlemagne and Clovis and Vercingétorix), revealing as he turned the master item of his appearance – that his hair, greasy, grey and uncut, was held in a queue at the back of his head, in what?

In a rusted safety-pin.

He took it in that I was a writer from England, and at one point emerged from his now Carolingian, Merovingian and Gallo-Roman and Phoenician rhetoric (we gathered that his family had been here at all epochs), turned a sharp eye on me, and inquired if I knew Paul Getty? 'He's interested in my Rembrandts.' It did not look, as I say, as if there were anything inside the *château*, chairs, or Rembrandts, anything at all, except that face at the window, still staring and staring.

Well, in the end *M. le Marquis* showed us the chapel, medieval, but rather overcrowded with funereal bric-a-brac of the Second Empire. He was infinitely courteous, in brief moments when the ancestral egoism and the Phoenician nonsense abated – infinitely courteous. A grandee, passed by time, holding his pigtail in with a rusted safety-pin.

He has died since. I asked someone who knew him why he had become so poor and peculiar. No, it wasn't drink, it wasn't women, it was having inherited a 'fortune', as they used to say, insufficient to cope with a perpetual itch for cars, large cars, fast cars, different cars, sports cars, saloon cars, new cars, an overriding passion to drive about in something new.

❦

That Marquis in sodden gym shoes, and a good deal else here in France, and a good many other acquaintances and experiences, remind me of the man who always wished to remain where he was or where he had been, in Herman Melville's story; who was given the sack and was back again when the office re-opened, who always said 'I'd rather not.'

The *Académie française* would rather not admit this or that Franglais word into French (it's there already). France would rather not change. Though it cannot help changing.

Everywhere there is a little pocket of resistance, or of continued acquiescence in what is usual and correct. France resists – or doesn't welcome – changes in its Napoleonic system of education. A French archaeologist resists knowing what archaeology has been up to outside France. France resists disbelief in the medico-magical virtue of mineral waters (or does that come of the addiction of the French to the study of their poor alcoholized livers?). The tools in the Trôo workcave – or some of them – continue to be the same as the tools in use in the miniatures of a Book of Hours, a wooden framesaw in which tension is given to the blade by twisting rope, a crescent-shaped long-handled hook of the kind used in ambushing a party of Protestants in the days of Charles IX or a stray group of pilling Englishmen under Coeur-de-Lion; whereas the descendants of the pilling Englishmen have shown an extraordinary restless plasticity, which they continue to show, if in a more than usually half-conscious or undirected way.

❦

Sunday on the Loir; green boats drawn in under willows, unmoving fishermen in orange waterproofs: reflected orange

on the water: rain, no fish, the orange reflections dimpled
by the rain. In between-whiles the sun comes out, orioles say a
loriot or two.

༄

On a lilac bush in the garden every leaf has been serrated by a
leaf-cutting bee. Leaning on the hedge alongside there is a
long-handled billhook, of that vicious shape I have just mentioned, the blade a crescent moon with a spur at the back (I
have been using it to hack at elm-suckers above a cave). The
shapes bitten out by the leaf-cutting bees are identical, just as
taut, just as crescentic; they have the same vicious energy.

༄

The minister in Gide's *La Symphonie pastorale* talks of his wife's
mistrust of every effort of the soul – well, let's change that and
say of the mind – to discover in Christianity 'something else
than the domestication of our instincts'. The beast domesti-
cated. Cats will scratch, when they are frightened or when
they don't understand. So will people in Trôo, or my Wiltshire
village. A very gentle *paysan* here suddenly says over a glass
of *rosé* he would shoot strikers or sit-in students. This same
gentle *paysan*'s in-laws had all their claws out when his wife
died, over this and that which had belonged to her. She had
promised this set of spoons, that set of crockery. His face was
slapped before she was buried, as he stood in front of the tall
fruit-wood *armoire* which contained the spoons and the coffee.
The quarrel continues – they pass and don't talk – and will
only die away slowly, almost imperceptibly.

Still, it is some advantage when the instincts are domesti-
cated, when people a little more disciplined by education and
ideas and notions of behaviour don't say or don't quite formu-
late even to themselves what they really feel, or don't act or
break out as they would like to; and that, or the degree of
gentillesse de coeur we encounter in this valley, can be chalked up,
I suppose, to the cumulative, if now less obvious, influence of
Christianity.

Elsewhere it would not be Christianity, but another religion.

All the same remember Swift ironically rebutting his
ironic suggestion that abolishing Sunday (along with Christ-

ianity *in toto*) would give a clear gain of one day of trade, business and pleasure in every seven days.

'Are fewer Claps got upon Sundays than other days?'

༷

I hear the bell. Another funeral. The *curé* usefully ritualizing and softening death (for the living) as he ritualizes the seriousness of being born and of getting married. Why should he suppose he is wanted in between?

༷

'Literary criticism,' says the editor of a series of 'modern judgements' on fortunately for themselves dead authors, 'has only recently come of age as an academic discipline, and the intellectual activity that, a hundred years ago, went into theological discussion, now finds its most natural outlet in the critical essay.'

O my God! (which I feel to be the right expletive) O my Paul! O my Leavis, patron saint of academic critics, newly emancipated, from the very lower middle class! As if I didn't remember how the theological books went from wall after wall at threepence a yard when the contents of my father's vicarage were sold. Threepence a yard – tomorrow – for university selection, university elevation, university denigration of poems and poets of today.

༷

Gentillesse de coeur – it's a nice phrase for a nice quality. They have it here up and down the valley, and on the farms, and in the shops. The occasional encounter with opposite qualities gives a shock: we were once treated with a sharp lack of *gentillesse de coeur* by a local innkeeper – but it was explained to us that he came from Paris. Maurice puts this more than amiability down to vineyards, down to wine. Some of it – or the forms of it, another matter – may have sunk down through the social liquid, dense and opaque, from the 'upper classes'; but I would think another source has been mutual poverty and mutual interdependence, in a climate which does its best to help with its own friendliness.

57

Yeats wrote of the two meritorious classes, whose members could be themselves, the aristocrats who have everything and so desire nothing, and the poor who have nothing to lose. A little barmy of him. Aristocrats seem to me uncommonly vulgar as a rule, the most unoriginating of groups. Look at the contents, Tudor to High Victorian, of so many of their grand houses, now open to us all for two half-crowns. But if Yeats found an aristocrat, or a female aristocrat, who wrote poetry, then the poetry must be good; so he admired the evidently flat verse of the Duchess of Wellington and the evidently ridiculous verse of Edith Sitwell. His Gaeltacht poor, without the wine, without the climate, certainly had good things in common with the poor here on the edges of Touraine.

But wouldn't a cool look now make him revise both of his estimates?

What happens to the poor when they begin to have something to lose, and when the something increases and increases – and what happens to that *gentillesse de coeur*?

Try America, try England, though we haven't gone so far. Tomorrow try the Russians and the French. They begin to have more to lose in France, but when de Gaulle frightens them with a nasty rasp in his old voice on the radio (after giving them a little more in answer to their threats), they think they are going to lose their little all, like Čapek's dung-beetle, and they rush and give the Gaullistes an absolute majority. One could call it rather Gadarene. But I wish I could see how some social virtues and generosities are going to survive the required supersession of poverty.

꒰꒰ꕤ꒱꒱

J. wants an acacia with pink flowers. It is quite an obsessive longing. On the way into the shops and the market stalls at Montoire we pass a little domain which someone has evidently prepared for his retirement. The gate is always locked. A stream runs round the garden, and in this stream there are trout. The closed shutters, the doors, are all newly painted. The grass is green to artificiality, every blade seeming separate from every other blade. The shrubs are young and healthy; and among them, blessed among them, is this acacia with pink flowers, pink like the face of Helen in that *cassone* panel in the

National Gallery which used to be ascribed to Gozzoli, Helen
being carried off on the shoulder of Paris.

'The pink acacia is out,' says J.

If she could, she would go in and triumphantly carry it
away on her shoulder. The rape of the pink acacia.

෴

The Poetry Book Society has – kindly, I know – recommended
my new book of poems for summer reading by its members or
subscribers. The society publishes a bulletin in which as a
preliminary or an accompaniment 'chosen' or 'recommended'
poets are enticed to contribute some guiding thoughts or
some comments about their poems, or poetry.

Can I pass off the following:

The proper place for writers of poems to appear, in strict relation
to themselves as poem writers, is in their poems.

Exegi monumentum is acceptable, if rash, in a poem.

Five paragraphs or a single paragraph beginning *I believe, I do not
wish, I am, I write because*, are unacceptable and indecent.

Poetry is, Poetry will become are presumptuous.

About one's poems the pronouncements that *I play in a mountain
corner on a scrannel pipe*, and *I play with myself in a confessional box
without a curtain so that everyone can see the spasm on my face*, are self-
advertising, equally.

No warlocking, no astrologizing.

Attaching to one's public self a proletarian form of a Christian name
is writing one's ad or wearing one's Order of Merit at an art auction
where one's own pictures are up for sale.

At a poetry Festival or a writers' conference Hesiod, or Coleridge,
or Pasternak, are not likely to be encountered.

Poetry, poem – each word inclines to presumption in regard to oneself. Even more so *poet*.

I regret – but not much – a snobbery in these sentences.

I regret such relation as these sentences have or must have to the
I myself of the poems which the selectors of the Poetry Book Society
are recommending.

If I could concisely explain poems or me or my poems, probably I should not write them.

Allow me to say, Mind your own business; which will be reading my poems, if you wish to.

ᴄ✿ᴄ

But it does do no harm to recall – recall isn't the word, to see again – the Muses on Helicon; and the shining places where they danced. They were honest. We know – Hesiod made them remark – how to say many false things which look as if they were true, but we know how to tell the truth when we want to.

Hesiod saw the Muses in the half mists of Helicon and Olympus, Pierre de Ronsard saw the Muses in these fields and woods, Arnold, yes, school inspector Arnold, borrowed words out of the *Theogony* for them and almost managed to see them round Cumnor and near lashers and with their feet in the orchids, Early Purple. They became real, the Muses, all nine of them, together; not to be approached, or individually or too pertly scrutinized. Their dance places do begin to hover and shine – a fine state of things – on the edges of the mind. But their dance places are not picnic places. 'Not here, O Apollo,' etc.

Not among the empty oily sharp sardine-tins, O reviewers.

ᴄ✿ᴄ

Searching out *polissoirs* in the cool of afternoon or evening has become one of our pursuits, with the aid of a list published by the archaeological society at Vendôme. They take us into woods, blackthorn thickets, sweet corn forests, wildernesses without shade, into parishes and plain areas we should other-wise never visit.

But I haven't explained. A *polissoir* is a neolithic polishing or sharpening stone, created by the relentless sharpening, smooth-ing and polishing of flint cutting tools. Instead of 'stone' I should say boulder, huge lumps of puddingstone or sarsen, above or nearly level with the ground. There are hundreds of these polishing boulders round the Beauce, between Vendôme and Chartres, there are a good many round Vendôme. Hun-dreds have been destoyed, many have been removed.

English archaeology doesn't explain this huge abundance of *polissoirs* in France and their extreme scarcity in England (I know of two French-type *polissoirs* among the sarsen boulders near Avebury, and a few probably ancient *polissoirs* built into church walls). But in our *polissoir* hunting I think less of the economico-archaeological problems of axe and sharpening boulders than of the surprise of the absolute smoothness of the long regular grooves, the *rainures*, after four thousand or five thousand years of exposure.

French antiquaries love *polissoirs*, and I suppose we should borrow their vocabulary of *polissoir*, *rainure*, and *cuvette* (bowl or basin, since a perfect *polissoir* will have a shallow dish or basin depression in the rock alongside the grooves), and their convention of indicating the grooves, in archaeological bulletins and pamphlets, with long outlines, like the convex outlines of an elongated stone axe or a lens.

The local names divide as a rule between St Martin and the Devil – Devil's Scratch, Devil's Stone, Devil's Stoup, St Martin's Pint, St Martin's Well, St Martin's Steps.

✎

Landowners were given to removing *polissoirs* to their parks, their terraces, or to the gravelled courtyard outside the antiquarian society's museum. There are *polissoirs* in the courtyard of the museum at Vendôme, in the old cloister-garth between the museum and the flying buttresses of La Trinité. There are *polissoirs* by the gate as you go into the museum at Châteaudun (which owns the most charming collection of birds formalized out of science into pretty arrangements on gilded perches).

Last year a big firm making agricultural machines established a small factory or service depot in one of the villages out on our southern sector of the Beauce. They spent money in the village, they put grass and a kerb round the Romanesque church; and they wanted to transfer a huge *polissoir*, grooved all over, from beside a lane on the borders of the *commune*: it was to catch all eyes in the tidied centre of the village.

Paris said no: it was classified as a *monument historique*: it wasn't to be moved.

✎

Any two *polissoirs* are the same, however different. A poem, if it is good, is unique. It is a 'sweet' with peculiar lasting powers. Not too sweet, I hope. But I enjoy it, swallow it, absorb it – if it doesn't happen to be read by a poet on a British Council record. And I look in the box again weeks later, and it is still there. It returns like the cooked and eaten trout to the holy well.

❧

How lucky that atmosphere and light – neither of which is among the hard technicians of Disneyland – vary my phenomenal world for me, for my additionally variant self: Loir, cliffs, caves, swing of ivy, texture of fields.

❧

I wonder if deity and art, music as much as painting or making poems, don't originate in sparkle, glitter, crystal, refracted light, an abstracted portion of sun. Or of the electricity of the brain? The rock crystal which the aboriginal takes into his cave, and the sparkle of calcite? Also can art which retains none of that concentration and apparent mystery – initiate's mystery – of light remain of account?

Hopkins staring at the shine in the gravel, after rain. *Pearl*, *Paradise Lost*, Marlowe, Hölderlin, Pope, Hugo, Whitman, Wen-i-To, Pasternak, Ronsard, Dante beside Virgil. The dancing places which shine, in Hesiod. 'Immortal diamond'.

❧

Quick drive to Le Mans, through sandy forest where thrift grows by the road in natural borders of pink. I read not long ago that the grandmama of Somerset Maugham survived as a widow by writing children's books in France – in Le Mans. An English widow without money, and without looks, I would guess. That fits Le Mans; where everybody seems to be running after francs too absorbedly to notice how shabby their city is; if they catch up with the francs, they don't spend them – on Le Mans. It is full of grey corners apt for grey English Victorian widows in reduced circumstances.

Freeman the historian gave the authorities of Le Mans a splendid pounding for their habit of wholesale demolition, destroying twelfth-century buildings, cutting through the Roman walls, and cutting the brutal chasm of a road – a road I hate and am rather afraid of – right through the ancient centre.

'Perhaps there is some stuck-up Mayor or Prefect who would think himself a great man if he could make Le Mans as ugly and uninteresting as the dreary modern streets of Rouen or of Paris itself. It is at all events certain that M. Haussman was not long ago seen in Le Mans, and such a presence at such a time is frightfully ominous. . . . When the Roman walls of Le Mans are not spared, nothing can be safe. All that can be done is for those in whose eyes antiquity is not a crime to run to and fro over the world as fast as may be, and see all that they can while anything is left.'

I like another sentence. There was an ancient hospital Freeman could not go into: it was built by a King of England (Le Mans is Henry II's town): he was all the more indignant.

'A fine hospital, the work of Henry the Second, is now perverted to some military purpose, and some military tom-foolery forbids examination.'

These French! These generals and colonels! *La Gloire!* These countrymen of Daumier's!

And those English grandees of the educated middle class of the High Nineteenth Century!

༈

Freeman noticed the menhir built into the corner of the great cathedral of St Julien of Le Mans – an odd, rather human-shaped stone with the natural appearance of drapery. A Celtic god? A kind of Thor Stone like the one alongside a medieval cross in the Oxfordshire hamlet of Taston? A stone dropped by Taranis the Hairy, god of the Gauls, god of bang and flash? Or Taranis himself? Continuity in change, at any rate.

༈

In one of the drab open places in Le Mans I watched the pre-paration for bedding out. It was like horticultural cuisine, like the preparation of a splendid cake in rich layers of dung and earth, the stratification visible, dark green, lighter brown, until the earth was tamped down to the edge of the border. Not a dollop of dung, not a grain of earth wasted or allowed to spill on to the tarmac.

✼

Just outside our *commune*, at Vieux Artins on the flood plain of the Loir, there is an abandoned church (you can see into the ruined nave only by climbing a ladder thoughtfully placed in the blackthorns against a window). A hundred yards away the Roman crossed the river by a bridge which a flood destroyed in 1555, and it is said that in Roman days this church was preceded by a temple of Jupiter, in which a cracking wonder was performed by that St Julien of Le Mans, Apostle of Normandy. He was reputedly – like St Martin of Tours – a well-born Roman; and from Le Mans he came down to our portion of the Loir valley (most of which used to be in the diocese of Le Mans) to deal with its obstinately heathen Romans or Romanized Gauls. At Vieux Artins he found this temple in which the statue of Jupiter (mightn't Jupiter have been Taranis the Hairy again?) stood up among a crowd of lesser idols. St Julien prayed, Jupiter fell to bits; and out of the bits there came a most unpleasant dragon, which at once ate several of the company; at this point St Julien, rather late, made the sign of the Cross, and the dragon disappeared; and the people of the valley of the Loir were all converted; and have been Christian ever since.

St Julien should have broken up the menhir now tucked between the corner buttresses of his cathedral; or perhaps it is a manifestation of evil which St Julien petrified; perhaps it is a fossilized priest of the heathens.

✼

In China when they first made pottery vessels in place of bronze ones, under the Han emperors, they glazed them to look like bronze and gave them fixed pottery handles in relief which looked like the old loose handles, ring handles, of bronze. Early cars looked like carriages. Early electric fires – no, electric fires which are still in shops – are made to look like coal fires. Vieux Artins keeps a temple and changes gods. Make new ideas *look* like old ones, and nobody is upset. Parsons now say God, and mean Ethics.

ᴄ✿ᴗ

I mentioned Daumier. That most irritating of French towns, Blois (which is the departmental town of Loir-et-Cher) has mounted an exhibition in the *château* in honour of that most dangerous draughtsman. Nearly five hundred lithographs. *Superbe épreuve du 2ᵉ état. Noter les expressions, crédules, pour ce bon bourgeois parisien*, etc.

The catalogue – the catalogue of a Daumier exhibition – begins with a preface by M. le Maire de Blois, in which – not a word about Daumier – he praises Blois for promoting *réalisations artistiques de cette importance*, and the man who arranged the exhibition for his ardour and his great competence in the artistic domain.

It is a Daumier drawing, this preface. After which, on the walls, Daumier is a bit trimmed. Perhaps there weren't proofs sufficiently *superbe* and *rarissime* of the most biting lithographs, political or domestic or legal. This is de Gaulle's France (anti-Gaullist strike notices on every wall and hoarding) in which one must not get too close to the knuckle of the mayors and the prefects and all the Parisian owners of houses in the country which are shuttered for ten months of the year behind their lime trees; all the Gaullistes who don't intend to give away a centime more of money or power or possibility than they have to.

De Gaulle is even in the catalogue. Every section has its text, frequently from Baudelaire. One section introduces itself with

'*DAUMIER, c'est de l'Histoire . . .*'
Ch. de Gaulle.

Well, it is lucky they never met. Think of Daumier's de Gaulle, companion to his *Gargantua*, his Louis-Philippe of 1831, which is in the exhibition.

But then the politics of 1831 are safely past.

ᴄ✿ᴗ

Perhaps I was being malicious. But it did seem to me that the middle-class art fanciers of Blois were going from lithograph to lithograph with unduly po faces, as if they were catching themselves in looking-glasses. They didn't giggle or smile. One of them was in pink; fair hair spiralling up like a tower of Babel on top of her head. She was false-young, a Daumier elongation, with pinched, hard, narrow Daumier features. She didn't laugh.

Another, a man, a kind of middle-aging bourgeois beatnik in soft shoes, was purest Daumier, blessed with one of those faces he creates which resemble the ridgy back of an oyster shell. He didn't laugh.

What about a Daumier bust of de Gaulle? He wouldn't laugh, either, when he came face to face with it.

❧

My dislike of Blois. Traffic coming across the Loire. Traffic at right angles coming from Paris and Orléans. Navigating the traffic on hot afternoons in July. Boredom in room after room of the *château* of Louis XII and François Ier. The dirty state of the books (and their dullness) in the one bookshop, which I can never find. In Blois one might be expected to think of young Wordsworth making love there to Annette Vallon. It is something I never remember until afterwards. Blois is all traffic, and the clattery porcupine of King Louis on the *château* walls, and Denis Papin with his pressure cooker, both in bronze at the top of the steps (and even that he invented in London, cooking pigeons in it for Pepys and Evelyn and other wise men of the Royal Society).

I only forget the porcupine quills of Blois when I reach the terrace of the *château*, past the elegant fountain (dry, cracked, repaired, filled with ivy and ice-cream papers), past the horse chestnuts in flower, white and *pâtissier's* pink, when I look out on to the roofs, the Balzacian attics, the washing, the open-work towers of St-Nicolas, and as much as can be seen of the Loire.

Greed: you used to be able to walk in through the main gateway, across the courtyard, past the great spiral staircase,

under the chestnuts, to this *terrasse du Foix* – for nothing.
Now you are diverted through a wicket, for cash.

✧

Specialities of Blois, according to the guidebook: *objets
reproduisants les motifs d'ornementation du château.*

✧

The miraculously black-hatted pomp of Chambord isn't so far
away on the other bank: of which *château* Arthur Young,
improver and eulogist of turnips, wrote: 'I could not help
thinking, that if the king of France ever formed the idea of
establishing one compleat and perfect farm under the turnip
culture of England, here is the place for it. Let him assign the
chateau for the residence of the director and all his attendants;
and the barracks, which are now applied to no use whatever,
for stalls for cattle. . . . What comparison between the utility
of such an establishment, and that of a much greater expence
applied here at present for supporting a wretched haras [stud],
which has not a tendancy but to mischief!'
    Arthur Young came here in September 1787. He admired
Chambord; and was moved to his opinion of Chambord as
headquarters of a turnip project only by what he saw from the
roof – a flat uninteresting prospect of a park, great tracts of
which were, as they still are, 'waste or under heath, etc. or at
least a very imperfect cultivation'.

✧

How do I explain the difference between Blois and Tours on
the same river? Tours does leave a sense of pleasure behind
not entirely accounted for by any detail of itself or its houses
or its enormous history. I am partial to hairy wild boar hanging
there in the market. Also to the gardens there outside the art
gallery, bedded scarlet, yellow and blue. Also to the bracket
fungi on a dead tree in Mantegna's picture upstairs in the
gallery.
    My friend Ben Nicholson was at Tours in 1911, when he
was seventeen or eighteen. When he came to Trôo last summer,

more than fifty years later (in a fast car rightly called, he said,
Ben's Mercedes, not Mercedes-Benz) he wanted to see again
the islands imposed on the Loire: a double imposition, trees
imposed on the sand, the sandy islands imposed on the wide
flow: he made the Loire and its islands sound like his own
reliefs. And I remember that Landor was at Tours; as well as
Ronsard, at St-Cosme, dancing as well as dying. Three clear-
edged artists.

> Poet! I like not mealy fruit; give me
> Freshness and crispness and solidity;
> Apples are none the better overripe,
> And prime buck venison I prefer to tripe.

⌒⁊❋⁊⌒

After seeing Ben back to his hotel at Trôo one warm night I
recall walking home and hearing with extra pleasure one of the
special noises of Trôo.

If you are a way off, this noise could be described as the
slow hitting of a soft anvil. It is unfamiliar enough to English
hearing, anyway, to be worth a note. When I was first at
Trôo I used to listen to it from the cape-like end of our small
terrace. I could not make it out at all, coming up the cliff, a
faintly metallic noise, mellow, if with a suggestion of artificiality.

A clear night, with three-quarters of a moon, early summer,
and here is this soft anvilling again – which is, in fact, the
noise of natterjack toads in unhurried conversation about their
annually required sex. There are several dampish folds in the
cliff, in the gardens, more exactly, on the steep descent between the Rue Haute and the main road which runs more or
less at river level. Also several springs or at least trickles,
some of them dammed into a pool.

This is the natterjack territory.

When you hear them closer, from immediately below the
Rue Haute, the noise they make loses a bit of its anvil character,
and becomes the note of a bell, a peculiar bell, let's say, of
great sweetness, making a note which seems quite round, quite
globular, gentle, charmingly complete, one little globe of

68

music answering another. Sometimes the globe of music seems to divide into gentler globes. It is a bit like music by Satie.

ᕯᔆᕯ

How many words have Greenland Eskimos for different parts of seals, different aspects of seals, different products of the seal? More than 150, I think I have read; and I would like to see a French wine or alcohol vocabulary – no, not of the words used by wine journalists in the *Observer* or the *Sunday Times* or English gentlemen restaurant-keepers who have become knowing about wines (for which they overcharge grossly in their often uncomfortable and unworthy restaurants), but the words, local, provincial, and all, to do with vines, grapes, wine-presses, casks, caves, tools, etcetera.

One could begin with bottles – since I have spent an early summer day cleaning out bottles and bottling wine. For us in England a bottle is a bottle – a large bottle, a small bottle. For my neighbours in Trôo a bottle, according to shape or capacity, is a *champenoise*, a champagne bottle, dark green, holding eighty centilitres, much in demand because of its strength; a *bordelaise*, a Bordeaux bottle, which has more pronounced shoulders, and holds about sixty-six centilitres; a *parisienne*, a Paris bottle, same capacity, but slimmer in outline; and a *fillette* or *chopine*, a half-bottle holding a *chopine* or thirty-three centilitres. French country people maintain a stronger suspicion of all shop-keepers (they weren't so dependent on them two generations ago), and all bistro keepers, and voice their opinion of them. Talking about the *fillette* or *chopine*, Maurice observed with dislike that in the cafés the *fillette* was cut down from thirty-three to twenty-eight centilitres, of course.

By the look of them I could imagine that some of the bottles uncorked in an evening's drinking outside the caves were made in a woodland glasshouse two centuries ago. Maurice held up such a bottle, thick, sturdy, and made by hand, and remarked that it was a *bouteille vieille comme Hérode*. I acquired a hundred or more of these thick old bottles from a seldom used cave – filthy they were and crusted inside – the first time we bought a cask of red wine for bottling. How many times had they been filled and refilled?

Add to the bottle vocabulary the words for the bottle's

69

anatomy: its *cul*, its re-entrant arse, its *ventre* or belly, its *goulot* or neck; and the *bague*, the ring round the *goulot*, large and wide on these old bottles, which has the double function of strengthening the cork end and preventing a newly washed or a wine-wet bottle slipping through the fingers.

And what about all the country-wide words for cask, *fût* merely one of them, words indicating the various sizes and shapes of cask?

꿈

Over ninety in the shade (does my 'ninety' mark my age? Over whatever that is in centigrade, in the shade) one sees the point of wine. Maurice was saying that in his young years, the hard years of poverty, peasant-labourers such as his father could not always afford to eat the eggs their few hens gave them or the butter from the one cow. The eggs and butter were sold, to buy the two staples of flour and a little wine.

꿈

I would like another vocabulary of terms to do with bread, which has the same Eskimo-seal importance in local life – partly from the old tradition of poverty? It would start with a full list of the different breads. Factory bread has not yet come to Trôo. People discuss this or that *boulanger*, almost as if he were a bullfighter. Maurice's wife didn't like bread made in Trôo (where one baker, on the Rue Haute, bakes in what used to be the chapel of St-Gabriel the Archangel: a mutilated or weather-worn Archangel continues to occupy a niche in the rock above his door); she swore by the *boulanger* of Ternay, the *commune* of Ronsard's Croixval; Mme Champy, the keeper of the *tabac* and general stores on the Rue Haute, likes to have her bread from Sougé, two or three miles down the river.

Of our two bakers, the excellent one down on the Rue Basse bakes and sells the following kinds, shapes and sizes:

    gros pain, large oblong loaves, which keep; and go out especially to the farms. This is the *pain de quatre livres*, 4 lbs.

    pain, the largest of the long thin loaves of white bread, *un pain d'un livre*, half a kilo.

    baguette, next size down from the *pain* (I notice that if you turn up *baguette* in the *Concise Oxford French Dictionary* you

are told that is means a dowser's wand, a ramrod, the stick of a rocket, a fillet in architecture, and a drum-stick. No mention of bread).
ficelle or *flûte*, the thinnest of the long thin loaves.

As well as these ordinary breads he makes *pain complet*, toughish but good wholemeal bread in loaves of one kilo, and various fancy breads, *pain gruau*, of fine white flour, *pain de mie*, soft light crumbly bread, *pain au lait*, *pain mousseline*, soft yellow bread baked tall like a chef's hat, much the same as his *brioches*, baked in small tins, and his *pain brioché*, baked in long tins. Also he makes *croissants* – all these breads (and more) in one small country bakery, though the fancy breads are made only for the weekend.

And rye bread, black bread, *pain de seigle*, *pain noir*, coming nowadays from Brittany, can be bought in the market at Montoire every week.

ᕙᔑᕗ

Yet it can only be within memory that the *boulanger*'s trade impinged much on the people outside the towns. As in many parts of England, one can see bread-ovens bulging out of the cottages – of the kind with an opening on one side of the hearth, which were heated with a fire of twigs (from faggots) kindled inside the oven. Then the ashes were swept out and the bread inserted, and cooked with a declining heat, like coddling eggs. Bread was baked house by house in this way – with flour milled in the *commune* – much more recently here than in most parts of England. Also every village house – so underfurnished by English rural standards – makes an antique treasure of its rectangular wooden *maie*, or lidded kneading-trough. The *maie*, often of cherry wood or walnut, quite handsomely put together – for a long life – by one of the carpenters of the *commune*, symbolizes time past for everyone, the time of grandparents, great-grandparents. Antique dealers pounce on these kneading-troughs at sales, and repair the holes, and squeeze putty into the cracks, and charge the earth for them.

One must think the *boulanger* a stage between the oven and the factory. On with the sliced loaf, in waxed paper.

ᕙᔑᕗ

I wrote this about bread and ovens and the *boulanger* when the over-heated June air was like the inside of a bread oven, and began sizzling towards a storm; between bread and storm I was reminded of the now popular tradition of affairs with the *boulanger*'s wife (the *boulanger* bakes at night, and by day he sleeps or is out with his van) by Anatole France's account of the flash Harry who had his affair with the very beautiful young wife of a country baker, only to meet a peculiar death when he was escaping from justice: he got himself into a hollow tree, and couldn't get out.

Everyone supposed that he was clean away, until the tree was split by lightning some time after, revealing his skeleton.

৵ৡৡৡ

In France nothing is wasted, in the thriftiness of a poor country. Down on the other Loire, on the high ground above another chalk cliff pierced with cave-houses, we climbed to see an extra large dolmen or passage grave. The *boulanger* had made it his bakehouse.

৵ৡৡৡ

How long is France, at least rural France, going to maintain local or individual modes of supply? If many have gone, many remain. My neighbour's father in the village of Lunay a few miles away (where he digs the graves and does other such jobs in the *commune*) killed a pig last week. The travelling *charcutier* was in attendance, and the son's share included a ham and black puddings (he gave us some of the black puddings, which were admirably spiced, and gentle in texture). The ham he is smoking, over – or up a little chimney in the rock above – a very slow sullen fire of heaped sawdust. Rolled and tied round with string and hitched to the top end of a pole which goes up at an angle and keeps it well clear of the heat of the fire, the ham will bathe in the rising smoke for a month. The chimney and the hearth and the small room or space in front were specially built – or built and hewn out of the rock – for smoking meat, perhaps a hundred or two hundred years ago.

In his kitchen he has a fridge, an electric mixer and coffee grinder, and shiny modern surfaces. Across his garden he is in the Middle Ages.

ↂ

For lunch twelve snails, black puddings, cider (which is made here, as well as wine) and a *barquette*, under the lime tree. The temperature is right, there is a little wind, the shadowed side of the tree isn't over warm. I become too sleepy to eat, see white cloud approaching over the cliff behind sprays of elm, and shall soon be fast asleep. J. remarks that this is the way babies fall asleep on breasts, warm, full of food, and content.

Hum of an insect, hum of a car, at about the same pitch. I shut my eyes, still at table, and a red colour forms and spreads: I bend my head a little and spread a hand across my forehead, thumb one side, fingers the other, and behind the eyelids or in front of the brain the red changes to a cool dark green with vague islands of darkest blue.

I hear the clack of the sifter from the Moulin Papillon – and go to sleep.

ↂ

'This book, *Journal du Voleur*, pursuit of the Impossible Nothingness' – Jean Genet. Pursuit is active. Maybe I evade Impossible Nothingness by being here, by pursuing facts, experiences; noting the colours between me and my closed eyelids; feeling the day's warmth in the morning in pyjamas, through pyjamas, as I wouldn't dare do in cold Wiltshire; putting on a comfortable shirt and trousers of selective ignorance, not knowing, not having to know too much of *here*. I fancy I experience here the briefest – certainly the briefest – moments of Possible Nothingness.

ↂ

Statement in the catalogue which has just arrived of Ben's latest exhibition, at Basel (his seventy-fifth year), that there is an 'unlimited source of life of which mankind has so far discovered only the merest fraction, we are hardly even at the beginning'. Supply of livingness, I suppose that means, but not outside 'nature'. I think one discovers a fraction of this merest fraction by changing one's whereabouts, in place and culture and sense of now and the past, changing one's angle of view for a while – Wiltshire to Trôo.

But also another of his statements: 'Both my parents were painters and I can remember my mother remarking that when she'd listened to a lot of art-talk it made her want to go and scrub the kitchen table. I think my reliefs are not unlike scrubbing the much scarred wooden kitchen table.'

✔✿✔

The convention of the rectangular canvas, which is the formalization of the visioned space around one's two eyes, upsets Ben, as a limitation. This – not their naïvety – is one reason why he has admired Sunday painters (real ones, for whom painting is days on, and far from every seventh day off, far from Sunday) who combine their marks on a piece of cardboard, a torn box lid, front and then back, if there is nothing else to hand; why he has admired the painters who used bark or body or rock.

There is a very real point here which reconciles me, almost, to canting Museums of Modern Art exalting a new painter on shoe-box lids.

✔✿✔

Ben to my daughter, aged eight. 'Why is beetroot called beetroot? Because the last words from the drowning lover before the water covered his red, red nose, were *Be true to me.*'

He used to repeat this in front of his own children. 'Oh, Ben, not that again!'

✔✿✔

More of Daumier. The great strike of the summer of 1968 against de Gaulle or the Gaullistes means that there are no Paris papers in the village, only the Blois edition of *La Nouvelle République*, which has an account of the private view of the Daumier lithographs and sculptures. *Plus qu'un banale mani-*

74

festation d'inauguration ce fut une passionante conférence-visite, attended by:

Of course various mayors and councillors.
The Bishop's Vicar-General
The Chief Engineer of Waters and Forests
The Chief Engineer of Roads and Bridges
The Police Superintendent
The Head Postmaster
The Station-Master
The President of the White Butterflies
The Director of the Agricultural Mutual Benefit Society

The worthies of Blois attending a thrilling lecture, listening to *une éblouissante causerie* – on Daumier. Then they all slipped back into the frames.

Still, I suppose Vice should pay its tributes to Virtue. Across the three columns in *La Nouvelle République* there wasn't a Daumier, but a photo of the Important Persons, three deep.

༒

I showed Maurice the catalogue of this Daumier exhibition at Blois, and, since he had met Ben Nicholson and liked him, the catalogue of Ben's exhibition. Books are something he has no occasion to use, and I doubt if he has ever been in a museum or a picture gallery. He took the point of Daumier's lithographs, laughed, shared Daumier's humanity (the friends and relations drinking after a funeral and one of them saying *Je n'ai jamais tant ri qu'à l'enterrement de la fille à Bourdin.*) Then he turned over the pages of Ben's catalogue, curious to see what made him a celebrated or rich artist. No comments. No link of recognition between himself and cut-out shapes in low tones of blue and green and grey. Indifference, but no indignation. The plates were tipped in along the top edge. This took Maurice's eye. I saw him lift up a plate to discover what was on the other side, or underneath.

༒

Worried by sand everywhere in the car after fetching a small load from the builder's merchant. Maurice comes out of the house with the bellows and as he begins to blow away the sand from each join and corner, remarks 'Jeffrie, we are given *une tête pour réfléchir.*'

✥

There are books, either more or less local or local which I know to exist, and find it impossible to buy. One is by Laumonier, Ronsard's editor – *Ronsard et sa province*, Paris, 1909. I never find it, at any price, in a *bouquiniste*'s shop. Others are histories of towns or parishes, as of Montoire or Trôo. The prize for me will be finding the only parts ever published of a *Monographie de Trôo*, by Alexandre de Salies, 1878, with drawings of exteriors and interiors of Trôo.

The possibilities are, that secondhand bookshop at Blois (in which I always hope to come across a book inscribed by Wordsworth to Annette Vallon), one or other of the two *bouquinistes* at Tours, a bookshop at Angers, or perhaps a sale. Bookshops at Nantes, or Caen, would be too far away. The scattered French *bouquinistes* confine themselves very much to their own provinces in this respect; they are little interested – knowing their customers – in books about a locality miles away in the next department.

Local books must have been printed in very small editions for a very small educated or interested number of strictly local readers.

✥

Looked inside an abandoned car – one of several arranged neatly in an orchard of dying apple trees up a hillside, along a parish road which has a faded No Entry sign at each end. Something moved along in a pool of water where the driver's feet had rested – it was brown, perhaps a beetle, but it looked as if it was moving in its own home. Also there were mosquito larvae jerking in the water. Life at any rate. And little crystalline nuggets of broken windscreen.

✥

Two of the neighbouring villages, one up the plain, on a shoulder of brown earth, above Ronsard's river the Braye, one next door along the cliff, the Loir, and the main road, are

Bonneveau and St-Quentin. After a time one does become curious about the past, if not the present, even of villages like these two, which seem to lack personality despite the hundreds of years of their existence.

Each has an undistinguished church – they cannot be apprehended and personalized on that account – and Bonneveau's church is no more plastered or elegant or tidy inside than a decaying stable. In each village there seems no history to be touched; all the more true of St-Quentin, which is less than a pause along the *route nationale*.

Then one day I heard Maurice, as he worked, singing something, in which I could hear 'St-Quentin', two lines only, again and again:

> *A St-Quentin il y a trois putains*
> *Et il y a pas moyens d'y mettre la main.*

Another time I asked him about Bonneveau, where again there are less than half a dozen houses round the church, I asked him about the small *château* (there is at least an old *château* there) which I had just been shown by the farmer who lives in it (potatoes in the tower rooms, grain, onions and all sorts in the grand saloon on the first floor. I hope, but I doubt it, that the farmer thought I was an international banker about to offer him a good price for his *château*, which I proposed to restore forthwith).

'Bonneveau?' said Maurice.

> *'Bonneveau, bonne vallée,*
> *Plus de putains que de cheminées.'*

More tarts than chimneys. Trôo on its neighbours: my village is better than your village.

Bonneveau – not on account of its girls – does scrape into guidebooks. They say the kind of vaguely grand things about it which the French seem to like and which you cannot very well prove or disprove – that a noble Gallo-Roman, Gaianus, built *un magnifique palais* there, which was destroyed by the Franks; that a great battle took place at Bonneveau, between Frank and Gaul; that Childebert, son of Clovis, built a castle there, where he minted his coins in the sixth century.

⋯⋯

I used to look in Bonneveau's stable-like church at a gilded baroque saint who was slowly being worm-eaten below the knees. He was upright the first year, had toppled to his side the second year, and had gone the third year.

Very well. He wasn't art, he was a cult object.

༩༩

Coming down a remote valley in Italy, where friars remain two a penny, I was once flagged for a lift by a Franciscan. He climbed in, he took everything as his due, it was very hot, and he rolled up the window (without asking), and he smelt. God how he smelt, like cheese. I had twenty-five miles of this spiritual bully. In the Loir valley I know of a *curé* who walks into the hardly well-to-do homes of his parishioners, when the family are about to eat, and says that he would like to eat with them. They are polite, they do not refuse, and somebody in the family goes without.

I am God's particular servant, serving you: feed this sheep. But it is bullying, and it is resented.

༩༩

Swift: 'I never saw, heard, nor read, that the clergy were beloved in any nation where Christianity was the religion of the country. Nothing can render them popular but some degree of persecution.' Accurate; though he could have added that it is often the fault of the clerics.

༩༩

A friend who has a passion for words and names and peculiarities of language – and puns – used to make much of the existence of the French delicacy called *pet-de-nonne*, Nun's Fart. I thought he had made it up. I should have known better. *Pets-de-nonne*, I read in a book of *pâtisserie familiale*, 'little rounded fritters of choux paste, walnut-sized pieces of which are dropped into hot oil'. Each swells into – exactly – a light puff, golden brown. 'Drain and sprinkle with icing sugar.' There you are, the delicate fart of a nun made manifest. Levity and delicacy.

༩༩

P. H. Reaney's book on the origin of English surnames has a
medieval note about Rolland le Pettour or Roland le Fartere
who held land in Hemmingstone in Suffolk 'by serjeanty of
appearing before the King every year on Christmas Day to do
a jump, a whistle and a fart' (*unum saltum et unum siffletum et
unum bumbulum*). I mentioned this – it is really hard to resist
unum bumbulum – in reviewing Reaney's book for an English
magazine, and it was politely removed from the proof.

❧

Tome VIII of *Contributions au Folklore de la Beauce*, Vol. 3,
Dictons, Propos et Rubriques, Paris, 1966, devotes a brief section
to *Le Pet . . . et Ses Suites* (referring, as one would expect, to
that Beauceron peasant nicknamed Jésus-Christ who farts with
such grandeur in Zola's novel *La Terre*). On the Beauce they
say to someone up on a roof, up a tree, on a rick, or up a
ladder, 'You'll hear the apostles farting up there'; after which
M. Marcel-Robbillard, author of this volume, mentions that
round Chartres they repeat a conversation between the long
figures of St Peter, St Andrew, St Thomas, St Philip and St
Matthew in the south doorway of the cathedral:

St Peter: Nasty smell about.
St Andrew: Someone's farted.
St Thomas: It's not me.
St Philip: It's him.
St Matthew: It just escaped (or 'I didn't do it on purpose').

The peasants and the ribald against the *curé* again? Like
German schoolchildren against Schiller and Goethe in a
rhyme about Schiller farting a delicate trill and Goethe farting
like a flute. The rhymes are *Schiller-Triller, Goethe-Flöter*.
I mentioned the *pets-de-nonne* to Maurice: but then words
are symbols – the *pet* had become lost, for him, in the *pâtisserie*.

❧

A pleasant noise in this old-fashioned and I think I must say
still backward France: the clip-clop of hooves drawing a trap,
which comes up at this moment from the other side of the

river. I prefer horse-droppings on the road to smears of oil on parking places; a preference – they look nicer – not a sentiment.

೮ﯝೲ

Backwardness and emptiness: aren't these the classic holiday attractions for the holiday-makers of the English professional or moneyed classes? For the educated? I suppose so – spreading from Tennyson's Merlin-haunted Tintagel in the 1850s to the anthropologist's village under the Himalayas in the 1960s.

೮ﯝೲ

A journey to Candes, then Angers. Realized with some regret that so much of our small Loir is fenced off, or inaccessible beyond deep meadows, whereas the grand Loire is open again and again down to its beaches of sand or shingle. Fences cannot be pushed up to the edge of a river which floods on such a scale.

Lunch on a grass bank, a flood bank covered in winter. Plovers, sandpipers, yellow wagtails about. The grass bending and reflecting. Wild roses, cotton from poplars. Sallows, pines. Olive colour of the sallows, great pine cones polished like new furniture, dropping dark-winged seeds. Wind and blue river, hundreds of spread shells of fresh-water mussels.

No pearls, no pearls, in any of them.

೮ﯝೲ

Light – here at Trôo I should call it a medium light, between the haziness of Normandy or England and the hardly obstructed light of the Mediterranean or North Africa. There is a gable on Trôo church above the south chapel, one slope of this gable begins with a small seated lion, grey, with yellow lichen on his head, flanks and tail. This morning when I came up from the cave-houses I could see, from about thirty feet below, each parallel furrow carved to indicate his mane.

೮ﯝೲ

People talk of the quality of light in France – and in East Anglia – as conducive to painting, or rather they talk negatively and declare that the haziness of light in most of England (where you can't be more than fifty miles from the sea) negates painting. I am sceptical. The quality of light isn't much better in Normandy, and how many French painters were Norman or painted in Norman forests, and not only along the Normandy coast? The way painting has gone in my lifetime does suggest (but correctly, altogether?) that a painter could make good pictures if he grew up, and continued to live, in a room without shutters or skylight, – or light at all, except the kind you switch on. (In 'tactile' days didn't Collingwood the Oxford philosopher and aesthetician talk of painting as an activity more or less of the blind? – which actually was a bit asinine, a bit beyond claims which do have some validity.)

Au fond I suppose the factors which maintain paintings in one country rather than another are history, tradition, persistence of a self-renewing changing standard, combined with the luck of genetics – allowing, let's say, the births, in the same country, within two hundred years, of a Hubert Robert, a Corot, a Monet, a Bonnard.

ᘒᘍᘒ

Each landscape painter tells us about aspects of landscape which *exist*: he favours and celebrates them and manipulates them especially. I stood dressing in the cave passage of our house this morning and found my eyes caught, while taking in the grey-greenness of the Loir prospect below our terrace, by a single tree in mid-vision, out in a field, illuminated by the eight o'clock sun.

Other trees formed a right angle of black shadow beyond and to each side of this single tree; it seemed – well, not that I could see round this isolated tree, this small green-grey *isola bella*, but that space, air, light, continued on the other side of it: the tree – I suppose it was a mile away – was thick, solid, three-dimensional, yet with a sharp outline.

It is that much drier here than in England: air can be *seen through* more easily. (Face-flannels dry in it more quickly, too.) So solidities are more solid, outlines sharper, colours more colourful, low tints more alive and cherishing, all of which must at any rate encourage painting.

All the same, with distracting halation cut off from my

eyes by the cave arch, I was seeing Corot-France in that tree and that deep perspective, in Corot-colour (that green-grey, or blue-grey, or wheat-colour), in Corot-touchability. True. But then the other Frances are also true, Bonnard-France, Sisley-France, Pissarro-France, Cézanne-France. And whatever one may argue about the innerness of painting now externalized, this revelation of the various visual qualities of our world is a lasting value in art. Also it is a gift of mastery alone, of an especial grace; ameliorating, comforting.

Here it is Ronsard-France, in this Loir valley downwards from Vendôme, landscape or world in an early phase, in spite of nymphs, Pan and the Muses. Every landscape quality Ronsard felt adds up, in his Loir poems, to their peculiar happiness of effect. Sixteenth-century consciousness lacked certain recognitions. These followed, these in our turn we begin to find old hat. But true recognitions remain true.

The happiness, the extreme happiness of local apprehension, i.e. of experience for which there is no substitute, in Ronsard's various poems of the Loir – in the *Ode on Choosing his Sepulchre*, in the poem against the woodmen felling Gâtine, in the sounds and rhythms used by him to think of local visitations from Apollo and Dionysos and local frequentation by the Nine:

O happy land,
   The Muses' home is here
Bright with the beauty
   Of the sky and year.

On you with hand unsparing
   From their full store
Happiness and Plenty
   All their favours pour.

The two slopes which immure you
   Are strong and do not fail
To protect you always
   From the grumbling gale.

Mother of demigods,
  On one the blest Gâtine
Raises to the sky
  Her painted head of green,

And on the other flourishes
Fruitful vine on vine
Whose liquor is a match
  For the sweet Anjou wine.

The tardy Loir conducts
  Her most meandering flow
Of waters through your meadows
  Bright as they are slow,

Making with the humour
  Distilled from its fat mud
All the land it travels through
  Very rich and good . . .

I have cheated a little in one stanza, Ronsard with decent truth
having said that the Loir wines from this neighbourhood need
scarcely envy the wines of Anjou. Correct.

And on the other flourishes
Fruitful vine on vine
Whose liquor almost matches
  The sweet Anjou wine.

⤜⁕⤛

A mark of particular felicity – the kind of Loir detail not in
Ronsard of course, and impossible – overtly – on canvas: I had
just finished writing that last note when the sound of golden
orioles came up from the poplars by the river – second hearing
this summer. Since one seldom sees the bright yellow of the
orioles, the round or bubbling happiness of the noise they
make, the disembodied *loriot, loriot, oriole, oriole*, can be taken
as the special sound of a river landscape. Nightingales I know
too much about, and disregard them at night: the proper
sounds here are by day the orioles, which arrive just before the

cherries ripen, and by night the little bells or bubbles of music from the natterjacks.

ぐ我ン

An analogy for Ronsard and the Loir, and La Possonnière: William Morris and the Thames and Kelmscott Manor, except that Morris was not so firm a poet. I think I now detect in that last of the stanzas I translated from *Louanges de Vendômois*, in my version I mean, a trace of Morris's song in *The Hollow Land*:

> Christ keep the Hollow Land
>   Through the sweet spring-tide
> When the apple-blossoms bless
>   The lowly bent hill side.
>
> Christ keep the Hollow Land
>   All the summer-tide.
> Still we cannot understand
>   Where the waters glide.
>
> Only dimly seeing them
>   Coldly slipping through
> Many green-lipp'd cavern mouths,
>   Where the hills are blue.

Curious how some poems, some cadences, edge into one's self without being invited, then stay there so satisfyingly.

ぐ我ン

The contrary thing: even in this happy land the poor have been murdered, and brutes have tortured other brutes. Witness the castles, the ruined *châteaux forts* along the river, the Frenchmen's Lavardin bristling on the other side of the river against the motte of Trôo and the more or less hidden vestiges of the enceinte wall of Richard Coeur-de-Lion's castle. In a book of French songs I bought in a sale at a doctor's house out on the Beauce (I need to write something about the Beauce, which is so much another world) I found this, which I did not know:

> *Gentil duc de Lorraine, prince de grand renom*
> *Tu as la renommée jusquès delà les monts,*

84

Et toi et tes gens d'armes et tous tes compagnons,
Du premier coup qu'il frappe abatit les donjons;
Tirez, tirez, bombardes, serpentines, canons.
'Nous sommes gentilshommes: prenez-nous à rançon.'
'Vous mentez par la gorge, vous n'êtes que larrons,
Et violeurs de femmes, et brûleurs de maisons:
Vous en aurez la corde par-dessus le menton,
Et entendrez matines au chant des oisillons,
Et entendrez la messe que les corbeaux diront.'

I doubt if you could distinguish gentle from brutes in castle warfare (or any warfare? of any age?). All depends on who did the talking – or the taking – and either way you were liable to feel, as long as feeling lasted, that rope under your chin as you dangled over the captured battlements and heard the mass of the crows.

Who was brute, who was gentle in Mercadier's warfare, or in Henry V's siege of Rouen in 1417? 'The English began hanging their prisoners where the townspeople could see them; the French retaliated by drowning theirs in sacks in the Seine.'

Massacre of captured garrisons was common, or if the knights were spared, massacre of everyone else.

Then at the end of the fifteenth century down go the *châteaux forts* to the new bombards and serpentines and cannon. And the country houses begin, and Loys Ronsard, father of our Ronsard, whose legless effigy collects dirt in Couture church, has those words *Voluptati et Gratiis* cut into the pallid stone of La Possonnière: To Pleasure and the young goddesses of spring, roses, dancing, and grace of body and spirit. And Ronsard the son can have the vision of the valley of happiness – and can see the Muses, friends of the Graces, dancing here to the harmony of his own poems.

৵৵৵

The contrary thing: even in this happy land the poor have died around the roads and villages from famine. In 1662, after a bad harvest the summer before, they weakened through the autumn and winter, they began to die in the spring. They dragged themselves from the villages into Montoire, from

Trôo, Les Hayes, Fontaine, Les Hermites, Lavardin, Poncé, Prunay, hoping for something to eat in the town. They died on the streets, old women, old men, children, widows, they crept into barns and stables and were found dead in the morning, they died near the public bake-house.

Du 23 juin. Un pauvre homme dit Grosmoulu, de Trôo, et un pauvre garçon de Prunay.

Du 24 juin. Deux enfants d'Aveline, du Tertre.

Du 30 juin. La fille Martin, des Hermites, morte en la grange de M. Villebazin.

Dying of starvation in the spring and the best summer month. But famine is then at its worst: nothing has yet grown, everything is used up. It must have been the paradox of famine in Europe: dying when everything else begins a new life.

ᚳᚱᚨᚠᚾᚩ

And I should remember the church, the *butte*, the burnings, the hangings and the wars of Protestant versus Catholic here on Ronsard's own doorstep, bloody and nasty, when the Muses were at last condescending to the meadows of the Loir. The wheel of all this country revolves round the strong, shadowed twelfth-century tower of Trôo church. You look up, you see the tower on the edge of the cliff and alongside it the cut off cone of the *butte*, the motte of the original castle. Both are dark against the sky, and it is on the *butte* that men were burned and hanged.

Michel Garrault, a canon of this collegial church of Trôo in Ronsard's time, left a chronicle of his years on the hill top. Two thieves robbed the church in 1559. One of them was broken on the wheel at Montoire. 'His companion called Julien Hazon was hanged on top of the great motte of Trôo.' He must have been visible, like a drawing by Victor Hugo, from up and down and across the valley. Eleven years before, the canon had seen a heretic burnt on the *butte*, the smoke curling into a January sky. Another heretic, a woolcomber, had been hanged on the *butte* a few months later for saying that the Pope was Antichrist. Protestants.

But then the Protestants plundered Trôo church and were in

86

power for more than a dozen years. Perhaps they burned Catholics on the motte?

❧

Episcopal scarlet outside the grey church for a confirmation last Sunday – a peony grandeur. I think there are still churchy people at Trôo who would not mind an *auto-da-fé* on the motte and a hanging or two. There are churchy people who would hang or burn Maurice. Or they could have a grand burning of members (last trace of the Revolution) of *La Société des Rationalistes et des Libres Penseurs du Val du Loir*. I was once taken to see the president of this society, and drank cider with him in the bare living-room of his isolated farmhouse.

❧

I should have said that the heretic on the motte was burnt *à petit feu*, slowly grilled, so that he could savour his own death.

When I was up on the motte yesterday, on a June evening after rain, which brought out the scent of the acacia flowers, it struck me that the burners and the about to be burned must have felt the overpowering presence of the church alongside, it is so near, so bulky. Were you burned, or hanged, back to the church and the cross and the weathercock and salvation, or facing them?

O crux ave spes unica.

I must ask the *curé* who is brisk and takes photographs, and orders one into photographical positions or compositions for a *son et lumière* programme he is compiling. He might have been rather good at organizing the fires. He has brisked up the church, put an historical pamphlet on sale – no mention of burnings or hangings – and put up an account of the martyrdom of St Mammès, St Mimé, St Mamas, alongside the statue of this martyr who holds his bowels in his hand, and is venerated for upset insides.

❧

Bourdelle designed the solid war memorial, the cenotaph, between the church and the *butte*, under the horse chestnut trees. So this open space is rather grandly called the Place Bourdelle. They have put a notice up here which points downhill and says

À RUE HAUTE

DEMEURES TROGLODYTES

PAR LES ESCALIERS

At the bottom of the hill there is another notice pointing upwards and saying

TRÔO

CITÉ TROGLODYTE

A visitor who had puffed up and then down by the look of him, stopped and asked me 'Where do I find the *demeures troglodytes*?'

Well, where does he find them? They are mostly abandoned; and if they haven't fallen in and are still used as tool sheds, they are likely to be well hidden by fences, or bushes or houses built in front of them.

In the real troglodyte days Trôo-glodytes were decidedly against advertising themselves. The archeologues of Le Mans, in 1904, made Trôo the object of their yearly outing. They visited the church, then came down the *escaliers*, the steps or wooden-stepped paths. Reaching a cave-house one of them levelled his camera 'at a woman and her two indigenous urchins'. The cave woman swore at the city gent and shooed him away, leaving the archeologues to discuss a grave legal point, 'Had a photographer, on a public road, the right to photograph a citizenness of France against her will?'

⎯⚜⎯

It is said that the language authorities want to deprive Trôo of its circumflex. Hands off, I should say if I was the mayor. The circumflex may be mysterious and indefensible, but it is part of Trôo. My theory is that it dropped on to that first o from the church – it is a repetition of the black-slated circumflex which caps the tower of Trôo church. Circumflex on top, Trôo church tower comes into view in a thousand situations, like Fuji in Hokusai's woodcuts. It will suddenly appear between the uprights of a corn-cob drier, a *séchoir*, it will look

88

at you through a gap. It is a black pyramid over a hill, it grows out of the ground as you approach. It is blue from a distance, sleeping over the landscape. I shall produce one day *A Hundred Views of the Tower of Trôo Church*.

⚬⚘⚬

Once instead of that circumflex a very tall steeple rose from the tower. Magnificent it must have been on the cliff, all the more the centre of the huge world. Lightning brought it down in 1737. The churchwardens cut an inscription about this into the wall of the church.

High Summer

Two splendid moments of Bonnard-France. Last autumn, coming off the Beauce, after hunting for neolithic *polissoirs* or polishing stones, on to the main road going westwards towards Trôo, from Vendôme, driving up a short incline into an entire blaze of orange – black road and then across it, driving up to it, this blaze of sunsetting orange.

Then today, a grilling day in June. When the heat died away, and it was cool enough to walk, we explored low cornfields and lower gravel meadows along the Loir reaching the bank at last through grass, sickly wild 'asparagus', brambles, nettles and barbed wire (have shares in a French barbed wire firm – five strands always used where one will do).

On the other clearer bank ugly summer fishing-houses in constructivist shapes, on stilts of concrete.

Yes, but behind them a great band, again, of sunsetting orange above a long band of purple escarpment.

If this was Bonnard-France, it was a sight Ronsard must often have seen from Couture, a mile or two downstream.

Now in the centuries before we were fully conscious or verbally conscious of such colour blazes, such visual splendours, what did men say to each other when they occurred? I presume people noticed them, but did they notice them mutually, and what did they say? Nothing?

It is hard to think so.

༻❀༺

Anyhow, isn't our modern ability of seeing more than we need, hearing more than we need, being sensitive to more than we require, isn't it something that may interfere with the simplicity of grace, or its effectiveness? Isn't it perhaps on the way out? Or being transferred only to the utilities of science?

I think of two special visions of yellow, late June yellow, here in Loir-et-Cher: why should I record them? But here goes, as I first wrote them down:

1. 'Cow-wheat in the woods on the way to Bessé forming a substantial, total, yet very delicate floor of pale green and flecks of yellow: dominant in big patches. Never such a carpet in England?'

2. 'Beyond Montrouveau on the way to Tours, always some fields with corn marigold. This year one field in which the yolk-yellow filled a far corner, thinning out into the green corn.'

I would suppose that Ronsard or Chaucer – or even Coleridge and Wordsworth – wouldn't have recognized the separateness, the identity, either of cow-wheat or corn marigold.

What use for others can I make of them, or can any other poet or writer make of them, sensibly? None?

I suppose that *all* our sensual experience, every brilliant or intimate scrap of it, can fill out and enrich our necessarily limited particularization. How many experiences of green or yellow can coalesce into the line which says 'green' or 'yellow'?

How many poets – especially American ones – have no sensual texture?

⁓⁂⁓

The not quite detestable, or the decreasingly detestable Ronnie Appleyard, of Kingsley Amis's *I want It Now*, inhabitant of citified England, television show-man, drives through woods in the American fall, sees oak, buckeye, dogwood, maple, magnolia, a squirrel, two blue jays, a bird he can't name, and a small brown shiny snake, and thinks to himself the following thought, that there are, after all, times 'when the consensus about Nature being all balls could be too sweeping'.

But then he is on his way back to his new and newly woken up, or at last stimulated girl, who meets him in the bedroom door in her underclothes. *Sex*, nature in her pants, is tuning up the senses.

Sex does tune up the senses like that, it can wipe the wind-

94

screen, or the lens. But I don't confuse the lens and the Loir.

⋯✺⋯

After copulation poems are conceived – by male poets. How commonly is that so? It is not a fact made visible by the hoarded work sheets of those in whom the poems are conceived.

⋯✺⋯

Ronsard liked *bocage*, which could be more abundant in Loir-et-Cher. So do I – land with undercover, or scrub, and an occasional tree, in which you don't feel the tightness or the exclusiveness of property; scrub in which there are glades, and juniper bushes, and orchids. It translates, not into solemnity or calm (forest); not into serenity or content (wide meadows or corn land), but into a measure of intimacy and secrecy which are required in enormous France.

⋯✺⋯

Fords are another item of translatable environment. We reached Trôo just in time for the last fords. Each time we come back another one has been neatly piped, the gravel, the sand, the banks of watercress have gone. Till a summer ago three fords had to be crossed on the rough lane up to Maurice's vineyard, all three in a hamlet.

A road meets its opposite, its contradiction. That is a ford. Each ford is a break, or a pause.

Usually there is space by a ford. *The Stanzas of the Graves*, Welsh englynion of the ninth or tenth century, locate the graves of several of the fighting men they commemorate, by a ford: space enough at a ford to bury someone caught and killed when brown flood water slowed the flight of his party.

> Whose grave is it with head downhill
> At the Ford of the Tribute Stone?
> Rhun's grave, Alun Dyfed's son.

There could be a collection of the prose and poetry of fords, to be read by appreciators from backward counties and countries.

95

The fords here, such as are left, are small and shallow – if usually with space for a picnic. In June, in July, the stream dries up, leaving only the yellow flints.

ᘓᕯᘒ

Seeing the head, the face of a hoped for visitor appearing above the edge of our terrace, observing a slow smile before his first speech. Two pleasures of Trôo.

ᘓᕯᘒ

> *Je suis opiniastre, indiscret, fantastique,*
> *Farouche, soupçonneux, triste et melancolique,*
> *Content et non content, mal propre, et mal courtois:*
> *Au reste craignant Dieu, les princes et les lois,*
> *Né d'assez bon esprit, de nature assez bonne,*
> *Qui pour rien ne voudroit avoir faché personne:*
> *Voylà mon naturel, mon Grevin, et je croy*
> *Que tous ceux de mon art ont tels vices que moy.*

I pushed this across the table and asked J. if she agreed with Ronsard. She asked what he meant by *propre*?

Women do have a greater pleasure in baths.

The poets I most object to have a very different defect. They strut. They think of themselves as very masculine, and as commanders, or creatures of tough habit (how splendid to be tough and lyrical, to be an amateur boxing champion under the balcony of Juliet). An art official who goes round recording poets reading their own poems gave me some particulars. I think he said he had recorded as many as sixty English poets (which gave me an official ranking, No. 61): he went to festivals, and mentioned poets I had heard of – just – who drank at these junketings and at once wanted to knock someone down, preferably another poet whose poems and person they did not care for. Or they become touchy over women.

ᘓᕯᘒ

The stallionizing of Roy Campbell. The Roy one liked – but then he was young – wrote of *New Statesman* competitions and

Whoring out a withered Muse
To judge the limericks in the reviews,

and, though the paint was a little crude, of zebras and lilies. The acceptable Roy explodes, for instance in the two lines of his poem on fishing-boats at Martigues:

Around the quays, kicked off in twos,
The Four Winds dry their wooden shoes,

or in the first lines of his *Tristan da Cunha*, snoring in the foam, the wind, the spray. The unacceptable Campbell goes on and on, a Hugo devoid of Hugo's combination of force, tenderness, surprise, and intelligence; an automaton forgetting his master Baudelaire's sardonic remark that poets write long poems because they are incapable of writing short ones.

Roy took to God, rifles, Franco and he-man homo-baiting (if he considered the homos red or the reds homo); and the sap drained and dried away, the swank of the mechanical couplets increased.

༄

If anyone disapproved in public of this Campbell Mark II, characters of an opposite etiolation, academic waifs and shrinkers who would like to ride stallions in Spain or on the Camargue and can hardly ride beach donkeys, or more than campus or quad donkeys, came to his defence in pained correspondence.

༄

It was this Campbell Mark II, rejected by his old friend Wyndham Lewis because of his increasing stupidity and prance, that I knew; or was it the Mark III, inclining to St John of the Cross? At any rate, the quiet and sly and in this case the charming vicariously succumbing once more to the violent, it was the Campbell for whom Desmond MacCarthy had found a job in the Talks Department of the B.B.C. MacCarthy then asked for him on a rather window-dressing committee – a Literary Advisory Committee, which met in Broadcasting House under his gossipy chairmanship. Roy was – for the

wrong rather than the right reasons – an inept producer of
talks and a useless committee member. To the discussion he
now and again contributed a grunt, a *bêtise*, a bluster. His face
was distinctly saurian at this time, dull eyes, a mouth with lips
turned in, an expression of malignancy rather cancelled by
sloth. The committee met grandly in a controller's office,
dinner coming first. Once there was nothing to open the metal-
capped bottles of ginger ale to go with the gin. Roy seized a
bottle, wedged the cap between the drawer and the wood (very
nice senior staff's veneer) of the controller's desk, and succeeded
only in scoring the desk with a ragged scratch all the way up.

He fell out with me on account of something I had written
about the poems of his friend Edith Sitwell (she had given him
her fatal blessing) and something I had broadcast about a
review – by Desmond, whom he called his 'daddy' – of Auden's
selection from Tennyson. Desmond's had been a prejudiced
impercipience, and I had quoted (though without mentioning
him) 'You chorus of indolent reviewers'.

‿❊❀❊‿

The result was an incident which has begun to sneak, in an
entirely false form, into literary reminiscence.

On my way from Broadcasting House to have a coffee,
I encountered Roy in a ten-gallon hat stalking up the pavement.
He raised a knobkerry, and threatened to crack it down on me
(for 'insulting his daddy'). I dissuaded him, and he stalked on –
that was all – to his office; from which (or so I have been told)
he sent a telegram to Dame Sitwell boasting of a victorious
assault on her old critical assailant. 'You should have dissuaded
him with a kick in the balls,' said Anthony West, as we drank
coffee a few minutes later.

The Campbell I have described is present in his style. I
prefer the vices, and the style, of Ronsard, let us say, the con-
cern for art, not attitudes. Roy, Ted, Al, black boots.

‿❊❀❊‿

I do not despise associations: they are not exactly *what is*,
but they do put you in touch with *what was* for other people,

98

for painters and poets; and I agree with Vaughan, up to a
point:

Poets – like angels – where they once appear
Hallow the place, and each succeeding year
Add rev'rence to't, such as at length doth give
This aged faith, that there their genii live.

If Ronsard isn't to be escaped around Trôo, there is also the
naïf painter André Bauchant. His widow died this year (1968)
in Montoire, where he died himself ten years ago, and I am
told there are about a hundred pictures by him in various houses
in and around the town. Le Corbusier 'discovered' him or
his paintings, or both, in Bauchant's flower shop at Château-
Renault a few miles from Montoire. Some of his pictures are
certainly full of humpy tiresome shapes, tiresomely arranged in
drawing and colour. The flower paintings are better, as they
should be, and some of the tree paintings, since he knew
trees (he started life growing poplars in straight lines) and
flowers. I would say that once you know the countryside of
the Bas-Vendômois and Bauchant's paintings, even at their
most preposterous, you recognize each in the other. The
Quatorze Juillet picture in the Musée d'Art Moderne in Paris,
tricolours flying, people dancing, might be a painting of the
main square at Montoire; and many more pictures do have the
rather quiet tones of this river and chalk-rock scenery and of
its poplars on parade.

Which is no more than to be expected.

I mean to go and see what is visible in this sense at La
Blutière, the little farm in the valley below Château-Renault to
which Bauchant moved so that neighbours wouldn't be upset
by the screaming of his first wife, when she went off her head. I
suppose the madness and the paintings, circumstance and
refuge (let us say the sweetness of the flower paintings), are
also related.

༺༒༻

In the stationer's at Montoire I found a pamphlet on Ronsard's
forest of Gâtine or Gastines (which in his childhood stretched
most of the way from the escarpment above his father's manor-
house to Bauchant's Château-Renault). It was an account of

the bounds of the forest and why and when it was cleared – an enlarged footnote, you might say, to Ronsard's lament for the felling of the trees. Pedantic. But after reading the pamphlet I went to explore the remnants of the forest near the Ronsard home and near that Croixval where he wrote some of his best poems. The exploration wasn't worth it. I was bitten by a mosquito on the edge of the lake, there were few large trees, notices said *Chasse gardée*, and I met no satyrs, Pans or dryads.

ᕦᕤ

What if the *chasseurs* from Paris put up a dryad? Unnecessary question. They would shoot.

ᕦᕤ

Still I had visited the last considerable piece of that woodland in which Ronsard says he first heard the humming arrow of Apollo. He had known it all his life, and the wholesale clearances began only after he had come to be prior of Croixval:

> Forest, high home of woodland birds,
> the solitary stag and the light roe-deer will no more
> graze in your shadows; and your green mane
> will scatter light of the summer sun no more
> and the amorous shepherd no more lean
> against a tree and blow into his four-holed flageolet,
> his sheepdog at his feet, his crook beside him,
> and tell of the ardours of his fair Janette.
> All will be mute, Echo will lose her voice:
> You will be fields, and where your trees
> stand now, whose broken shade stirs slowly,
> you'll feel the share, the coulter and the plough; you'll lose
> your silence, lose your Satyrs and your Pans, the does
> will no more hide their fawns in you.

I like 'You will be fields.' Most of the old forest is fields and farms, with a scattering of forest names: Les Essarts, the Clearings, Plessis, the fenced enclosure (fenced against deer), Les Hermites, where there were medieval hermits among the trees, La Ferrière where there were forges, using forest charcoal,

Gault, which means woodland, and La Touche or Les Touches, a pre-Latin name meaning clearings again.

❧

I think the fields or farms are not very good ones. Gastines, from an Old French *gastine*, is not an uncommon name, equivalent to Landes, with the same meaning of uncultivated or uncultivable land. This forest Ronsard made known beyond its merits, was like most forests, land which in the Middle Ages at least was not likely to repay clearing and ploughing.

> Goodbye, old forest, goodbye, you sacred heads,
> revered so long with tablets and with flowers,
> who can no longer shield with your sweet cool
> greenery the thirsty traveller from the burning air.

From a distance scraps of a forest which has been cleared often seem to coalesce into a black fixed line. It is so with Gâtine, which does look like a long black forest even now, when it is seen from heights above Trôo or from the *butte*.

❧

At Lavardin, there is a Saturday and Sunday horse show, in a meadow by the Loire, on the Montoire side of the medieval bridge and in view of the tooth-stumps of Lavardin castle.

Very red coats on very fine horses on a very green meadow.

Added to the show was a small art exhibition, in a vaulted thirteenth-century chamber under the *mairie*; a chance for local piety – the only act of such piety I have encountered – towards Bauchant. An exhibition of horses. Horse lithographs by Picasso. Circus horses by Dufy, active round rumps; a watercolour by Dufy of the paddock at Epsom. I could not imagine racehorses by Bauchant; and in two of his three pictures there were cart-horses. In the third, four quite lively horses drew an *auriga*, a Roman chariot, racing along the valley of the Loir.

'Why a chariot, M. Bauchant?

'Ah you see, there were Romans at Montoire.'

❧

Le Cheval Blanc, the better of the cart-horse pictures, contained a horse and a foal, childishly drawn, as part of a tall cool landscape which wasn't at all childish. Dark greens filled most of the picture under a blue slaty sky. Ochre cliffs divided the green and blue, and the composition included a barn criss-crossed with timbers. A piece of grave imagination. The date was 1923. Was that before anyone told Bauchant he was a painter?

✺

Sat and drank beer afterwards at Montoire's new bathing-place, in a landscape which is nearly a replica of Bauchant's personal and average virtue, and the nature of the Vendômois: in the typical structure of his paintings, Bauchant's typical clouds of cottonwool, Bauchant's bottom-rounded trees and bushes, his tones of grey-green, taking a touch of blue as the day passes into evening.

✺

Discovering the classics, Ronsard made a spring near his home into a Fons Bandusiae – of the mind. I've looked for that as well, the Fontaine Bellerie of his two odes (the first of them a fairly straight adaptation of Horace).

Was I going to discover a fountain, a real bubbling spring – or a creep of water into a *lavoir*, a washing place, a washing pool dirty from detergents and farmers' shirts?

> Silvery living spring
> Whose glittering stream
> Runs tardily and gives
> New life to the dying field.

Alors Bellerie voit se pencher sur sa face ondoyante un clair visage d'enfant qui rit et s'émerveille; et, par un prodige soudain, une source de poésie qui ne tarira plus, jaillit en même temps dans l'âme vive et joyeuse, dans l'âme naïve et rêveuse du petit petit Pierre de Ronsard; which is M. l'abbé Plat, speaking for the *Société archéologique du Vendômois* at the celebrations of the fourth centenary of the birth of Ronsard in 1924.

But I knew I should find a *lavoir*. The Fontaine Bellerie is down a lane at Vauméan, about a mile from La Possonnière, under the same escarpment. A damp hole choked, yes, with willow branches and flags of yellow iris. That is the spring, the *source*, in a green dell, with a farmhouse on either side. It does not bubble, it isn't crystal, it soaks under the lane into the detergent-grey pool of a *lavoir*.

> Silvery living spring,
> Whose glittering stream
> Runs tardily and gives
> New life to the dying field,
>
> When economical summer
> Reaps the bosom of Ceres bare
> And the air groans in measure
> With the beaten corn,
>
> May all who drink of you
> Or bring their herds
> To graze your edges green
> Worship you always,
>
> May the uncovered moon
> At midnight always see
> In the deep glen nymphs dance
> And dance by your retreat . . .

⌒⋇⌒

Omitting the greyness, it wasn't too bad, it was a pretty *lavoir*. I saw it at half-past seven on a brilliant 23rd of June. A child was kneeling in the middle of the lane cutting grass for rabbits with a small sickle of the kind which looks so pre-industrial and medieval. There was enough wind to move a few poplars planted round the pool, to move the whitish top surface of a wall of barley which came up to the bank. A hound-dog rolled on the grass, natterjacks had started calling. From the pool I followed the *fuite lente et tardive* round a corner till I looked over fields divided only by differences of crop. Then came the roofs and the spire of Couture, then the grey willows of the Loir, in low but still strong sunlight.

⌒⋇⌒

Remembering the abbé and the canons and the mayors and the sub-prefects all bowing to each other at the Ronsard celebrations, I must record that this landscape from Couture upstream towards Trôo was the scene also rendered memorable for ever in the Souvenir of those fourth centenary jollities in 1924. Added to the eminent locals, the participants included a prince from Rumania, a member of the *Académie française*, a member of the *Académie des Inscriptions et Belles-Lettres*, Ronsard's editors from Paris, and a deputy representing the Minister of Education, all there 'to associate the government of the Republic with this glorification of the great French poet'. They all made speeches – which are reprinted in the souvenir – first in Vendôme, then at Couture where they came for the unveiling of a bust of Ronsard, in the courtyard of the *mairie*, then at La Possonière itself. Each discourse is linked to the next in the souvenir by a morsel of recollection and description. The deputy spoke – *'Apollon, tôt ou tard, reconnait les siens. . . . Qui pénétrera le mystère des poètes?'* – and then: 'Scarcely had the last plaudits died away in the rue St-Jacques than the rumbling of innumerable motor-cars announced the departure of the official procession for Couture. A cloud of dust now stretches down the whole valley of the Loir, along the roads bordered with hedges. *C'est la gloire de Ronsard qui passe!'*

Perhaps the editor had been cued by the last words of the deputy's speech, a quotation about Ronsard having redis-covered the spark of eternal beauty in the dust of antiquity. Very French.

Even now? Yes, even now.

ↄ✲ↄ

Question, what happens, and how soon, to all the *lavoirs* of France, open to the sky or roofed over like a small barn, in half-a-million or a million corners and glens, when the washing-machine takes over; which it is doing?

Washing-machines are on show and sale at every Wednesday market in Montoire.

And used we to have such open air washing-places in England? Till when?

ↄ✲ↄ

I see the rotting mill wheel at St-Jacques, I imagine it turning, lapping, splashing, sparkling, and think of Marc Bloch's suggestion that water-mills, my old favourites since I was a small child, multiplied in the Middle Ages only because of the decline in slavery: there were no longer hands enough to do the work for nothing, without these expensive machines which had been invented long before.

Aren't machines in the house multiplying – to some extent – *pari passu* with the decline of semi-slavery or work for low wages?

Here they are coming in just that much slower than in England. It is the old women without a machine in their houses, except perhaps an electric coffee-mill, who still take in the washing of the well-to-do or of Parisians down for the summer and for weekends. They pull the washing in a trailer – a *remorque* with bicycle wheels – down to the cold spring water of the washing place. They pull it up, these old dears, wet and heavy, to go out on the airing line.

The last generation to do without the washing-machine? And their daughters the first generation to do without the washing places, and their communal gossip?

∽◦❧◦∾

A poem of the *lavoirs*, of the washing places, beating the wet clothes on the grey oak board, with a *battoir*:

> *Pan pan, Margot au lavoir*
> *Pan pan, à coups de battoir,*
> *Va laver ton coeur*
> *Tout noir de douleur.*

Laver ton coeur – hearts will have to be slipped into the white washing-machine, along with enzyme detergent.

∽◦❧◦∾

Sociologists say – it is true evidently – that Saharan supplies of natural gas have greatly modified, greatly improved village existence in France. Cylinder gas gives light, where there is no electricity; it gives heat; it cooks. But it still has not put the woodmen of the Middle Ages out of work. The woods continue to be cut systematically, and kept in good order.

Trôo has two suppliers of gas, but corners and verges along the lanes and yards alongside houses are piled with supplementary stacks of wood which families have bought for the winter. The stacks stand against the cliff like huts or outhouses. In July the man with the circular saw arrives. His unit – saw, bench, wheels and engine in one – lumps into position. I like the noise when the saw continues to sear and tear through length after length of oak, elm, and chestnut. The noise is more than itself, it is part of the calendar of life in Trôo, it is the agreeable sound of a Labour of the Months still dividing the year; the *commune* continuing to live – to some degree – by its own territory.

The short logs fill the lane quicker than the housewife or widow can pull them away in her *remorque*. The lane is blocked. Other *remorques* and cars cannot pass. It is an inconvenience of the year which everyone accepts.

❧

But words have to be eaten. Ronsard's other spring, the one he dedicated to his – if 'his' is exactly right – Hélène de Surgères, the Hélène of *Quand vous serez bien vieille, au soir à la chandelle*, in two sonnets and a set of stanzas for three voices, exists indisputably, up the side-valley from Croixval, of which Ronsard became prior *in commendam* in 1566; and it does well up gently, strongly and cleanly – *comme un beau Cristal, toujours tranquille et nette* – into a square stone basin; it does flow away audibly, even at midsummer (even if it fills a *lavoir*, where the washer of clothing kneels under a roof of galvanized iron).

First Voice. Moon, whose dress is starry light,
    In the hot days guard this spring,
    Protect it always from the heat and frost,
    Fill it with dew, and let it mirror you.

Second Voice. After a thousand years a shepherd gossiping about
    My loves will tell the nymphs round here how once
    A man of Vendômois died for a Santongean girl,
    And that his wraithe still rambles in these woods.

Poet. Young men, sing no more. Vesper already orders us
  To fold our flocks: the wolves are now abroad.
  Tomorrow in the cool we'll come again with other
  Company and dance here on these banks once more.

  Spring, meanwhile accept this holy wine
  I throw in you from this full cup.
  Be called always Helen's spring
  And in your waters guard my faith and love.

It is edged, this spring so unusual for one of the chalky valleys
around Trôo, with the most vivid watercress (see Ronsard's
poem *La Salade*, written at Croixval); and the water, though it
bubbles up under a hill of rocky chalk, doesn't taste of iron
like other springs of the neighbourhood, and isn't hard
(*'jamais calcaire*,' said the old lady of the cottage alongside, who
explained in rather a pleased way that Hélène was the reverend
prior's mistress – which she wasn't, body to body, the so
chaste Saintongeoise, as his poems to her make clear, with so much
pain); and the identification, I repeat, really is indisputable
the moment one adds up the clues in Ronsard's verse.

He says in one of the two sonnets that you fall in love here if
several conditions are fulfilled: you must drink the water, you
must sleep in a dark cave which opens into the neighbouring
hill, and – a little more or less Christian for a change – you
must pray to St Germain, guardian of the neighbourhood.

The 'cave' is there, a square-entried, rather ominous, huge
underground quarry, above the spring, with shoulders of rock
left to hold up the roof; and St Germain is – or was – there as
well.

Before and after Ronsard, this spring was St Germain's
spring.

Sixty years ago there used to be a wooden statue of St
Germain hoisted up nearby into an unusually large hazel-nut
tree (of which the stumps remain). Mothers took bottles of
the water – better than Vichy, said the old lady, and cheaper –

and dosed their children with it when they were ill. When they recovered, they brought offerings, a child's shirt, or socks, or trousers, and hung them on St Germain's nut-tree.

ゃゕゕ

Who added the clues up and identified the spring? I am glad to say the identification was published, in 1924, in the bulletin of that estimable but not always inspired *Société archéologique du Vendômois*, by a certain Mlle Lombard. And referring to the *Bulletin de la Societé de Sciences et Arts du Saumurois*, from Saumur on the feminine and large Loire, for April 1937, I find that owing to the efforts of the courteous *sous-préfet* of the department of Loir-et-Cher, the Vendômois society was then about to be pious and buy that other spring, that sluggish and grey Fontaine Bellerie or Belle-Iris near La Possonnière, a deal which can never have been completed.

You can go by in a car, or walk past, without benefit of a sign to either spring (which, though I wouldn't say it is uncommendable, is just a little odd once more, when you think of Pierre de Ronsard's real eminence, and when you review in mind that dust-cloud of the glory of Ronsard and all those Ronsardisants associating their egos in public with the glorification of the great poet of France, and never reading him, I would suspect, in private).

ゃゕゕ

I may be credulous, but I think that when conventions were more the rule, poets – or good poets – liked to make an equation of the conventional and the actual or the experienced: they liked to have the actual, the personal, inside the conventional; which is something academics disregard.

Here at the spring let's consider first a matter of sheep and shepherd, then the question of love and Ronsard.

Sheep (I hear a common don saying Baa! But let that pass): In the first of his two sonnets about the spring and Hélène, shepherds are told to keep their curly white-wooled flocks from cropping the flowers which grow around the spring. To the satisfied-looking, rather beautiful, very talkative old dear of seventy-five who lives at the spring, I happened to remark on the size of the barn next to her cottage. She replied it was on account of sheep: there used to be many sheep in the valley, her cottage had been a shepherd's cottage, sheep had been wintered in the barn.

Then Ronsard and bodies. Certainly Ronsard was forty-two, an old forty-two, when he became prior of Croixval; he was forty-five when he met Hélène (she was twenty-five), and fifty-four when the poems about her were first published. Also his troubles included gout as well as deafness and malaria. Also Hélène de Surgères, a royal lady-in-waiting, seems to have been both difficult and silly. (Read the letter Ronsard wrote from Croixval to his friend Scevole de Sainte-Marthe, who was seeing the *Sonnets pour Hélène* and the rest of his poems through the press, in 1578, away in Paris: she talked twaddle, she knew nothing about poetry, and the order of the poems was *not* to be changed to suit her ideas.)

Ronsard may never have had much from her, he may have had nothing; but against scholars who prate too much about ideality of love in renaissance sonnet sequences I'd set Graham Greene remarking wryly, in late middle age, that there is no better aphrodisiac for attracting women – and young ones – than being famous.

This deaf middle-aged poet at any rate indulged himself in dreams of Hélène lying without clothes in his arms, in the long winter nights (in the sonnet which begins *Ces longues nuicts d'hyver*, and comes immediately before *Quand vous serez bien vieille*); an indulgence – however unhavable *she* may have been – which he can hardly have been making up from memories of his bald teddy-bear.

꒰꒱

There must have been some talk of dressing up the spring with marble. 'If she wants to' – Ronsard to Scevole de Sainte-Marthe again – 'she can have some kind of design in marble round the spring. But you know what women's resolutions are worth: they last a day, and women are so mean by nature that they won't spend half-a-crown on something beautiful.'

꒰꒱

The psychology fits, I would say. Ronsard wasn't going to spend anything either: he had done his job by the spring, and by Hélène too. He preferred its watercress.

(Brief note about that 'cave' or ancient stone-mine above Hélène's spring, where would-be lovers have to pass the night. It is full of old ploughs, old carts – and fleas. After my last visit I had four ravening fleas tramping about in my trousers, unquestionably lean for want of students of Ronsard.)

⌘

This question again of whether Ronsard bedded his women (to which the obvious answer remains, some, yes, others, no) is complicated by thinking of Ronsard as a priest.

My old lady by Hélène's spring thought of him as a priest and prior. And I wrongly talked of him a few pages ago as 'reverend'. Prior he was, in a way – at any rate, he enjoyed the revenue of priories; priest he was not. He was tonsured when he was young, and that is as far towards priesthood as he ever went.

Being tonsured – I take this on the authority of French scholars, and I hope they are not quibbling – amounted to less than a first degree; it was a preliminary to orders. If your hair was cut and your crown polished (and no doubt Ronsard quickly grew his hair again), you were still a layman. And with this preliminary behind you, there was less obstacle to your happy receipt of a benefice, and its revenues, or several benefices, and several dollops of revenue, without having to perform any clerical functions.

With Ronsard it was a worldly preparation for a younger son without an inheritance.

⌘

So I am glad to have that out of the way. Ronsard wasn't a priest (unlike his follower Robert Herrick, but then I am pretty sure that Herrick never penetrated as far as the curtains of any girl's bed), he cannot be sneered at as an amorous cleric, or a clericized lover, or a semi-clericized poet. He was as free as the rest of us to fall in love – as he did, in and out. He could have married, as he didn't (and still have enjoyed his priories *in commendam*, even if it would have meant being non-resident or keeping a Mme de Ronsard elsewhere).

He shows off about his love affairs. All right, we are the beneficiaries. He discovered, and he said, that he wrote better, with more voice and spirit and invention, when he was in love. It is a recipe which works.

I suppose his bedded girls were the ones, or some of them, in between Cassandra (that pretty object must have been physically out of reach) and the unobtainable but very desirable, if silly, Hélène –

> *. . . je pens*
> *Que pour aimer beaucoup j'ai peu de recompense.*

Hélène was the last fling out of his early old age (if I said 'middle-aged' a while back, remember he was not only deaf and subject to gout, but yellow, grey-haired, and with bad teeth, by this time).

In between, don't forget (as if one could) Genèvre, whom he first saw when he was bathing naked in the Seine and she was pirouetting on the sandy edge of the river. Genèvre and others –

> So I pursue each girl today who comes my way,
> She may be black-haired or she may be blond,
> Feeling no fixity of love inside me
> I take what girls my luck may find me.

The priestly canard circulated in his own time, and he told those who sniffed and criticized, in his nicer way, that they could drop dead. Protestants – but it wouldn't have been only Protestants? – complained of him: they asked why he wrote more about love than about Jesus; to which Ronsard replied that he was what he was, and had a clear conscience.

⤙✤⤚

To be sure Ronsard wouldn't have cared for the way literary moles have identified the actual persons who were behind Cassandra, Astrée, Marie, etcetera, or for our discovery that Hélène was a little bitch and a fool.

That letter Ronsard wrote to his friend about Hélène, and

the spring, and the order of his poems, was only found in 1923. Perhaps it shouldn't have survived.

Quand vous serez bien vieille, When you are old and grey and full of sleep, And nodding by the fire – perhaps we should have been left thinking that she was beyond doubt as admirable, and large-hearted, as she was pretty, and desirable, and unmakable.

In Yeats's version of the sonnet Hélène is changed to Maud Gonne. 'My devotion,' Yeats said of Maud Gonne, 'might as well have been offered to an image in a milliner's window or to a statue in a museum.'

⋟⋞

When a very big storm moves over the plain and threatens the corn and the vines with hail, suddenly, between claps and flashes, one hears a miniature unechoing clap, and up goes a rocket, a quickly dying line of grey wavers and climbs against the puce of the thunder-clouds.

Maurice tells me that these rockets cost thirty to forty francs each, and I cannot think that sending them up is anything but pure magic, or impure science, which is the same thing. I cannot think they do any good.

Maurice rather surprised me by not seeing that the rockets were nonsense. If I told him about the processions in which the Sainte-Larme or Sacred Tear of Vendôme (*Jesus wept* – over Lazarus, and someone was at hand to catch the Tear, which made its way after ten centuries to La Trinité at Vendôme) used to be carried round to produce rain in a drought, his revolutionary old-socialist rationalism would agree that it was nonsense. Really it would be no defence to argue that the gap between the rockets and the clouds is a trifle less wide, or less obviously wide, than the gap between the Sainte-Larme and the clouds. But rockets look like science.

⋟⋞

I would like to read the sales literature on rockets and vines. But no, I'm not grumbling again about backward or pretentious France. I like the rockets. I also like the Sainte-Larme – or the idea of the Sainte-Larme, since it didn't survive the Revolution. But if it had survived, if it were still inside its

112

phial, and if the phial were still inside its *châsse*, and if the *châsse* were still inside La Trinité, wouldn't the clerics of Vendôme be delighted? And wouldn't they still be parading this symbol of divine compassion, this worker of miracles, and object of pilgrimage?

Just the other day – a village priest in his vestments, girls in white socks, stick-leaning widows in black – we were held up for rather an enjoyable twenty minutes on a *route nationale* in Poitou while the patronal relics went by.

༩ྂ

When I have mentioned bits and pieces of saints to Catholics of some intelligence I have had a shifty answer. 'Well, yes, *we* ... but then the poor, in countries like Italy . . .' In other words they are advancing the hierarchical, ultra-right argument that the poor and ignorant are fixed that way, and always will be, and deserve to be.

༩ྂ

But sometimes mustn't relics be intellectually embarrassing? The relics of the Three Kings, whose existence is a juggle with New Testament words, in their *châsse* behind the high altar at Cologne? Relics of the eleven thousand Virgins of St Ursula?

And what about the clergy of the six or seven European churches who have, or had their cut of the Praeputium Christi, the Foreskin – standing for chastity, I would imagine?

༩ྂ

I shall call now on that Sainte-Larme of Vendôme to introduce one of the most peculiar men of our neighbourhood, the Abbé Jean-Baptiste Thiers, hammer of monks and superstition.

As a preliminary let me recount the steps by which the Tear was brought to Vendôme. According to the Benedictines of La Trinité, it was an angel who stood by when Jesus wept; as the Tear fell towards Lazarus the angel conjured a phial into being and trapped it. He gave phial and tear to Mary Magdalene, who by legend was the sister of Lazarus and Martha.

Lazarus, restored to life, and Martha and the Magdalene and St Maximin and St Cidoine and St Marcelle all travelled together to France. On her death-bed the Magdalene gave the Tear to St Maximin, who gave it to his cathedral at Aix; where it rested until Constantine the Great, collector of relics like his mother St Helena, took it to his Constantinople; where it rested until Michael the Paphlagonian, Emperor of the East, gave it to Geoffrey Martel, Count of Anjou and Vendôme, builder of the first stone fortifications of Trôo, and of the *butte* of Trôo, and ancestor of the Plantagenets; who gave it to his new abbey of La Trinité at Vendôme (which he founded in 1035); where it rested until the Revolution, when someone trod on it.

> *O Lachryma gloriosa*
> *Christi praeclarissima!*
> *Gemma coeli pretiosa*
> *Lymphaque purissima . . .*
> *Quae semper inviolata permansisti. Amen*

The Tear cured the blind as well as putting an end to droughts. The great day for its exhibition was what the monks of La Trinité called Lazarus Friday, in the fourth week of Lent. On this special day, on Trinity Sunday, and on the Sundays after Trinity, the blind and the bleary arrived to adore Madame la Sainte-Larme. (Mostly they owed their blindness to smallpox.)

Magistrates and aldermen would have a word with the monks when Madame la Sainte-Larme was required for ending a drought. 'The aldermen and justiciary of Vendôme came and asked' – on 19 June 1667, according to the chronicle of the abbey – 'that the Holy Tear should be carried in procession to bring rain. This was done with such total solemnity and altogether so joyfully that rain followed, against the expectations and opinion not only of the monks and clergy, but even of the heretics' (i.e. the Protestants), 'one of whom said loftily that if rain fell within three days, he would go to mass.

The rain did not delay, but all the same this heretic failed to keep his word.'

᪥

It was soon after that the Abbé Jean-Baptiste Thiers intervened. In 1699 and 1700 this energetic *curé* of a parish up on our plateau, on the other side of St-Calais, published two small books attacking the monks and ridiculing Madame la Sainte-Larme. It was a fake: the monks knew it was a fake. He told his parishioners that the Tear was a false relic; and that superstition was a sin: it disgusted him, on Lazarus Friday, La Trinité *en fête* and the bells ringing, to see the monks, the wealthiest people in their congregation, holding a collection plate up to the poor blind man or woman who was kissing the Tear, or the phial which contained it.

The Abbé wrote that many trustworthy people who had held the phial in their hands, had told him they could see no liquid inside; and he defied the monks to show that it contained anything like a tear, or was anything but a sham; about which their champion (the Benedictine historian Jean Mabillon), who had written a reply to his first assault, only attempted to deceive the credulous and amuse the vacuous – *amuser les idiots.*

Then, ninety-two years later, the Revolution having reached Vendôme, Madame la Sainte-Larme was removed from the abbey church, and lodged in the office of the public trustee of Vendôme, who hoped to restore it when times were more favourable. It was now, according to a local historian, that some revolutionary freethinker picked up the phial, threw it down and trod on it.

So the Tear of our Saviour was spilt and lost on an office floor.

᪥

In search of the character of the Abbé Thiers I looked him up in the *Biographie Universelle*, which declared him to have been learned, resourceful, and a collector of curious facts. Chartres was his first home and his original diocese, his parents were humble *Chartrains*, and with his *penchant irrésistible pour la*

115

polémique he began by attacking the canons and the Archdeacon of Chartres.

Against Maître Robert, the Archdeacon, he wrote a squib he called *La Sauce-Robert*, 1676. Against the canons he wrote *A Dissertation on Church Porches*, 1679, because the canons allowed two women of Chartres to sell holy items such as rosaries in the shelter of the porches of the cathedral. Against archdeacons again, and no doubt against the victim of *La Sauce-Robert*, he wrote *A Treatise on the Fleecing of Parish Priests, in which it is shown that archdeacons have no right to the goods and chattels of a deceased curé.*

The cathedral chapter obtained a warrant for the arrest of this horsefly. The constables arrived at his presbytery – he was *curé* then of Champrond-en-Gâtine, a dozen miles or so north-west of Proust's Illiers, not far from the source of the Loir – and found themselves politely received and entertained to lunch. It was a very cold winter day. Thiers had a quick look at their horses, and while they were lunching he sent his own horse to be shod with frost-nails.

Lunch over, the constables took their man and began the ride back to Chartres. They passed a frozen mere. Thiers broke away and rode out on the ice. Since their horses were shod with ordinary nails, the constables could not follow; and Thiers took himself off from the jurisdiction of the diocese of Chartres to the next door diocese of Le Mans.

There he was well received by the bishop, and given the rather more important cure of Vibraye; from which he continued to launch new bursts of polemic and unexpected knowledge against superstition and clerical misbehaviour.

⋯✳⋯

One was *A History of Perruques, in which one may discover their origin, their employment, their forms, as well as the improper misuse of perruques by the clergy.* Another was *A Treatise on Bells, and the Sanctity of the Offering of the Bread and Wine at Masses for the Dead, not to be confused with the bread and wine offered on tombs.* Also he wrote – though I think this was not published – *A Treatise against Carriages,* apparently as vehicles of sin, among them single-passenger carriages called 'Misanthropes' and carriages with wood instead of glass in the doors, by which sinners (archdeacons? canons?) were enabled to drive out unseen to their pleasures.

❧

He wrote a lucid French quite unclogged by waste products of personality.

Monsieur,
    Les maximes que vous tâchez d'inspirer aux Curez de vôtre Archidiaconé sont si fort opposées à celles que vous pratiquez, qu'il est impossible que vous fassiez aucun fruit dans vôtre Ministère à moins que vous ne changiez de conduite . . .

That is how he began *La Sauce-Robert* in his young days, against the Maître Robert whom he accused of pluralism, luxury, snootiness, vanity and vengefulness:

Comment osez-vous prescher aux Ecclesiastiques la modestie dans leurs logements et dans leurs meubles, vous qui êtes si superbement logé, et magnifiquement meublé? Vous qui avez des tapisseries de haute-luxe; des tableaux de prix, et des planchers parquetez; vous dont l'oratoire est garny de deux jolis lits de repos pour prier Dieu plus à votre aise, et orné de quantité de bijoux et de colifichets, plus convenables à des femmes du siècle qu'à un Prestre; vous qui vous poudrez sourvent les cheveux, et plus souvent à Paris qu'à Chartres, afin de sentir meilleur et de parôitre plus beau garçon.

It translates of its own accord.

He said his pronouncements were '*un peu fortes, âcres et picquants; mais c'est le propre de la Sauce-Robert*' (made with mustard and gherkins, and served – insult within insult – almost exclusively with pork) '*d'avoir ces qualitez, et la verité, selon S. Augustin, ne guérit que quand elle est amère.*'

I've now read other books by him and I discover that he combined his polemic with a kind of sweetness even – a sweetness of judging and writing in a clear way for a clear and good purpose. Nothing about him of the critical bully of the provinces of Academe, of critical masochism, no swallowing of the dust and gravel of a waste land.

❧

Salute. I have searched for you in libraries. Next year I must stop and search for you in Vibraye – for your relics.

❧

In Jean-Baptiste Thiers' writings against the Holy Tear of Vendôme I find some instruction on the Praeputium Christi. He observes that portions of it were treasured in St John Lateran in Rome, in Antwerp, at the abbey of St Médard, near Soissons (where Abelard was imprisoned), at the abbey of Coulombs, north of Chartres and the abbey of Charroux, in Vienne (which Charlemagne founded). Wallis Budge gives an extended list of preputian localities in his book on amulets and magic: he adds Paris, Bruges, Boulogne, Besançon, Nancy, Metz, Le Puy, Conques, Hildesheim, and Calcutta. But he doesn't talk about the theological difficulties. Thiers says that the claim to have the foreskin of Christ is ridiculous and that the Benedictines anyway do not attend to learned Catholics on the matter: there was a Circumcision, yes; but the Jesuit philosopher Suarez, and long before him the compiler of *The Golden Legend*, positively stated that Christ rose from the dead perfect, and with foreskin intact.

❧

Apart from University libraries filled with the scribbling paper of English poets, the newest chapel I know of author relics is in Blackwell's bookshop at Oxford – a corner on the way to histology, theology, and oriental books, occupied by the desk John Masefield used in his house on Boar's Hill. Various Masefield items inhabit the desk, a small grey pig, an owl – Blinky the Owl from his book *The Midnight Folk*. But not his bones.

How fortunate if I had the skull of St Thomas Eliot to dispose of – like the despot of the Morea, according to Gibbon, escaping after the fall of Constantinople with the head of St Andrew!

'On the conquest of the Morea the despot escaped to Corfu, and from thence to Italy, with some naked adherents: his name, his sufferings, and the head of the apostle St Andrew entitled him to the hospitality of the Vatican.'

Scene: The customs shed, New York
Customs Officer. Have you anything to declare?
Myself. Nothing.
Customs Officer. What have you got in that bag?

Myself, opening the velvet bag. A skull.

Customs Officer. Whose skull's that? Yorick's?

Myself. It is not, it is the skull of St Thomas Stearns Eliot, re-furbished by St Ezra Loomis Pound.

Customs Officer. Where are you taking it?

Myself. To the Lockwood Memorial Library, Buffalo, for dollars.

ᭇᩳᩁᩁᩂ

Where is Claudel? I wait for miracles at Claudel's tomb, for Claudel's canonization.

ᭇᩳᩁᩁᩂ

La Trinité at Vendôme began in fact with shooting stars, and not with a tear in a phial. A good story. Geoffroy Martel was in his castle on the high ground across the Loir – or rather he was out on the terrace at night, when he saw three stars, a trinity of stars, falling out of the sky. An injunction evidently. The stars seemed to come down in a field across the river, where a spring bubbled up.

So there he built La Trinité.

ᭇᩳᩁᩁᩂ

Am I right that the upward current of air along the cliff saves us from the cumulus clouds and lightning? The fateful point of storms in the summer does seem to move along the plain on the far side of the river or along the plateau above and behind.

But we cowered last night under the ceiling tiles and slates. The flashes, then one violet flash in particular, seemed to be just outside the window.

I thought, well, that discharge should have hit somewhere on the brow of the cliff, or higher up. I thought perhaps it had hit the spire of Trôo church again after 240 years.

This morning there was no spire – on Montoire church, three miles away in the flat of the valley; or rather there was only the burnt and sagging skeleton of a spire and a scatter of black slates on the pavement. But the noise of the Montoire flash would have taken fifteen seconds to reach us – five seconds a mile. So one grand flash and several others must have earthed themselves pretty close.

Rain hammers down on the cliff, and an hour afterwards the surface is dry. A car can travel on the lanes.

❧

We had an undergraduate from the Sorbonne here, just after the storm, a medical student. He was like Maurice, he was quite convinced that the rockets stopped the hail, or transformed the hail, or diverted the hail, above vineyards.

❧

Trôo is sited admirably to get the best from the world. North winds, west winds, and in most parts of the village south-west winds (all winds not very strong as a rule) hardly touch the houses set back against the cliff; and when everyone lived under-ground, the shelter must have been absolute. In the summer, the houses along the Rue Haute, the old road of the stone-mines, which lifted traffic through the village and along the valley above the level of the floods, are often too hot, and the street is then a scrabble of heat and dust. The heat can be hard to endure. Again life would have been cool in the old subterranean days, before the four-square houses began to be built.

I went into the market at Montoire one windy afternoon (exceptional, a summer day with quite a high wind). The gusts were so strong that customers had to hold on to the awning along the fish stall, though it was weighted with a massive stone at each end. Back in Trôo a few minutes later, I was in quiet-ness, out of the wind. The poplars across the river were bending and tossing.

❧

Who said that strong winds are the breath of the Devil? Trôo's perfection is not so much days without wind as days like today of slight intermittent breeze, warm even in the shade, warm all round on either side of a few clouds. I walk out, pyjamas on, into the day. It is already caressing. I feel the day on my bare stomach. It won't burn. All day we shall enjoy nothingness of a high order. The breeze will go on just swinging the pea leaves of the acacia, just swaying the white flowers.

Curiously – since one doesn't associate wind and stained glass – it was at Chartres yesterday that I first realized the force of the famous winds off the Beauce, which would set the mill sails racing and sometimes tear a mill off its main-post. Often there isn't enough wind on the Beauce to make the corn breathe and bend, but yesterday a hot Beauceron wind, a hot gale, pushed on the cathedral, on the carved figures, and made it difficult to open the doors.

The great figures show how well the stone was chosen. In the paper there was a picture of workmen carefully lowering the long Angel of the Sun-Dial from the south tower. The angel has been weakened by eight centuries of exposure to rain and frost and wind off the Beauce, and is going to join already de-mounted carvings of the Queen of Sheba and a King of Judah in the crypt.

But the angel was no more than weakened and pitted. His features and his surface of feathers were plain enough.

⋘※⋙

Occasionally for a day, two days, at mid-summer the wind sets south-west and brings low cloud from the Atlantic. It rains, or else the humidity increases unbearably until the problems of life press at the back of the eyes. This is alien to Trôo, which is in one of the dryer areas of France; and when a proper day, an ordinary day, returns, beginning with a few clouds which are white, and which then diminish, and seem motionless, and finally disappear before mid-day, and when everything across the river plain reassumes its exact outline and its palpability, and its shadows, then Trôo is Oblomovka – in spite of a work-ing week of six days. The illusion is inescapable; in their houses one can imagine the people of Trôo, like Oblomov's people, kneeling down at night and saying 'Thank you, God, that nothing happened today; and please let nothing happen to-morrow.'

⋘※⋙

I have just read it again, that chapter in *Oblomov* called 'Oblo-mov's Dream', and it really is Trôo down to a stir of the wil-lows along the river, down to a warm whiff of honeysuckle from the arbour of the café along the Rue Haute (the café be-longs to a well-to-do carpenter of great skill. He can turn out an oak table, or a window frame, firm and exact to a millimetre. In the arbour of his café the benches and the shabby tables wobble as if they were going to collapse any second on to the dust floor. Should it be otherwise in Oblomovka?).

An Oxford don has just published a book interpreting Ron-sard's intermittent vision and version of the Golden Age of classical literature as a realm in his mind which he could enter for happiness and comfort, extrapolated from the forest, the valley, the Loir, the wine caves – 'a daydream, as if the way he spent his time on a fine day in the forest could be extended to an entire way of life. For a few hours one could wander or rest under the trees . . . until one had the illusion of being part of that world for ever.'

So she ended her book with a 'map of the Ronsard country'.

Doesn't everyone need his Trôo, his Oblomovka, his Gol-den Age? Isn't it just a little ridiculous and masochistic to see the committed, and the earnest readers of Orwell, rooting up their guilt and bulldozing and flattening their Oblomovkas (and of course leaving the dead tree stumps all over the place in a dry disgusting tangle)?

Actually for some people here, this lazy peace is not altogether an illusion. Monsieur Henri and his wife sit at their front door in the evening, on the hard Rue Haute, as if on a balustraded cliff. They sit in a cool warmth, since the sun drops behind the cliff in the late afternoon; they see the river underneath them, not the ochre bluff above them and behind them.

Monsieur Henri is a very big man, who hasn't shrunk, though he has just celebrated his eightieth birthday. 'I retired twenty-seven years ago,' he said, giving J. a four-leafed clover he had found in his garden on the other side of the Loir. He was a petty-officer in the submarine service. Since retiring he has had twenty-seven years of pension, health, fishing, banter, good humour, and companionship.

His sister once showed me a brown photograph of Henri and Marie on their wedding-day She had her arm in his, a small woman against his height: he was bending slightly towards her, in naval uniform, lovingly, a little condescendingly, like Sisley bending towards his wife, in the portrait of the two of them by Renoir.

They are as close to each other as they could be. No children, no grandchildren. My daughter used to be called in, on her morning journey to school along the Rue Haute or her return journey, for a biscuit or a sweet handed to her by this small, now goitred old lady, who has tender eyes and whose movements are small and rather timid. An elderly dove.

Human doves do exist.

❧

There was no need for anything; life flowed on like a quiet river, and all that remained for them was to sit on the bank watching the inevitable events that presented themselves, uncalled for, to everyone in his turn.

❧

Who said, or says that strong winds are the breath of the Devil? I remember now. It is the gypsies, French gypsies: they say that the wind is the Devil's sneezing or farting. No people could be more concerned for windless mornings, days, and evenings.

❧

Came, in searching for a very low or lowly *polissoir* on the Beauce, to a pompous, unlowly memorial, by itself in the hedgeless corn. I guessed the word *gloire* would occur in the inscription. I guessed it would mark a defeat. It did: a defeat in 1870, by the Prussians.

Here there had been a *jour de gloire*. Here – refresh yourself in the wordage of that Papuan whoop the *Marseillaise* – the impure blood of Germans had helped to fertilize France: *Marchons, marchons, qu'un sang impur abreuve nos sillons.*

123

O the defeats, glory, blood, speeches, prefects, mayors, inscriptions, the habit of having wars and then losing wars, Caesar to Hitler, and bobbing up for *la gloire* again. Mars in Gallo-Roman Gaul was worshipped 'under fifty-nine different titles' – a multiplicity of tribal gods subsumed in one imperial god of war.

✧❋✧

Gloire-victoire: there exist rhymes, accidents of language, which do positive harm. *Les enfants de la patrie* haven't noticed that in French – and in every other language – glory rhymes with defeat.

✧❋✧

Or have they, at last? In all its extensions (do you remember *C'est la gloire de Ronsard qui passe?*) *la gloire* is said to be dying off: we French disperse to our holidays, with pay, with our fishing rods, our newly acquired cornflower-blue tents, our fibre-glass boats.

But *la gloire* is certainly around still in speeches, in news-papers.

✧❋✧

We came also to Oradour early last year – by accident – on our way from Trôo to the Dordogne. Very calming on a long journey: silent ruins, streets of silent grass, notices asking for silence, the sewing-machines twisted with fire, but now red and rusty, in the houses which Germans set on fire, before burning the people.

How *normal* the nude trees are and the snowed roofs, and the snowed pollards of willow, in Bruegel's 'Massacre of the Innocents'!

Then next day in the square of our village in the Dordogne, between four rows of the *tricolore*, the children on this anniversary of Armistice Day (the French Armistice Day) carried spring flowers and sang the *Marseillaise* – battalions, victory, death, glory; and M. le Maire pinned a red Legion of Honour to the coat lapel of a one-legged ex-sergeant with grey hairs.

Let us learn to manage our rotten ribs.

✧❋✧

124

The *Éléphant Fritz* – some day, some wet sad day I shall visit
Tours and the art museum in the old palace of the bishops, and
the stuffed *Éléphant Fritz* will have gone.

He will have gone because someone will have realized that
Fritz, among his comrades, images the French kind of stuffed
pomposity.

His comrades: motionless and dry in his stable, staring out at
the cedar over the heads of the children who come to admire
him, Fritz enjoys the comradeship of a bust of Marshal Foch
(on the ground); a plaster deity back to Fritz and face to the
wall, wearing as chlamys a dirty, torn length of dust sheeting;
a plaster cast of a *poilu* of the First World War supporting a
wounded *poilu* whose arm is thick with plaster bandages; a
white goddess or nymph, arm broken off in round section at the
wrist, seated on a headless cow (or could it be Zeus as bull?);
the huge head and shoulders of the Minotaur (Picassoesque); a
brace of classical hounds; a classical he-goat; and the horizontal
extremities of an otherwise invisible hero lying under Fritz's
backside.

Muck lies everywhere, candy packets, flat spoons from ices,
bits of cloth, bits of packing-case.

The plaster tusks which protruded from Fritz (who took the
real ones? Barnum and Bailey, one each, back to America, when
the circus presented dead Fritz to the city? the Mayor? the
Bishop? the Museum Director?) have broken away, leaving
ragged jags of white. His plaster mouth, painted red for truth,
is broken and the more evidently untrue.

But oh Fritz, your solid official stance, your little false eyes,
your solitary dry teat, showing askew between the pillars of
your dry legs!

Mon général, staring at the littleness of things.

❧

I have managed at last to read *Le Loir angevin*, a poem in six
idylls by Pierre de Loyer. He lived miles away downstream, at
Huillé (or at least that is where he was born) not far from
Angers and the meeting of the Loir and the Sarthe, and he was
a man of Ronsard's class. Ronsard was his admiration, twenty-
six years older than himself; which explains this poem – not
quite as bad, or as remote, as I expected it would be – about

his own lengths of the river. He complimented elderly Ronsard, who

> *fera résonner d'une amoreuse plainte*
> *Braye, La Possonnière, et sa Gastine saincte,*

and Ronsard complimented him in rather a poor epigram which he placed at the beginning of his one book of verse (it came out in 1579) which contains these idylls about the Loir.

When he wrote *Le Loir angevin* this Pierre de Loyer, Seigneur de la Brosse, was in his twenties. He liked fishing, for upper class fishes like the trout:

> Of common fish I shall not tell
> Which in the Loir and store-ponds dwell,
> The carp, the pike, the tench and perch,
> For which the lower classes search.

(Perhaps that is a slightly unfair parody. But what did he think of Ronsard hoping to catch a large coarse bony barbel from deep water under a willow stump?) He liked shooting, and he writes a bird catalogue, part real, part conventional, about swans and flocks of cranes in the autumn, about

> Egret, plover, teal and loon,
> Heron, coot and duck and drake,
> Which in the depth of winter make
> This river their retreat.

He was loving the river of familiarity, via Ronsard – and via du Bellay, whom he imitates in his poem:

> *O mon fleuve du Loir, qu'heureuses sont tes sources,*
> *Qu'heureux tes calmes flots, et qu'heureuses tes courses*

– and when he regarded meadows, woods, copses, cornfields along the river, the thing which pleased him most was the slow passage of the Loir

> Winding here and there across
> The flat, and flowing deeply
> With a gentle noise.

The Loir loops, has islands, willows, poplars, pretty bathing-places and an impressionist look of tranquillity, as it approaches

Angers, from Durtal, then past Pierre de Loyer's Huillé, then round two great curves of an S to Seiches.

But this Loir of Anjou lacks the Ronsardian cliffs and caves.

の菜の

The past lying about in the present like old bits of dry straw. In the hot sunlight in Montoire I stand to read auction sale notices on the hoarding, printed on scarlet, yellow and green posters. I notice that a farmstead and fields are being sold by the authorities of the Hospital, that the barn among the buildings is classified (so hands off, whoever buys) as an historic monument.

La Madeleine, the farmstead is called; and there at the farm was the old, old Montoirean hospital of the Middle Ages, the old *maladrerie*, the Lazarus house of the town, the hospital for the diseased poor a kilometre and a half outside the old Montoire and the enceinte of its castle. I have often noticed the chapel-barn, it is Romanesque, it has a cracked apsidal end, and a corbel-table of weathered heads, it is stuffed, one can see through double doors, with old farm rubbish.

When was the lazar-house translated into the urban hospital and humanely moved right into the town, round the corner from the hoarding?

The brief answer is that at the very end of the seventeenth century several old *maladreries* of the neighbourhood were combined in the one *hôtel-Dieu* of Montoire. They included La Madeleine, and the *hôtel-Dieu* or *maladrerie* of Trôo, which was dedicated, not to the Magdalene, but to St Catherine. In the same way that *maladrerie* of Trôo was placed outside the line of the old town defences. It is there still, a large roofless set of walls, again Romanesque of the twelfth century, a dull grey ruin disinfected of ancient diseases, and of identity.

の菜の

I drove home past La Madeleine. A lime-tree is still in flower between the barn and the farmer's house. This reminded me of going to see Grünewald's red spotted green Christ at Colmar in the Unterlinden Museum, Christ continuing to rot inside while the limes outside above the pavement did their best to give a perfume to existence.

Grünewald's Christ was for a *maladrerie*, it was painted for an Alsatian house of the Antonites, the hospitallers of the order of St Anthony of Vienne. Inmates saw him in the chapel, outer panel of an altar-piece which opened and spread to an ultimate revelation of St Anthony's saintliness and glory; and I have always supposed that these sick were regarding a Christ crucified to death, as they might be themselves before long, by St Anthony's Fire, the disease of the saint's special care – erysipelas, the Rose, the Fire of St Anthony because it was cured by St Anthony's intercession, or so men had begun to think first of all in the eleventh century; the disease of poverty and dirt (St Anthony never washed) which attacked the old and underfed in winter (St Anthony's feast is 17 January); the disease which was common enough round Trôo – and everywhere else – in Grünewald's time. In that Virgilian hymn he wrote to St Blaise, Ronsard made the family fathers of Montrouveau beg St Blaise to guard them from St Anthony's Fire, from gangrenous erysipelas, which ate into their bodies. He called it by Virgil's name (see the *Georgics*, Book III), the *feu sacré*, the *sacer ignis*, the accursed fire.

Ronsard must have written his hymn about sixty years after Grünewald specialized in his Christs pricked by thorns, and speckled with angry pits and spots.

⎰⎱

Grünewald was moved by pity, and by mystic visions or mystical accounts of visions of the crucified Christ? Perhaps.

But wasn't he fascinated by violence and corruption to the point of indulging them? Isn't he really the nastiest of painters, not because of the violence or corruption he paints, but because of the nasty realism of his way of painting it, because of his mirror quality, even if his mirror is a distorting and twisting one like a mirror on a fair ground? Doesn't he do 'what the beast inside him wills him to do'?

I do not believe Grünewald is exalting for us, whatever may be said (by Malraux, for example, *passim*, in *Les Voix de silence*). I've been glad to drive out of Colmar; and I think I see a similar nasty realism and commonness of vision, of style, in pictures, as a consequence corrupt rather than tragic, by Francis Bacon.

CR

Yet when it is nearly dark at Montoire, that dearest and neatest of little towns, on warm October evenings, the old *maladrerie* seems to have opened its door, and sicked back some of its sad people into the streets – out shopping when they won't be too visible in the half-light.

I have been surprised by this more than once. A woman who is noseless, and has lost more than her nose; a crippled woman hunched over and given a sideways twist, who finds it difficult to get the change back into her purse; anonymous Bruegel figures shamed into hiding themselves in the half-dark because of the modern gloss – but that isn't fair, it is more than a gloss – of health and prosperity upon life, from which they are excluded. They are signed – that is the emphasis – by their poverty, their old clothes, and their disease.

But then in France there is so much façade, doctors and chemists are greedy, the health service is lopsided. Masons are busy renewing, but old Bruegel buildings sag and are crippled and are in use behind a gaudiness of plastic buckets and blue 'camping gaz' containers.

In poorer countries the diseased poor don't have to hide, they have to beg, like that vast dropsical female beggar who had her position a few years ago in the passage into the physic garden at Padua, in the shade, six feet from the full sun. If visitors to the garden did not give alms to her satisfaction, she staged a monstrous booming fart, her defiance.

CR

Bruegel – on second thoughts Bruegel vis-a-vis Bacon or Grünewald. I believe Bruegel always; and feel blessed by him, by his beggars and his demons and his *Triumph of Death*, and his snow, by what Malraux would call his accent and his oneness.

CR

A Trôo evening (29 June)
After great heat and a day of entirely empty blue sky. Searching for the
Roman road from Tours, supposed to have crossed the river at Vieux
Artins by the Roman settlement and temple, then to have bent through
half a right angle for Paris – for Lutetia. Have found no accurate
identification. So made for a point north of escarpment and of Trôo
church where a lane and the boundary of the commune coincide on the
map, this lane with a break or two continuing, though not exactly
straight, for miles over dry terrain, to N.E.

Light still brilliant at 7.30. Followed lane or track into a wood,
past field where farmer was planting mangolds, then past wheat field
('field': no, patches of open landscape). There in the wood (intimidatingly
black after the brilliance of light) a wide agger began almost at once,
raised between ditches; and continued half a mile to head of a small
valley, out in sun again just beyond the wood. The Roman road then
sank a little, became hollow, and rose, and plunged on, a green band of
tall grass through endless oats and wheat, on and on, the agger weathered,
almost flat.

Honeysuckle.

Piles of soil dug out by nesting wasps, where the agger was worn away
to a deep layer of flints: each pile of earth-grains brightest orange against
the duller earth and round the black spot of entrance to the burrow.

Blazing end to the wood tunnel, then the sunlight still hot on my
westward cheek. And shining through poppy petals.

The farmer gone. Alone in outsized world of evening sun. Inside of
the car – car key not lost – hotter than on some middays.

ᡄᡓᢁᡛᢩ

A Trôo morning.

Switching the transistor to L, for the Long Wave English news,
7.30. This is sadism on ultra-fine mornings – hearing that rain
is coming in from the (English) west or that cricket has been
washed out. It is masochism, too, hearing those wriggling
ponces of the spoken word, the disc-jockeys, smarming out
their birthday greetings, and interspersing greetings and chatter
about themselves with self-pitying songs about love. 'Long
time no see,' says the morning's ponce, or 'best of British luck';
and I walk out in pyjamas, and pee on the gravel, and count the
number of Morning Glories.

ᡄᡓᢁᡛᢩ

If I have put the plants in early enough, there will be too many to count. Not surprising that seeds of Morning Glory are supposed to give a hallucinatory drug. The flowers have a hallucinatory colour. I like them better than anything which grows and spreads into the sun. Morning Glory – if you are English – stands for being Elsewhere: in the Midi, in America. The blood-blue prodigality of the blossom. In Connecticut one autumn Sunday morning Anthony West drove me down a sprout land track (where you could see the stone walls of seventeenth or eighteenth century fields under a renewed army of sprouts, of saplings and small trees) to a frame farm-house occupied by a New York painter and his wife. They weren't up. We never saw them. But the white-boarded front of the house was netted, in that light of all the world's light, with Morning Glories – five hundred or more flowers for that one day.

It is a good moment when the year's Morning Glory plants begin to clasp and climb, a better moment when the buds are ready to untwist.

⟡⟡⟡

Have been looking rather more – as far as books here allowed – into Roman roads. There is nothing for France, for Gaul, like Margary's two volumes which survey the Roman roads of Britain. But then the able men who constructed the eighteenth century highways of France – on Roman principles, deliberately, owing to the happy finding and analysis of a stretch of Roman road in a garden at Rheims early in the seventeenth century – must have used the old more or less straight Roman lines wherever they could, and this would now be a snag in the way of an accurate mapping of the Roman network.

Old vestiges would have been covered very often. Here and there around Trôo, or out on the Beauce, I find isolated stretches marked, on the generally uninformative French maps, *Ancienne Voie Romane, Voie de Jules César*, etc. But the Institut Géographique National, the mapping authority, has still to be much excited by archaeology. The Institut must like its maps to be – I was going to say practical and of use to the military, but some of the 1 in 50,000 maps, which continue on sale and which were revised and printed in the late forties, are more or

131

less indecipherable, on account of bad and crowded lettering and an underlying forest of hatching.

Very old fashioned. I think they must have been intended to confuse invaders, possibly allies as well.

A good passage-grave will be marked – no, it may be marked: and recent editions were not above printing the words *Pierres Druidiques* against such neolithic tombs. The Institut still seems more interested in marking every genteel *château* (like an English eighteenth-century road map marking every country house).

So I am little farther with local Roman roads, such as that one I mentioned going from Tours via Trôo to Paris.

I tried Maurice. That extraordinary man, so hunched and knotted from hard work and early poverty, came up as usual with the unexpected. Yes, he knew the section of Roman road from the river along the north border of the *commune*, which curls up the escarpment, and round, not far from his wine cave and his vines. 'Measure Roman roads,' Maurice said, 'and you will find them seven metres wide, ditch to ditch – in the woods, where the plough hasn't eaten them'; a measurement pretty well correct for those woodland lengths of the Tours–Paris road. I should have asked Maurice how he arrived at the seven metres, if he had paced them out himself?

France has its *strata* or 'street' names, such as our Stratton, Stratford. I have looked for *strata* names round here, for an Etraye, L'Etrat, Estrée, but no luck.

Lighten our darkness we beseech thee, O realization of absurdity?

We love each other – so we unite our inescapable rucksacks of *omnia vanitas*? But the colloquialism 'So what?' (which used to be so common a few years ago) does not reckon with the assuagements of our absurdity, however brief.

I explore the Roman road to Paris. Absurdity is assuaged, absurdly.

I examine another length of the Roman road where it crosses the open plateau. It is a boundary here between parishes, it is little used. Filled with grass and defined by a straightness of shadow, and emphasized by this twisty tarred road which cuts across it, how deeply and suddenly, left and right, going on and on, and how absurdly, it expresses human intention.

But then I have been reading portions of Ionesco's journal, (including Ionesco on his childhood near Laval).

❧

Maurice likes all the world to have been *bien élevé*: everyone should treat everyone else properly, foreigners such as ourselves should be treated properly (and vice versa). But of course, it does have to be admitted that there are, without doubt, certain pigs, unfortunately.

He was upset by an experience we had a week ago on the road back to Trôo from Chartres. Petrol was low. I had forgotten to fill up, and it wasn't at all certain that we had petrol enough to take us up the cliff, or as far as the petrol pump at Trôo before it was locked up for the night. So it was necessary to go steadily and smoothly to the point, five miles ahead, from which we could free wheel, if we had to, down to the pump; and now, as we turned an abrupt corner, ahead of us was a farmer, driving his cows and two goats back to grass.

It looked as if there wasn't an opening through the barbed wire right or left for nearly a mile. We went slow, the needle wagged to E. Broad verges extended on either side, so why didn't the farmer guide his beasts off the road for a minute (which is the usual thing in France, from a combination of more courteous manners and fear of damage to cows, sheep, etc.).

The farmer didn't look round. Perhaps he was stone-deaf. He continued not to look round. After two hundred, then three hundred yards in petrol-drinking low gear, I tried a deprecative electric hoot; which had the properly electric result of spinning the farmer round, sending his arms and his stick into the air, setting his legs apart in a war-dance, and releasing an explosion of exceedingly rough words. I hooted again, loud, the farmer

133

gesticulated and jumped again, we threw words back as accurately pronounced as possible.

The farmer turned his back and trudged. So we crept another half mile. Then the two goats, and the cows, and the farmer turned into a meadow.

The petrol wasn't quite used up, and we did, after all, reach the petrol pump.

Maurice cross-examined me to fix the identity of this farmer who was not *bien élevé*, then decided that he was a well-known pig, living, fortunately, but as might be expected, outside the *commune* of Trôo. He practically apologized on behalf of the people of France.

✿

I haven't told Maurice the sequel, three afternoons ago. We went out on the same road, searching for the point where it is crossed by that Roman road from Tours to Chartres, we left the car in the blaze of the evening sunshine, and noticed a man half a mile further on – half a mile nearer our rencontre with the farmer and his cows – hoeing between rows of sweet corn.

Our farmer? But he couldn't be recognized that far off.

Taking a large-scale map, we vanished along a track at right angles, bordering a wood.

As we returned under the oaks twenty minutes later, I noticed someone step quickly into the hedge from the long grass of the track, just round a corner.

Our farmer? Don't be silly.

But it was. We marched on, mixing trepidation with dignity. We passed him, his back slyly turned to us, or half turned to us, in a field. He came out behind us, wheeling a bicycle. He followed us out to the road. I walked ahead a little (*that* wasn't very brave), I had the car key ready; and we felt safer behind window and windscreen. The farmer climbed on to his bike and cycled back to his hot field of maize.

Harmless? A pointless trepidation? 'British tourists struck down.' But weren't we two to one? I considered his side of the occasion. He had been puzzled. What has a car stopped for down there? The same car, that foreign car, same colour, same roof-rack. It is those foreigners. There is nothing out here, what are they up to?

So he cycles down; he sees a man and a woman – but an elderly man – walk off into a wood. He carries a map – just why are they walking off to the wood?

꿏

Yes. But this is the only time so far in this wide foreign countryside when an action by a man has made me uneasy or uncomfortable. We drove on, we looked for another length of the Roman road very much further on, very much elsewhere. I was uncomfortable for the rest of the day.

꿏

J. recalled my formula for the problem of man and woman together with a bull. The man doesn't turn and face the bull – he's not a matador – while the woman escapes. They both run – in opposite directions, for opposite fences, thus leaving the bull in a split state of confusion and indecision.

She suspects a flaw in this solution.

It is certain that one of the two gets away.

꿏

To reach the lane from our terrace to the Rue Basse and some of the shops I have to walk past a dell of grass sloping back and down to three wine caves of antiquity. A neighbour stacks wood on the edges of the dell, where it waits for the peripatetic log-cutter. Another neighbour cuts the grass for rabbits. The dell is comfortably shaded by trees, and in the cool, deep in a corner, I noticed an oldish man, curled up, asleep, like a cat.

This worried me a little. Children, including my child, are free of the lanes of Trôo, and pass the dell and wood stacks on their school journey. Maurice was consulted. No, the sleeping man is everybody's friend. Very intelligent, said Maurice, you can talk to him about anything. *Très bien élevé.*

In winter he holes up in a farm. In spring, summer, autumn, he is on the tramp. Very clean, said Maurice. He goes to the public baths at Montoire, he gets the nuns at Montoire to keep his clothes together and washed. Everyone likes him, you can talk to him about anything.

He follows the same itinerary each year, and in the dell he spends one or two nights every summer. Was he ever married? Yes. When did he start tramping? In middle age, some time after his wife died: he was lonely.

༺༉༻

A good expression, *les grenouilles de bénitier*, frogs of the holy water stoup, for the old women in black, who fuss round the church and the *curé* and do the flowers. I nourish perpetually a desire to own an oblong or oval *bénitier*, on a pillar, baroque, of the seventeenth century, and look hopefully, but without success, in junk yards and antique shops. For washing one's hands before lunch, under a lime tree.

༺༉༻

Statues of saints carved and coloured with an appealing naïvety (seventeenth or early eighteenth century statues) rot on their feet, or thin ankles or thin knees, in the churches round here – like that baroque saint I used to regard with so much envy in the church at Bonneveau. The worm eats through their feet and they fall; they are put up again, and the worm eats through their ankles, and so on, until they lie on their sides, gradually collapsing into worm dust.

Does the *curé* – dust to dust and ashes to ashes – give them an honourable burial or an honourable burning at last?

Down the valley, and not far from La Possonière, Ronsard's house, there used to be a very smart antique shop, for those about to furnish a restored *château*. The proprietor told me, in a tone wistful for profits, that the loft above the nave of the church at Couture was full of rotting statues and service books for plain-chant. I suppose the priest would say that sanctified objects, even if rejected, should rot in sanctified peace. It is logical. Maurice remarked that if it wasn't so (and if there weren't heavy penalties for the unauthorized sale of church property), the priests would sell the lot.

༺༉༻

This seller of antiques lived on a charming platform of gardens backing against a low length of chalk cliff, pierced with wine caves. Appropriately it was La Denisière – see Ronsard's *Hymn to Bacchus*, where he gives the wine god a new title, Bacchus of Vendômois, and says that on his wild course through the world he camped his army on the left bank of the Loir, that the fresh earth felt his tread and was suddenly made fertile, and bore vines thick with grape and foliage:

> Your own hand layered there
> A high hill now named, from your name Denys,
> La Denysière

Denys is the familiar form for Dionysos, so La Denisière does mean the place of someone named Denys, Denis, or Dionysos.

Does every Denis or Dennis realize that his name comes from Dionysos – even if by way of St Denis, the great cephalophore, the patron of France and of Paris?

I knew a Methodist and a teetotaller, very strict, very upright, who taught at the Working Mens' College. His name was Dennis. I wish I had realized its meaning: Dionysos, teetotaller, without wild girls.

> Over the light blue hills
> There came a noise of revellers.

He ought to have changed his unChristian Christian name. So should St Denis.

༺༻

As I must have said, the patron saint of the *collégiale*, the great church of Trôo, is St Martin of Tours. The church has rather an engaging statue of him on horseback, with the beggar.

Why did St Martin cut his cloak in two and give only half of it to the cold beggar, instead of giving him the whole cloak, undivided?

Ask *la grande bourgeoisie* of France, who don't intend to give away more than a quarter of the cloak if they can help it. St Martin is the commonest of all the patron saints of France.

༺༻

Maurice plunged up the lane in his blue van and took out a barbel he had caught this morning in the Loir, down at St Jacques. It weighed about two pounds.

Ronsard in his *Gayetez*:

> If you allow me to lift clear
> Upon my shaking rod
> The plump barbel
> Which swims here,
> In this deep hole below
> The willow stump, I swear
> Never again, Naiads
> Of the deep water,
> To come fishing here;
> The eternal sign of which shall be
> My coracle, my nets,
> My lines, hung up
> To you on this grey willow tree.

Where, I asked Maurice (who had used a net and not a rod), do you find barbel?

'In deep water, in under the willows.'

❧

Barbel, four grey beardlets or barbels hanging from its mouth, isn't the best fish we get from the Loir. It is all bones and tastes flat and watery. We are given carp, tench, eels – especially eels which Maurice has taught us to grill in short lengths over a cindery fire of vine twigs.

❧

The French must forgive me for a theory I have that various excellent things of French life spring from the quite uncommon ugliness of the French. In Europe I think I have been conscious of little people as ugly, or uglier, only in the Rhineland (observe opera-goers at Bonn, togged up, in the foyer during the interval). But then in the Rhineland they never seem to have noticed their ugliness, so the same consequences have not flowed.

Which consequences? That the French have developed – in Paris – style and elegance in women's clothing. They have had to, to make something of shrewish little figures. Also that the French have developed the most intriguing scents in the world, to inject allure into the unalluring. Perhaps the ugliness of French women has contributed to that pronounced *gentillesse de coeur*? And to French cooking?

'For God's sake, cook!' as a variant of the husband's despairing remark to the great soprano, 'For God's sake, sing!' – as he woke up to her in the morning?

Waiting at Chartres, on the long or rather slow train journey from Trôo to Paris, we tested, not the theory but the ugliness, by observing all the people, the women especially, who crowded up the stairs out of the subway, after the factories closed. No match for them except in the foyer of the opera house at Bonn. And I cannot allege that the valley of the Loir is inhabited exactly by nymphs and dryads of the first Ronsardian exquisiteness, as one sees them in the Wednesday market at Montoire, or at some 'do' in one of the villages, *Quand je vous vois, ma mortelle Déesse*, etc.

Compare children of Viking descent, walking to school in the morning, in the Cherbourg peninsula. Long, graceful bodies, capped with fair hair. Not the dark little Gauls who hid from Caesar in their caves.

❧

No, I am wrong about dark little Gauls. Caesar talks of small Romans, and large Gauls looking down and despising Roman stature. After all, the Franks came from eastward of the Rhine, they were Germans, and Franks and Gauls melted into each other hereabouts in the sixth century. I must put the littleness and ugliness down to the French, not the Gallic share in the mix. The German share, the dominant share.

❧

At a Sunday afternoon farm sale, in sunshine under the baked hills. Little farmers, little farmers' little wives, the broad, the square, the sparse, the wet (decidedly – there is a bar in one of the sheds), the dry, including the little farmer like a bee, whom we call on in autumn with our honey bucket. Among them, above them, above waggons, a pair of super de Gaulles, a pair of Eiffel Towers, twin brothers about six foot eight tall, known – Gaul among Frank – as *Les Deux Mètres*.

To talk to *Les Deux Mètres* other people had to stick their chins in the air, *Les Deux Mètres* lowering chin to chest.

❧

We do have one enormous farmer in Trôo, six foot two or three, middle-aged, with a hard belly sloping down and out-wards. He likes women and gives J. a long, cool stare from the high seat of his tractor. A Gaul, not a Frank. A girl from the Sorbonne was taken up to see him, in his farmhouse along the old enceinte wall of the castle, by her own large Anglo-French father. She was awestruck. '*Mais c'est un Dieu de la Terre! Et il est plus grand que toi, mon père.*'

For us he is now the *Dieu de la Terre*.

❧

I shall also call him Taurius the Gaul, for that bull belly. Every village up and down the river which isn't named after a saint is named after a Gaul – a Gaullish owner romanized, with a Latin *-us* tacked to him, or with a name borrowed from the conquerors. There was Taurius, Silvus, Navus, Lunus, Calus, Turnus, Cornelius, Artinius, owners of this ordered landscape of the river levels and the alluvium.

Cornelius out of that list owned Cornille, where Maurice has his vineyard. Does it help me to suppose that Cornelius got tipsy in the same evening sunshine with the same wine from the same slopes?

And there is Poncé, downstream, where they make studio pottery in the stables of the *château* which is perhaps the site of the domanial house, if not of Pilate, then of Pontius, gallicized, romanized, germanized, christianized, republicanized, Com-mon-marketized.

When Taurius the Gaul, Earth God, came down on his tractor pulling a barrel of herbicide to spray the shrubs over his wine cave, he stopped at the cave for a minute, then asked if he could do the spraying from our terrace, the nearest accessible point. Spraying over, he advanced on us, great sweat-dark chest, great sweat-dark belly, primitive *Bos primogenius*, with a bottle of his white wine (explaining the short visit to his cave). We sat, we drank, we regarded the Gaullish landscape.

Taurius had observed decorum: a favour had been granted, a favour had been balanced or acknowledged with a sharing of wine.

⋴⋗⋇⋖⋽

According to Rabelais it was Gargantua's mare which cleared the Beauce. She was so enraged by horseflies in a forest near Orléans, five and thirty leagues long and seventeen in breadth, that she laid about her with her tail and swished flies and trees away, reducing the forest to a plain champaign field 'which Gargantua took great pleasure to behold, and said to his company no more than this: *Je trouve beau ce* (I find this pretty); whereupon that country hath been ever since that time called Beauce.'

I am with Gargantua: I find the Beauce beautiful, or at any rate some adjective which would amount to spatially entranc-ing, or having a personality of space, texture and light. 'For a first visit to Chartres, choose some pleasant morning when the lights are soft, for one wants to be welcome, and the cathedral has moods, at times severe. At best, the Beauce is a country none too gay.' That – Henry Adams, in *Mont-Saint-Michel and Chartres* – is how most people respond; they would applaud if I admitted there's nothing at all of *beau* in Beauce (supposedly from an ancient pre-Latin word *belsa*, a plateau).

⋴⋗⋇⋖⋽

In the Bas-Vendômois, villages, intimacy, slopes, corners, paths, hedges, lanes, fruit trees overhead.

On the Beauce, villages where one looks for the signpost, where one does not stay (or stay longer than is required to find the key of the church and examine the rough country baroque of its altars); villages from which one looks out to an horizon all round.

I like the contrast, and write this after an extra sun-bath and space-bath in the centre of the Beauce. Left early to see as much

141

as possible – dolmens, *polissoirs*, etc. – in the cool. A first men-hir and dolmen, together, couldn't be reached because of wheat above waist level, could be observed only. Then we found a long grass track, smooth, going from one small grey dolmen to another. Light, wheat, brown soil, intense red patches of Napoleon clover, vermilion rather than red, oases-in-reverse of desert in endless fertility, i.e. of leached desert limestone with small pines and gorse, and shallow quarries, stones newly excavated and yellow-white in the neatest rec-tangular piles.

Wind moving the wheat. Larks. Black spires of churches, white water-towers. Blue pimpernel by the track. Not-to-be-seen quails sibilitating in the wheat. Now and again sweet corn watered from giant sprinklers. Then more grizzled boulders, scored with irregular holes, adding up to another low dolmen leaning against a tangle of sallows.

Not a few of Gargantua's mare's horseflies.

༺⳽⳼༻

Our farthest point was a dolmen in endless wheat along another desiccated track, in the *commune* of Neuvy-en-Dunois (this only fourteen or fifteen miles from Romilly-sur-Aigre, the Rogne of Zola's *La Terre*). We reached it, climbed on it, through bram-bles, felt the long *polissoir* grooves in the capstone, which were hot, looked to the black dead windmill on the horizon; and realized that in all this light, all this unclouded France, there wasn't a blade of shadow for a midday meal. Each of our shadows was only a foot away from our feet. We ate and drank excellently, if too warmly, on the side of the car away from the sun, having rigged up two umbrellas and two chairs to con-trive at least a small maximum of shadow across half the table, half of ourselves, and all of a thermos of *rosé*.

Our faces, necks, hands, arms, as ochre as the ground.

༺⳽⳼༻

Nottonville is the Beauceron village, or village neighbourhood, I should try on someone who finds the great plateau a huge nothing. It isn't quite typical. A slow stream is lost here in reeds of a valley which is only a depression. Stream led to settlement; flint and puddingstone led to industry and tombs.

This Nottonville neighbourhood has twenty-four *polissoirs* and three dolmens.

I've found one of the *polissoirs* in fierce heat, in an island of space in the corn, another under bolts of October rain when my shoes were doubled with mud. One of the *polissoirs* is the Devil's Stoup, one of the dolmens is Gargantua's Quoit (Gargantua having been about in the popular mind before Rabelais).

Nottonville has also:

Its sense of being lost, its suggestivity, its tumbled cottages, its name (which means either Nanto's villa, Nanto's farm estate, Nanto having been a Gallo-Roman proprietor; or else the farm estate of the *nantos*, or valley), two Roman roads, and a grange; (also that over-swollen monument of glory and defeat on a field where the French were drubbed by the Prussians).

I imagine it was the Benedictines of Bonneval, a few miles away on the Loir, who owned the grange. There it stands on the edge of Nottonville, alone, a tall huddle of late medieval buildings and barns, in use, surrounded with a high wall. Wall, gatehouse, decaying. A splendid knot of buildings, a granary of Beauceron wealth which should have put Nottonville into guidebooks. I might turn it, if I had millions, into a museum of the Beauce.

ᘓᔕᐽ

The open fields at the back of Trôo church having been shaved down to the stubble, our Earth God has built the last of his wheat stacks in the farmyard alongside the ruins of the Porte de Bessé. The hollow of this untidy yard is now peopled with fat tea-cosies of wheat. Each tea-cosy has been crested with flowers. To warn away lightning – perhaps that was the original purpose of the flowers, though one sees in them now a poetry of relaxation, of taking it easy after the harvest. Wouldn't the farmer say 'Well, it's what we do'; wouldn't he feel something was wrong, like an open fly-button, if the stacks hadn't been crested with flowers? Ladders lean up against the tea-cosies.

ᘓᔕᐽ

I hate the exclusive company of the old, opinionated, and without hope, or the exclusive company of the young, opinionated, and without experience; and here where grandmothers are so active with grandchildren, the spectrum usually seems well mixed into something which can be called life. Families are made a necessary strong-point against poverty. Children are used to adults, not embarrassed in their company. The evident happiness and confidence of children here are two elements of *douceur de vivre*, within a setting of whatever hardness, meanness or narrowness. French education for the very young may be rather ridiculous, but at the annual prize-giving before the long summer holidays begin, everyone gets a prize. It is a ceremony I like. After lunch today, last Sunday in June, *M. le Maire* and his councillors – at Trôo they include a blacksmith and an ambassador (the mayor is a farmer) – will once more sit around in a degree of social majesty in the half-open shed, across the gravelled courtyard, the overflowing company getting as much shade as possible from old plane trees. Each councillor will present a prize in turn.

Reasons are discovered for every prize. One child, not over bright, never a candidate for the *prix d'excellence*, will have his book this afternoon for *assiduité*, another for *bonne volonté*, another for *camaraderie*, enviable qualities all of them. Up they will go to be kissed by the councillor, to kiss him in turn. They will walk back with bright eyes, and mothers will be consoled if not satisfied.

My daughter one year – since there are councillors and councillors, and breaths more and less mephitic, cheeks more and less prickly – hoped with fervency that her prize-giver would be François Fleau the blacksmith, a very lovable man. François it was, and she slightly injured the decorum of the situation by flinging both arms round her councillor's neck, hugging him with delight, then kissing him with less than the required formality.

꘎꘎꘎

July 1968. Three undergraduates here from Paris after the occupation – and evacuation – of the Sorbonne, not, it is true, seeing a great way in front of their own concerns. Their complaints, though, after the grand discovery that French education is backward and fraudulent, reminded me of Hugo's sonnet on the small talk of pretty women waltzing at a ball.

When? In July 1870:

> Force is all that matters. War is sacred. Hanging's a
> Good thing. We don't need too much knowledge. We must
> Build more prisons, and build fewer schools.

That spirit endures; though one would not think so after reading newspaper sermonettes recently on the need of change, reform and spiritual incentives. Or after hearing de Gaulle using the word 'participation'.

Dangerous, I should have thought. The Gaullistes or the Right in general cannot really mean that everyone should participate more, let us say, in economic control. But give an idea a name, and you give it a handle, a blade. If a 'participation' that does not proffer more weekly or monthly cash, fails to follow the naming, and the talk, of 'participation', then real participation may be demanded. Then it may be impossible to buy off the workers, as they have been bought off in America?

On the radio, tennis at Wimbledon, go-slow on British Railways, and Labour losing the seat which the reformer Sidney Silverman held for thirty-five years. After hearing this I crossed the Loir to St-Jacques, looked down, and saw a punt, painted blue, moored in shadow under the poplars. It was a working day, not Sunday (here in the country men work a six day week, outside the big concerns). Two men, one about thirty-three or thirty-four, one middle-aged, both middle-class, and well dressed, were sitting in the punt, in wicker armchairs. One was fishing, one was smoking, and regarding life, time, poplar leaves, and reflections in the water. Having escaped from poverty as a grind and a back-bender and wrist-thickener, having more regular money, people want still more regular money. Which is natural. Others have much more. Why shouldn't they join these others and do more sitting in the punt and more fishing – watching Wimbledon in fact, as well as on TV?

It's share genuinely, or buy. Which is all the present troubles are about, obscurely.

Melancholy, monotony: 'The view is extensive but monotonous.' That is fair, from guidebooks. I don't ask guidebooks
to feel the Beauce. I've tried enticing people, even the near and
dear, on to the Beauce. It does not often work. I've tried a good
polissoir on them, the sweet corn just coming up round it, wind
cold, sky cloudless, soil dusty or turned to earthenware.

No good. I've tried Beauce churches on my family, opening
the door to the crude colour-show inside, with a proprietor's
superiority (perhaps that was the trouble). No good at all.

Then I've ended by asking, in a pushful way, have you read
La Terre?

La Terre, yes, by Emile Zola, No. 15 in *Les Rougon-Macquarts,
Histoire naturelle et sociale d'une famille sous le Second Empire*,
published in 1887:

Spring: *La mer des céréales, roulante, profonde, sans bornes. . . .
Continuellement une ondulation succédait à une autre.*

Summer (the Beauce shaved by harvesters): *C'était l'époque
où la grande solitude triste de la Beauce s'égayait le plus* – harvesters
with sickles moving across it like insects – *Pas une fraîcheur de
feuillage, rien que l'ombre courte des hommes, à terre.*

Autumn: *Au moindre coup de vent des grandes poussières s'en-
volaient, couvrant les talus et les haies de leur cendre. Et le ciel bleu, le
soleil éclatant, n'étaient qu'une tristesse de plus, au-dessus de cette
désolation.*

Last words: *Des morts, des semences, et le pain poussait de la terre.*

༺✿༻

Zola came down and did earnest field work on the Beauce and
the Beaucerons. Rognes, his village of the brutalities and bes-
tialities of devotion to every obtainable square centimetre of
earth, is Romilly-sur-Aigre; his town, Cloyes, in which the
notary lives, the market-town of the villagers, is actually on our
river, on the Loir, upstream, not in Loir-et-Cher, but Eure-et-
Loir, astride the dangerous main road from Vendôme up to
Châteaudun, Chartres and Paris.

Could there be copies of *La Terre* in Romilly? (Or copies on
sale, paperback edition, in Cloyes, where I've only stopped to
buy *croissants* and a newspaper?) Do Romilly people know about

that champion farter nicknamed Jésus-Christ, about M. and Mme Charles, with their 300,000 francs saved from keeping a brothel in Chartres, in the Rue aux Juifs, two hundred yards from the cathedral, about their anaemic granddaughter who was given a religious upbringing in a convent at Châteaudun, by the Sisters of the Visitation, 'on the strictest of religious principles', before she took over the brothel on her own account, with a display of such excellent business sense? About the *Filles de la Vierge* who appear in church in Romilly-Rognes so often and so obviously big-bellied? And old Mother Caca collecting turds to make her vegetables grow so large and succulent?

The Romilly-Rognes people will have changed, thanks to greater prosperity – and machines. I imagine bellies still enlarge before marriage (as they do in every other village in the world, or at any rate in the non-contraceptive or semi-contraceptive world). But there are no flails, no seed bags, no reaping by hand, no standing in dung up to the waist; there are tractors instead of horses, there are muck-spreaders, combine-harvesters; gum boots instead of *sabots*, saloon-cars instead of covered traps, tarred roads instead of ribbons of white chalk going across the plain, to the diminuendo of telegraph poles.

But I cannot think Zola is exactly the patron-saint of the Beaucerons, or of Romilly-sur-Aigre, even if he knew the heat, hail, dust, cold, endlessness – all in his novel. An epic prairie, yes, with lyric patches, lyric intervals.

One French historian, follower of Marc Bloch, has been working for years on a history of this vast granary, which provided the cash for the high spires and the long carvings of Chartres. It is a book I want to read more than most.

⟢

I am glad to have known something of the Beauce, to have been deep inside the Beauce, wheat all around, on a day of small clouds, to have discovered many of its rural-baroque churches, before reading *La Terre*. Some of Zola's brutality might otherwise have seeped – I suppose – into my estimate, into my view of the landscape, and might have been hard to expunge.

The brutality I mean is not one of incident – the scythe blade in the pregnant belly of the raped girl, and so on: I repeat it is

Zola's brutality: Zola devises a special iron harrow, squared and rigid: he fits it over the necks of the people of the Beauce, they have to act according to this pattern of agricultural iron around their necks.

Zola's battery humans.

It is too much like saying – with the very strongest effect – that the French are licentious, that Americans are corrupt, that Germans are pigs, that lawyers are dishonest. At Trôo they say Beaucerons are stupid, brutish and mean. When they want to condemn one local tradesman for his shortcomings and his wife for her snootiness, they recall 'they're from the Beauce'; which isn't the level for a novelist. Haven't we each of us more room to be free, individual, distinct, inside our battery?

༈

Early July. *Châteaux*, or solid old-fashioned country houses are opening around France, grey owners are arriving, and daughters, and grandchildren – where from?

Of course from Paris; for which the rest of France, I shouldn't be the first to say, exists, somewhat on sufferance.

Leant this evening on the gates in front of the small Château de Fretay, which is miles from anywhere, down lanes, in the dullish country north of Trôo. It is a favourite of ours, a not very remarkable house, with a more or less modern visage of the usual pallid tone, veiling a hint of ancientness in two little towers, one at each end, and a moat.

We had walked up the long avenue of trees, a converted lane, which at last gives a view of the house – a neglected avenue: the hay between the trees had just been cut (a late season), and was being carried, behind a tractor. Then as we leant on the gates, we realized that the shutters and windows were open, for the first time this year; and we could see – exactly so, a grey narrow father, a grey mother, and a youngish woman standing in a room between the tall windows open at the back and the tall windows open at the front.

It seemed rude to stare as usual at the *château*, so we moved. A man was cutting the 'lawn', the long grass between ourselves and the room open to the air, with a hay-cutter attached to his tractor. I would guess he is the gardener, king of the demesne, uninterfered with, for most of the year: probably his wife comes

148

in and airs the *château* from time to time, and does the cooking while the family are so briefly in residence for the two months of summer (two months, then a month at the sea).

Grey thin father, grey short mother and neat-figured daughter walk from the room on to the edge of the lawn where the long grass now lay in swathes, then stroll across the lane into the seldom-seen vegetable garden, to discover how the soft fruit is doing under its nets.

Millions and millions of francs, and an infinite quantity of conceit of class and cash, are locked away behind the long grass and the grey shutters of such large, little-used country houses. In English: 'country house' (twentieth century): house you live in, in the country. In French: *maison de campagne*, house you go to from Paris, in the country, shut most of the year.

જ⁂ર

Down the avenue we had discovered an immense and exceptional *cormier*, or sorb tree. It was the middle one of three *cormiers* forming a little courtyard, as it seemed, to one side of the avenue, where a gate opened into a field. About ten feet from the ground the trunk flattened, yet bulged out on two sides, and divided into three towering branches.

Bark irregularly squared, small regularly arranged leaves, and a habit I shall call benign, make a sorb tree rising clear from the grass peculiarly attractive.

And the fruit. Promise of great quantity this year. We could see them still green, crowded on top of the tree, against the blue of the sky. They will lie and rot and waste on the grass here in October, tiny soft brown pears, full of sugar, delightful to eat, now seldom eaten or picked up by anyone, though some may go into making a liqueur with *eau de vie de marc*.

We mark living finds such as this on the map, a yellow blob in water-colour, circled in pen; a note in the margin.

જ⁂ર

Came this morning into Chartres, on the west side, from Illiers, after a drab journey through the Perche. This way in, the two spires have to be looked for, beyond three brutish slabs of no doubt clean and comfortable habitation in concrete, and one enormous round tower in concrete. Beyond this tower the

Romanesque *flèche* and the Gothic *flèche* are reduced to pencil ends. The road which circles round the old city was blocked with lorries, buses, cars slowly moving to or from Paris, by way – I had plenty of time to read the name – of what is now the Boulevard Charles Péguy.

A neo-Catholic patriotic rhapsodist stages a neo-Catholic restoration and celebrates the Virgin, her cathedral, and the Beauce. He is given his posthumous reward: his name affixed to half of a clattering boulevard misty with diesel smoke and petrol fumes. You drive from Paris through the Boulevard Clémenceau, into the Boulevard du Maréchal Foch into the Boulevard Jean Jaurès, over the river, then into the Boulevard Charles Péguy; where you stick for twenty minutes.

⤙✳⤚

The cathedral loses its power – its secondary power.

Its primary power, cathedral of the Virgin,

> *Consolatrix miserorum*
> *Suscitatrix mortuorum,*

it lost centuries ago. See Henry Adams on Chartres and thirteenth century investment in the power of the Queen of Heaven: the bourgeois satisfied himself 'that neither the road to Heaven nor Heaven itself had been made surer or brought nearer by an investment of capital which amounted to the best part of the wealth of France. Economically speaking, he became satisfied that his enormous money-investment had proved to be an almost total loss. . . . The efforts of the bourgeoisie and the peasantry to recover their property, so far as it was recoverable, have lasted to the present day.'

That was printed first in 1904; and the bourgeoisie and the peasants have recovered much more of their property since then; have let much more of the religious investment of the Middle Ages fall into ruins.

But then they don't greatly care for the secondary power, that *this* was our past, that this – *Consolatrix miserorum* – imaged a value active beyond the religion in which it was regenerated; that these porches, these carvings, this scarlet and blue, these two spires, are human victories rather more important than most.

That is the power the cathedral is losing; and keeping it alive is the problem of every old country with monuments.

'The first glimpse that is caught, and the first that was meant to be caught, is that of the two spires.' A poorly written sentence, but the spires do continue to be seen that way, as you come in from Paris, they continue standing up from the Beauce without obstacle in a dusty isolation. Ten years ago they stood in the same degree of isolation, without concrete blocks and towers in the way, as you followed the road in from Illiers.

In another ten years?

ᏹᏯᏹ

What a smart town hall gesture – how good they are at gestures – to put Boulevard Jean Jaurès (Boulevard Second International, Boulevard International Socialism) next to Boulevard Patriotic-Neo-Catholicism-cum-Poetry (Boulevard Charles Péguy). But they are only roads, and there's so much traffic, there are so many vehicles, and the vehicles are mostly lorries and industry, and nobody notices, and nobody cares.

ᏹᏯᏹ

Report in *Figaro*, A.D. 2106 – or before – of an operation akin to the shifting of the temples of Abu Simbel:

> *Successful removal of Old Christian Temple. Notre-Dame de Chartres taken stone by stone from the factory complex of Paris-Chartres (to make room for the new meat-market), and re-erected on a site forty miles away, in the last few unenclosed acres of the Beauce.*
>
> *Impressive ceremony of inauguration. Moving address by Emperor Charles III. 'Français, Françaises . . .', etc.*

ᏹᏯᏹ

Anticlerical, and against religion, mightn't Zola have had the grace, which doesn't mean the religious grace or more than the humanistic grace, to mention that Chartres was built out of the earth and the harvests, the muck and the crops, of the Beauce?

If not God, Art? A once eager search for meaning – even if the brothel of M. and Mme Charles came so close to the south porch, and the English tea-room?

Corot's quiet and great painting of the cathedral, art out of art out of muck.

❧

Heat at Trôo. Early July. Too hot for lizards to run. Though it's a dry heat, there was nothing to do all this morning, all this afternoon, but sit quite still in the cave, not even thinking; which would have meant thinking of heat. The sun leaves our house and goes behind trees at half-past four, and behind the cliff at five o'clock. It was still hot. When the sun was well down we put chairs and a table in the car, and drove up and along cart tracks to the highest point in the fields, on the plateau. There we set the table up and had supper by a solitary pear-tree, a huge, still very warm, now darkening sky all around.

❧

In the *Manyō Shū*, or *Collection of Myriad Leaves*, the very large, and oldest, anthology of Japanese poems, written between 660 and 760 of our era, there is a love poem by Hitomaro, which I know only from a translation into a Dutch sensibility, then out of that sensibility into bad English. Never mind, Hitomaro says that his dear love leant against him 'as the seaweed of the open sea rests on the waves'.

You never know when you are going to think of such things. I thought of Hitomaro's seaweed when I saw crabs and clams today resting on seaweed on the marvellous fish-stall in Montoire market – marvellous because the fish, brought from Nantes through the dark hours of the morning, are so fresh and various, smelling so much of the sea. Today they smelt of fish, it was so hot; and the seaweed had gone stiff and dry, where the crumbled ice wasn't melting into it. The stall, the seaweed, the black and red crabs which wheezed, gasped and foamed a little, or didn't move, still made me sea-conscious.

I want sea. I was born near sea.

If only, I think at this moment – we are having red mullet for supper – this cliff of Trôo looked down on the sea. But that would mean shacks and bungalows everywhere, not just a few along the river, half screened by willows. Or if only Trôo was no more than a French road hour – say thirty-five to forty miles – from the sea. But that would mean more wind, more rain, perhaps no vineyards.

It is dry, everything is dry. Everything once wet, like the slime on the mouth of the pipe into the rain-butt, has caked to hardness. Everything is hard and ochre.

⌇⌖⌇

The heat has slackened. But I would like to walk at once into real water, not into the warm clear soup of the Loir, not into our lukewarm azure bathing pool, newly erected at Bessé, but into surging sea water, brown seaweed rising with it and falling with it.

Colette's story *L'Entrave*: Brittany, the gorse slope to the Atlantic, then the sea rising up, as the woman, no longer so young, wades out, the sea 'encircling ankles, then knees, in two heavy icy bracelets'.

As if it wasn't for heat that one comes to Trôo; and for being alone, more or less.

⌇⌖⌇

I picked a handful of wild fennel on the cliff (to go with small white turnips, and smoked *jambon de pays*): the fennel was surrounded by its own scent, extracted, volatilized by the sun. The fennel immediately transferred its scent to my fingers. Lunch is over, but the scent is still there when I put my hand up to my face.

⌇⌖⌇

The heat – 3 p.m. – now comes round the trees and takes possession of black shadow. The cheek away from the sun also burns. But the root of a weed I pulled up is markedly cool and damp. Earth and stubble, and grass, now tones of a universal ochre.

⌇⌖⌇

From far above I have just witnessed the circumstances of someone falling from a boat and drowning in the Loir, on a

153

Sunday evening. Figures, just visible through the trees, ran up and down the bank, in the clear light. Unusual shouts and cries came up. A fire-engine arrived, bringing frogmen to find the body.

Then other boats and *pédalos* continued their coloured Sunday progression, under the blue willows of (early, not late) Corot, as though nothing had happened. 'The body' – as if it hadn't been permeated by a creature of sentience, in his own universe – how quickly one becomes a 'body'!

❧

The colour seen with most exciting clarity this summer in France: pallid mineral green of unripe spindle berries hanging on a bush in the wood, on the way back from tracking the Roman road.

The brightness of less bright colours: the test of light.

❧

The body of the young man – eighteen years old, over for a day's jaunt from St-Symphorien, at Tours – has been found, after three days deep in the warm soup of the Loir. Not by the frogmen, but by the men going to work this morning at the little factory half a mile downstream; they noticed the body floating, said Maurice, '*parmi les nénuphars,*' which sounded very poetical in English ears, as if *nénuphar* meant something rather more than water-lily. They brought his body up to the *mairie*. And he rated, for his whole life, four lines in the local edition of *La Nouvelle République*.

❧

Slow clouds, instead of clouds of a wild Atlanticism. Clouds without menace.

Movements without sound, or without appreciable sound. Birds too small to be heard, or moving in black across the sky too far off or too far up for their movement to be heard. Slow clouds again. Boats down on the river. Two perfect unities of noiselessness and movement.

154

Those sounds which come from very close, and are very small, or from a distance; which can be conveyed or concealed by the slight movements of air.

The clock, the mill. The hands are now revolved electrically, in silence, the mills are closed down. We are losing the sound of these first intimate, inoffensive machines.

Sounds (individual, recurrent, intermittent) allowed their identity; no scream too long, no pitch too high, no dominance going on and on.
The hen she is killing quickly dies.
The single aeroplane disappears.
The lorry rumbles away.
The audibility of the river returns.

St Amand, on the Beauce. Great fields of August sunflowers. Corn, and more stubble than corn. Gentle pink clover, then green where the clover has been cut, from the aftermath of clover leaves.

The Fall

Back in October, to a Bas-Vendômois of ochre and yellow. We have a game, if we drive somewhere, of counting the number of golden things, principally vegetable, and including pumpkins collected into a mound of solid golden bubbles. Also the *séchoirs* filled with maize, each farm now having its long vertical slab or slabs of bright yellow or orange. The luminosity, the exoticism, let's say the oriental elsewhereness of the yellow; as in Ronsard's sonnet *Sur la Naissance du Duc de Beaumont, fils aîné du Duc de Vendôme et Roi de Navarre.* Look coldly at his lines and you may think, how over artificial, how simple-minded to ask for a Gastines of lemons and oranges:

> *Que Gâtine aît tout le chef jaunissant*
> *De maint citron et mainte belle orange.*

But really the poem is less about a birthday than a day round here of October perfection: the trees of Gâtine are more brilliant than lemons and oranges; or the poem is less about brilliant trees and October perfection than about Ronsard himself.

> May Gâtine's head all yellow turn
> With lemons and fine oranges galore;
> May through our orchards fully flow
> All perfumes of all foreign lands;
>
> And may the Loir run milk, its green
> Rampart to a tapestry of emeralds change;
> And may the sand which settles
> In the Braye be sands of yellow gold;

Sky, rain down your scents and roses,
Drop, strong winds, to slightest breezes,
Sea, be calm, air filled with happiness!

Today my seigneur's heir is born;
Fates, a fair thread of honour spin him,
From earth to draughts of nectar in the sky.

ᇮᇮ

There is a dish of an American book, *The Golden Peaches of Samarkand*,[1] about the exotic goods enjoyed in T'ang China – falcons, peacocks, parrots, paradise drongos or kalavinka birds (supposed to be able to sing while still in the egg), sandal wood, purple gold, relics of the masters of Buddhism, cloves, myrobalans and mare's teat grapes. Lemons and oranges were exotics in that way to Ronsard, I imagine. In La Possonnière, or in Montoire market, they cannot have been everyday objects as early as that sonnet (which was written in 1551).

When he was old, or older, in the 1570s, Hélène de Surgères sent him some cypresses and orange trees, no doubt for his priory garden (though the orange trees would have been put under cover in winter), on the island in the Loire –

> *J'ay reçeu vos Cyprez, et vos Orangers verds,*
> *Le Cyprez est ma mort, l'Oranger signifie*
> *(Ou Phebus me deçoit) qu'après ma courte vie*
> *Une gentille odeur sortira de mes vers.*

But this is getting too pedantic. What I was going to say is that my American book begins with the potency of the charm of good things from elsewhere: 'Their real life is in the bright world of imagination, where we take our true holidays.'

Trôo is my bright world of imagination, where I take my true holidays; and in that world truth is more true and the real more real.

ᇮᇮ

If, says J., we win the Irish sweep, the Malta sweep, and the Pools – if, I add, we find that suddenly and for no reason at all

---

[1] By Edward Schafer, Professor of Oriental Languages at the University of California.

we've inherited all the oil millions of Paul Getty, and all his pictures by Rubens and Rembrandt – we will rebuild that great spire of Trôo church. Then we will give the whole landscape a push and watch it revolve all the more evidently around its axle.

I think we shall be too late. By that time (only just, things move slowly in rural France) our water-tower, our *château d'eau*, will have been built, and no spire could boss such a gleaming pillar of white concrete. A new *château d'eau* (I like that term) has taken possession lately of the whole huge horizon, or edge of the huge landscape, towards Vendôme. It is brilliant, six miles away, against thunder clouds.

When I come back from England, I ask about the *château d'eau*, which will at last mean running water. The well was dug years ago, two or three hundred yards behind the church. I am told 'The water is resting.' I am also told there is not enough money to go on and build the tower.

༖

October incident. Clicks of a ratchet – of a *pressoir* being screwed by its iron handle on to the squared mass of broken grapes – from a black cave in a ⊃-shaped embrasure of chalk in the woods. The scent of the grape juice. The clicks stop, a man comes out of the cave and climbs round and up into the woods, to relieve himself. While he is up there, I can hear the invisible spring of juice out of the press crooling into a cemented tank or pool inside the cave. A crash through the bushes, the man comes down again on the other side of the cave, pushing branches away with one hand, holding in the other two *ceps*, brown-capped, full, firm, still unsmeared by slugs, untunnelled by grubs, sturdily beautiful objects.

༖

On our hillside Maurice's grapes are not quite ready. Nor is Maurice: he is at work on the barrels, tightening the iron bands (barrels very dry), fitting new bungs and corks, crawling inside to fix little bundles of vine twigs across the bottom draining hole so that it won't be blocked by the *rosé* grapes (which are not pressed, but broken and stuffed direct into barrels).

✌︎❀︎❀︎✍

It is astonishing how long some of these thrifty *vignerons* – like Maurice – make the barrels serve, taking out rotten staves, fitting in new lengths of chestnut wood, wedging in lines of reed which swell and make the old joints wine-proof.

Today Maurice had just or had nearly finished the delicate job of repairing the up-ended base of an elderly barrel and wedging it into its groove, with lengths of reed. I had joined him outside his cave for a midday drink and picnic, and what should I do but plant my elbow on to the circle, which at once fell in. Maurice has good manners: he looked, he didn't even swear.

I drove off apologetically to his loft at St-Jacques in search of another bundle of reed.

✌︎❀︎❀︎✍

This cave, where I have spent many hours, in the summer season of drinking, and at the *vendange*, October by October, lies on the old (untarred) main road which goes down the valley from Trôo to Sougé alongside the modern *route nationale*. It looks like a farm lane – it is a lane between farm and farm, hamlet and hamlet; but it still serves as a local main thoroughfare. The baker comes this way, and many others; and often there is a line of vans or cars or tractors drawn into the side. The drivers are having a glass of *rosé* at the cave, whose proprietor emerges from the dark and the cobwebs with bottles and corkscrew and a load of witticisms. The fields flatten away to the trees which mark the Loir, or up river to the roots of the hill which is capped by Trôo church. Another bottle comes up. Another van arrives. Maurice speaks contemptuously of the land a few miles to the north where the vineyards give out, and cider replaces wine, and heaviness succeeds a Vendômois – and *rosé*-irrigated – lightness.

✌︎❀︎❀︎✍

162

Late in turning in our yellow world, the poplars along the Loir at last and suddenly go lemon; they look as if they gave off light, lighting up the river plain.

In the vineyards every leaf has turned yellow or red. The vine leaves which are red and shiny like thin lino or vinyl belong to the Gamay vines, ancient and universal yielders of a heavy crop, always blamed in books for indifferent quality. Maurice says one must have the very dark Gamay grapes if one's red wine is to show a good colour.

❧

The sound of the year's collected life, the sound of a spring of new wine, cool and sweetly delicious to drink, if loosening to the inside, will come in the next few days from tree-concealed cave after cave in these low hills along either side of the river.

The trough of Maurice's *pressoir*, in the mouth of his cave, has been cleaned out like a dish. The cogs of the *pressoir* have been oiled, the steel worm, down which the timbers are forced on to the pile of grapes, has been smeared with two handfuls of grease.

❧

A process still obscurely sacred, still obscurely to do with being extra alive.

So people come for the *vendange*. Maurice is a priest older than the *curé*. He wears a leather apron, down to his feet, a stiff cassock blackened with grape juice; from his cave he now emerges half-hidden under baskets – the small baskets he makes in the winter, which are to be emptied into the long carrier baskets, the dossers, the *hottes*, now waiting to be picked up and fitted on to the backs of young and strong volunteers.

More people arrive, young men, old women, girls. The sun dries off the grass, leaves drop from a bullace and a pear above the cave.

An Englishman can be aware of what will go on till night, he feels it is fascinating, in this unEnglish light. I doubt if he can have it inside him, really.

I have tried many times.

> Wines rest in cool caves, becoming fine,
> Says monsieur in his book, and clear.

Now look, how each warm vent of breeze
Loosens a patter of yellow pear

And plum leaves down. Now one by one
Two-legged black baskets come. Black
Beams on broken grapes press down.
Into that cool a spring of juice

Runs down. A spring to a pool; from which
A scent of now most old, new
Life floats back from under the ground
And hangs around.

I notice on Maurice's face, on and off all today, a particular
smile. His congregation works for him. He is happy in his
leather cassock and gum boots. The year's anxiety is over, he
has a fine day for his *vendange*. It has all happened again,
though he is getting old.

༄

She stands in a wooden tub which is black from grape skins
and grape juice, wearing blue jeans and a dark red shirt. The
jeans come in tight on a narrow waist. She is slender, she is
extremely vivid.

Young men, and other girls who are less pretty, stand round
her tub and throw grapes at her, which she tries to catch in her
mouth. Everyone laughs; and the *vendange* is over.

No, they are not rustic youths and maidens out of Keats and
cockneyism, or local young men and girls from Trôo: they are
down from Paris for a Saturday afternoon and a Sunday of
picking grapes; and the girl in the tub with the pretty grape-
smudged face, balancing, leaning forward, laughing, showing
bare flesh between shirt and jeans, is a tennis player from international tournaments.

Why not? She remains pretty, this remains an October
occasion of real grapes in real France. They have worked very
hard.

It is pleasanter to pick grapes than to pull sugar beets.

༄

A Humming-bird Hawkmoth came into the front room and
hovered from flower to pink flower of soapwort in a jug.

༄

Woods round Trôo at this moment are full of *trompettes de mort*, Wood Blewits, various *ceps, girolles, pieds de mouton* (i.e. *Hydnum repandum*), Fairy Club, Peziza, False Morel, hard, lacquered Ganoderma, Blushers, Death Caps, clumps of *Ramaria botrys*, otherwise *barbe de bique* or Nanny-goat's Beard. There is much local collecting and eating, especially of *cep, girolle, pied de mouton, barbe de bique*, and *trompette de mort*.

The *trompettes*, black trumpets rising from the earth, or the dead leaves, or from banks of green moss, are usually about when the grapes are picked.

They are mixed into the rabbit and pork pâtés for the supper which the owner of the vineyard gives to the tired pickers who have stripped the vines to the last bunch.

Men come out of the woods carrying grape-baskets piled black and grey with these mushrooms of the dead (subfusc relatives of the *girolle*) for this – I won't say festival of new wine, but thankoffering for a *vendange* completed.

⟡

The mist is getting thin, the corrugated fibre-glass which covers the verandah begins to squeak and creak overhead, as the sun strikes it. End of the first week of October, yes; but it will soon be too hot to sit here and think or write or move, or regard the Loir, framed in a picture corner between one upright of the verandah and the tight trunk of our lime tree.

⟡

One of Victor Hugo's long preachings in *Les Misérables* talks of the two problems of a country: 'First problem: to produce wealth. Second problem: to share it.' England, he says, creates wealth excellently and shares it badly, exists in monstrous opulence and monstrous wretchedness; and will therefore die of bankruptcy. A fair view from his eyrie of 1861. In spite of Toryism, hasn't England begun to share its wealth decently, isn't English socialism beginning to realize there must be wealth to share; and though it may be a near thing, aren't we going to avoid bankruptcy of thought and economics, after all?

And what about France now, the wealth beginning to pile up – and my old image of St Martin's cloak, sharing as little of the cloak as possible, still in operation? A Trôo child, two days ago, was white, miserable, listless; and had a sore on his face, another on his hand. The child's mother – she was also grape-picking yesterday and the day before – hesitated to go to the doctor in Montoire: the doctor would charge so much, the chemist would charge even more, for the medicine, if it was an antibiotic; she would have to pay the whole score, and wait for weeks until the percentage was refunded.

Actually she went. Didier, the child, has come round to play, duly antibioticized and smeared with gentian-violet.

As foretold, the bill was huge.

༺༒༻

I asked an intelligent girl down for the *vendange* (from Paris) her view of Ronsard. She hadn't one. He was a school poet, she had had enough of him. She preferred Aragon and Éluard, and René Char. It is really no wonder that in the flush of the sur-realist movement, in 1929, Aragon included Ronsard in his list of the ridiculous: 'Clowns one can think of: Julien Benda, M. Thiers, Goethe, Paul Fort, Abbé Bremond, the writer of *Rien que la terre*, Raymond Poincaré, Gyp, Pastor Soulié, André Maurois, Ronsard, Julien Benda most of all. Baron Seillières is more stableboy than clown. André Gide isn't a clown or a stableboy: he's a fucking bore.'

Ronsard, you could say, expresses hope, and satisfaction, even if momentary and evanescent; he respects society, and Aragon wedges him between a society author and a philoso-pher who sneaks off to a solution for the insoluble, for the bizarre accident of existence, in 'God'.

But wasn't Aragon attacking his decade's Ronsard, the builders of soft nests in Ronsard, the Ronsardisants, the gentry putting up his bust in the courtyard of the *mairie* (of all situations for the bust of a poet) at Couture?

C'est la gloire de Ronsard qui passe.

༺༒༻

Read Aragon, Breton, Éluard, Queneau, and the rest of them (when young) – again in Maurice Nadeau's *Histoire du Surréa-lisme* – writing to the Mayor and Councillors of Rimbaud's

Charleville, and to the President of the Society of the Poets or the Ardennes, etc., on their inauguration of a monument to Rimbaud at Charleville, in the Place de la Gare.

'Rimbaud? He allowed no one to salute the dead when he was about. He wrote 'Shit on God' on church walls . . .

'Rimbaud? He lived as you think men shouldn't live: he got drunk, he provoked fights, he slept under bridges, he had lice.'

Any of us could think of a hundred lit. and art occasions, Arts Council occasions, Westminster Abbey occasions, book page occasions, literary prize occasions, publishing occasions – all in the last year or two – when we should have been improved by the instantaneous insults and provocations of Aragon and Breton (when young).

༒

Do I shame myself by saying – by repeating – 'when young'?

༒

I examined that bust of Ronsard, at Couture. The *Mairie* and the village school occupy one dull building at the edge of the village, on the flat between the river and the *gentilhommière* of the Ronsards. The bust stands at right angles to the schoolroom (voice of the schoolmaster, shuffle of feet through the window) against a curtain, yes, of *laurels* now ugly and dying. The bust is the most positively unnoticeable object; and when deliberately noticed, it proves to be no more than a pinched and pallid copy in stone of a bust of Ronsard at Tours, I think, which has been copied over and over again.

O rare Pierre de Ronsard! It suggests nothing, this bust of you.

༒

Up to La Possonnière again, and past the house by a sunken lane to the plateau, through the woods which were a part of Gastines. No large trees any more, nothing but chestnut coppice above a richness of wet leaves. A large puddingstone here and there among the leaves. A tractor driven by a short wide man with a grin pulls grapes in barrels down from the plateau to a wine cave near the house, where the air smells of new wine.

I don't decline to observe the pinkish light as well on the pale façade of the house, on the inscriptions *Avant partir*, *Voluptati et Gratiis*, etc., or the pink clouds over the crocketed spire – added by Loys de Ronsard, Ronsard's father – of Couture church. I don't decline the sentimentality, or the agreeability, of thinking this dampish muddy evening in October to have been the kind of evening of the *vendange* which was often familiar to Ronsard.

Drove back by way of the Green Island. The river looks all the wider now they have cut down a thirty-three-year growth of poplars along one bank.

The owner of the white *château* down here by Ronsard's Island was the man – or so I am told – who introduced myxomatosis into France, and Europe.

❧

At Trôo you should see Mme Radet arriving early from her café on the Rue Haute, four hundred yards away, to collect any pears which may have been so misguided, so much without a sense of property, as to fall from her pear tree on to the public realm.

Let it be observed that the branches above the lane produce, for passers-by and their shopping nets, only hard little cooking pears (which nevertheless Mme Radet gathers up from the flints and the horse droppings). From the same tree branches grow the other way, *over* Mme Radet's field, which is closely barbwired against intrusion. These branches – from a graft – hang with juicy tawny pears which are good for eating.

The English driving through France are impressed by fruit trees along roads, but the impression changes when they try their teeth and tongues on the fruit littering the road or verge. The French are not fools.

❧

Pouff! Pouff! – from inside the unrisen mist of a Sunday morning in October; and then, dogs wet through, autumnal coloured wellingtons muddy – then nothing but one pigeon or one hare. Daudet's *Tartarin*: 'Stupid as the brute creation is, you can readily understand that, in time, it learnt some distrust.

'For five leagues around Tarascon' – and Trôo – 'forms, lairs, and burrows are empty, nesting-places abandoned. You'll not find a single quail or blackbird, one little leveret or the tiniest tit . . . Tarascon' – all France, one sometimes feels – 'is down in the black book of the world of fur and feather. The very birds of passage have ticked it off in their guidebooks.'

Maurice is down there in the mist, with his gun and his Breton spaniel.

ᘎᕼᕽᕽ

After Sunday lunch searched for two *polissoirs* in a peculiar part of the Beauce, the valley of the Brisse, a wide dip of land which looks old and melancholy; it is almost without features – or houses.

The first *polissoir* we should never have found without a workman who was cutting his way along a thicket of maize. He led us through the clattery stems of the maize straight to the rock, by a ditch, nearly grassed over and almost level with the ground. *Polissoir* boulders are often like this one, in four or five thousand years the boulder has sunk by its own weight or the ground has risen, or both.

The second *polissoir* took some finding, though we knew it was in a wood; which turned out to be a sick plantation, full of large white fungi drooping into grey, also full of puddingstones, among blackthorn. The one puddingstone with the polishing grooves, and a polishing basin, in a denseness of blackthorn, we discovered just in time when the sun was going down and sending orange slices of light between the tree trunks and through the thorns.

We cleaned moss and rot out of the grooves and felt their polish. The pleasure of finding this *polissoir* didn't prevent me from feeling autumnally alone and out on a limb, as we walked back to the car, across baked farm mud, in a foreign emptiness unmodified by familiarity or participation.

The autumnal die-away of a most brilliant Sunday morning and afternoon.

ᘎᕼᕽᕽ

I have never been out on this grey dish of land in the rain. And what must it look like, feel like, under snow?

J'avais, j'avais ce goût de vivre chez les hommes, et voici que la terre exhale son âme d'étrangère.

English poetry belongs to the intimate, where country can become a park or a garden at any minute. Very well, it likes to escape from the park – but in that it belongs to a park condition. A human inheritance.

And Americans are the abstract people who should capsule through space, who should grow red stubble of beards on the other side of the moon.

⤳⤲

To come home off the Beauce, without running out of petrol, to come up the flinty lane without a puncture, swing left, tyres spinning a little, wearing off the tread, to come to rest on the terrace outside the locked door, the key down in the irises! To light the lamp, and read, perhaps about *polissoirs* – or to read Perse or Hugo!

⤳⤲

Why – I find I am always asking this kind of question, and leaving it unanswered, or incompletely answered – why do I so much enjoy finding one of these neolithic polishing or sharpening stones, and – if necessary – pushing the muck out of its grooves, uncovering a polished furrow, a made-by-man furrow, continuing smooth with his energy?

I don't have to think of the people who squatted on these boulders pushing and pulling axes of honey flint forwards and backwards, and coating them again with a little sand and water. If I did I would have to think of the axemakers as savage, without tenderness, given to head-hunting, to shaping brain-balls, to cannibalism.

I think of them – I suppose – in a blurred way as peoplers of space (this grey emptiness so unlike anything in England) and of time so much before my time. I comfort myself when I feel along one of these silky-surfaced grooves worn across and into the rough naturalness of the stone. I don't – in *polissoirs*, in dolmens, in Iron Age camps – make communion with the

dead, except vaguely: I don't touch a work of art: I make a lair
for myself.

❧

October picnic, in tree shade, acacia and pine shade, on top of
the immense dolmen in the fields outside Mettray, a good break
in a shopping journey from Trôo to Tours.

In the 1920s an English admiral came here and estimated that
two of the three capstones weighed twenty-four tons each, and
that the big capstone in the middle weighed fifty-six tons.

On the side of this middle block I notice that someone has
drawn, very black in pencil, his girl friend, and himself with a
super-neolithic erection.

❧

The wasps of Trôo deserve a note. They are generally small,
few, and lacking in will. A wave or two of the hand, and they
go, even from jam on the table – if they get that far.

Common wasps? (If common, not pushing.) A different
species? At any rate they are not a nuisance. One would expect
the grape bunches to be crawling with wasps, when the *vendange* proceeds on a sunny day at the beginning of October.
But no, not as a rule.

Hornets – a fair number. So large, so surprising always, that
they look dangerous. But they have here, as at home, an admirable timidity, or lack of aggressiveness.

❧

Trôo gives me an owner's interest in Richard Coeur-de-Lion,
so I am glad to see that Malraux, as cultural minister, has now
cleared the convicts out of the Abbey of Fontevrault, where he
is – or was – buried. The convicts and the warders. A warder
unlocked the way into the abbey church with an extra shiny
key on a chain, and one glimpsed convicts before coming to
the Plantagenet effigies in the empty nave.

Richard, his father Henry II, and his mother, and the queen
of his brother and successor, King John Sans Terre – Queen
Victoria put in a claim to them: she asked if the effigies could

171

be brought from Fontevrault and allowed to join the other kings and queens of England in Westminster Abbey.

Rather grand of Queen Victoria, I used to consider. Her Plantagenet ancestors were as French as could be, and liked Touraine and Anjou, and sunshine, better than they liked England. But it was also rather insulting to have one's ancestors in prison; also in Victoria's day the convicts slept in the nave. Victoria's request was turned down by the Council-General of Maine-et-Loire.

✑

I believe in fact there is nothing of Richard in the abbey now except effigy and memory. He was divided after that gangrenous death, from his wound at Chalus. His heart went to the cathedral at Rouen. His insides went to Charlemagne's abbey at Charroux (near Poitiers), and his body – his body they did bury at Fontevrault. But in 1910 they tidied up the church and came on what was left of the various Plantagenets. An English book on the burial of hearts which I found in one of the two secondhand bookshops at Tours, declares that the 'ashes' of King Richard were then sent, after all, to Westminster; which I hope would have satisfied the Queen.

✑

The same book says that Richard's heart – reputed to have been extra large, a lion's heart (but is a lion's heart larger than a man's?) – was uncovered in its burial place in Rouen cathedral in 1838; then, in about the same preservation as his castle at Trôo – or rather better preservation, thin and dry like a leaf – it went to the Musée d'Antiquités at Rouen; where it was said to remain, in a purse of green silk.

Nice to think of, the dry leaf, in the green silk. But untrue. What they do have at Rouen is a little crystal box with some dust inside. It is inscribed 'Dust of the heart of Richard Coeur de Lion which I found 31 July 1838, under the paving of the sanctuary of the Cathedral. A. Deville.'

Right and proper, gone to dust. Even then the museum has only half the dust, mixed with powdered embalming spices and powdered silk: the other half (or could this have been the real

172

heart, unpowdered and 'thin as a leaf'?) was reburied in the cathedral in 1869 under a lead plaque, inscribed like the original plaque with a cross and

HIC: IACET:
COR: RICAR:
DI: REGIS:
    ANGLORUM:

It was found again, and buried again, when the bombed cathedral was repaired after the Second World War.

೭ఇ৵

I said something sarcastic about burying the embalmed penis of Casanova, or Don Juan, or Henry Miller, in the Lady Chapel.

'Well,' said J. 'It wouldn't be much good embalmed. And the heart *was* a poetic symbol.'

As if the phallus wasn't; and couldn't be described as nearer the heart of the matter?

೭ఇ৵

Had dinner yesterday evening in the cave house of the friend who took me on my first journey from Trôo to Fontevrault (which is miles away across both Loir and Loire). When we came near Chinon on that journey, he slowed down and said 'Which will you do' (we couldn't do both because we were expected to lunch in a remote village another fifty miles southwest) – 'will you have a bottle of Chinon here, on the Vienne, or will you stop and see the Plantagenets on the other side of the river at Fontevrault?'

I chose the Plantagenets. Then we drove on to lunch in a garden room, with a tiled floor, which opened on to grass shaded by greengage trees and a barn. We were given some of the headiest white – or rather yellow – wine I've encountered. We mumbled happily into sleep under the greengage trees. When the afternoon cooled and we came to, we carried on our heads from a cottage to the car an enormous grandfather clock, time horizontal, time like a bier, time arrested, three hundred yards through the sharp-edged shadows of the village street.

I watched the clock this evening, six years later, I watched its huge gilt pendulum decorated with reaping hooks and sheaves of corn (a country clock) swinging softly behind its glass door.

⌘

So far I cannot complain about the weakening of a body which has served me well for many years. I cannot complain, but I shall and I do. For one thing I am unable to drive so far as from Trôo to Fontevrault or Angers and come home again without feeling whacked. I think of Ronsard, retreating to Croixval, aged forty-five or fifty, unfortunate only in his body, deaf (he had been half deaf for years), thin, languid, yellow, worried by malaria; then, before he died, skinny, limp, and with no muscle.

He persists all the same in a mandorla of happiness (the mandorla being made by the intersection of the circles of matter and mind).

⌘

Think of Alexander Pope, and be thankful. He is another poet who might have persisted entirely in such a mandorla. He was happy – loved, and loving – in a country childhood about as genial as Ronsard's, also with forests, fields and river, until at twelve he caught spinal tuberculosis from infected milk; after which the sun inside him had to compete all his life with the black weather of headaches, neuralgia, insomnia, and, since he never grew, the agony of remaining diminutive except in mind. A large fine head on a curved little body, with meagre limbs. I brought a proof copy to Trôo of Peter Quennell's book on the first forty years of Pope's life. It blackens sunshine. Quennell writes that one should mark off the adult Pope's full height – four feet six inches – on a wall or door, and keep it in sight as one ponders his character.

I measured four foot six on the door jamb; and was appalled.

⌘

Two visions of this poet who should have been happy *au fond*. Pope in a brothel near the Haymarket. His friends think he will catch the clap if he stays longer with the girl. One of them throws open the door on him – 'where I found this little hasty

174

hero, like a terrible Tom Tit, pertly perching upon the Mount of Love . . . I fairly laid hold of his heels, and actually drew him down safe and sound from his danger'.

The second vision: I see him, diminutive, walking the Thames country around Twickenham, carrying pistols – in fear that he might be attacked by one of the men he had victimized so malevolently in *The Dunciad* – and accompanied by his Great Dane: homunculus and huge dog. But then: 'His littleness is his protection; no one shoots a wren.'

ଔଚଙ

I regret that I have never rented or owned a garden containing a mulberry. I have never planted one, yet I regard the mulberry as one of the Trees of Life.

Konstantin Paustovsky, that Communist Russian who continued and renewed the tradition of Aksakov's autobiographies: 'We travelled with no undue haste' – under the Caucasus mountains – 'enjoying the heat and the ripe mulberries. They were spread on the road like a thick carpet.'

The mulberry does not grow fast. But, like a willow pole, a fair sized branch will take if it is put into the ground. What owner of a mulberry will allow me to cut off a fair sized branch?

Generosity defined: 'He gave me a fair sized branch of his Tree of Life.'

ଔଚଙ

Getting older, I begin to *know* the different growth, densities, movement, etc. of different kinds of tree, which is something else than the smaller power of distinguishing one kind of tree from other kinds on sight. Upward branching, downward branching, subdivision of branching, trees with an angular angry branching (the apple, when left alone) or a peaceful branching, total textures due to different leaf arrangement, leaf size, leaf shape, leaf tone, volume of leafage, and so on.

Most good painters who concerned themselves incidentally or primarily with landscape, painted their trees right and recognizable by sheer perceptive power, or inability to refrain from seeing. There is a bistre drawing by Claude (in the Teyler Museum at Haarlem), a drawing of a wood in which the contour, the leaning, the branching, the angles of branch to trunk, the nature of the dead branches, the rooting, at once show the trees to be pines, without any less than broad detail, without any indication of pine needles.

It is an exercise to match one's power of recognizing trees against an artist's power of perceiving them. He will have the tree right; but see if you can put the right name to his rightness.

❧

I have never seen Ma Yüan's famous 'one corner' painting of a poet or a philosopher – I prefer poet, but perhaps poet is incorrect – gazing at the moon. It is often reproduced in plates not quite good enough or large enough to show one major detail, that from a pine tree above the poet, which grows in sharp angles out of the cliff, a tiny fan of three needles is falling through the air. I have just discovered this trio of pine needles in a larger photograph. They create silence. They push everything away. They belong to Trôo – which pushes everything away, and where there are no such pines – as well as to China. They double the affectivity of the picture.

❧

Good examples, too, these twelfth- or thirteenth-century paintings by Ma Yüan, of the 'realness' in convention: here's the convention of the one large pine, which Kuo Hsi in the *Great Message of Forests and Streams* demanded as a kind of regulator in mountain landscape, as 'the aged master' to be selected first so as to determine in the picture (as it does in that masterpiece by Ma Yüan) the lesser plants, stones, rocks.

The convention is obeyed, the aged master is none the less (or all the more?) a 'real' pine; like the 'real', physical, experienced, conventional love in the sonnets of *Astrophel and Stella*, for example; or of Ronsard.

❧

Some places have bad luck. You cannot imagine that Montoire was ever one of them.

When you look across the square at Montoire on a mild October afternoon, the edges of the horse-chestnut leaves yellow and many dampish-dark ochre leaves already on the gravel, this uncrowded small town exhibits such a quietness and sweetness, devoid now of holiday traffic, that you cannot imagine it was ever chosen for an act of infamy, with infamous consequences. At the now more or less abandoned railway station in 1940 old Marshal Pétain shook hands with Hitler after the fall of France, and promised that France would give in, and cooperate. So all France knew, and knows, of 'the handshake at Montoire'.

I remember my mother, who came from the Midlands, telling her children about Palmer 'the Rugeley murderer', and how – so notorious had he made their town – the Rugeley people asked the Home Secretary if the name of the town couldn't be changed? No, said the Home Secretary, who was Lord Palmerston, – not unless you rename it after me, and call it Palmer's Town.

Witty, no doubt. My mama liked the wit, but as a woman of her Victorian generation she didn't see the insolence, the way in which a Victorian statesman could twit mere common townspeople in a small Staffordshire town. His behaviour wouldn't do for a modern Home Secretary. A good thing too.

If Montoire feels uncomfortable – I am sure it does – about 'the handshake at Montoire', it has never had to suffer jokes about a change of name to Pétainville or Laval-sur-Loir.

༺ॐༀ

Meanwhile let it also be recorded of Montoire that its people are served by one of the best *charcutiers* of France (the say so is French, not mine). Try this M. Cureau's *saucisson en brioche*, his *pâté de foie*. See the confections this tall overworked artist with a stoop and a sad face carries out into his van for First Communion beanos in June. The worst days in Montoire are when a notice in the door says the shop is closed for a fortnight, while M. Cureau and his family take their annual holiday.

༺ॐༀ

I dreamt last night that Ben Nicholson was talking to me and others we had both known in Hampstead forty years ago. He was explaining what he called, in this dream, 'Islands on the coast of colour.'

177

Then I found myself in an oak tree with Ben's mama, James Pryde's sister (whom I never knew, though I know about her from Ben's writings, and his conversation, an enigmatic but impulsive woman who once walked into the Channel in a new Paris gown, in the moonlight, for a swim, with Orpen's wife). The oak was rather symmetrical, its leaves were formalized and not very thick. Ben called up that a cuckoo had flown into the oak: we both bent down and looked for it, and saw it several times, its back below us mottled with blue. Ben's mother leant forward again and shooed it a little, but this time she leant forward too much and over-balanced the tree, which fell slowly forward. We were neither of us frightened or harmed.

✥

Straight pewter measures with straight handles, in a set from a litre downwards, are standard in French antique shops, in Montoire, Vendôme, in the shops down the Rue de la Scellerie at Tours – everywhere. *Mazagrans*, too, for drinking coffee, tapering downwards, with no handle, with a simple design on perhaps a white glaze. They are deceptive, both measures and *mazagrans*, I mean they deceive the foreigner, who discovers them to be about five times as expensive as he thought they were going to be.

Social or economic historians should consider the French antique shop, and its pretentious paucity of dull goods, at a high price. In a shop in one of the small towns round here, or on a main road, there may be a good country cupboard, an *armoire* of cherry wood (one of the hold-alls of the farmhouse or cottage living-room), there may be a good chest or kneading-trough, and a piece or two of the soft earthenware, glazed brown outside, cream inside, with a band of yellow round the rim, which used to be common form in all poor households (sherds of it come to the surface in the garden). The rest will be rubbish, often the wormy rubbish of bygones – those wormy wooden screws from an old wine-press, or bits of gentility made in this century in imitation of the eighteenth century, or rough farm tables enormously expensive (feel for the repairer's putty still soft under the brown varnish), a fireback or two, a pot crane (painted silver), or a modern cast in imitation stone of a Gothic Virgin or a Romanesque apostle. The style of

178

living even in this agriculturally rich area has been too poor and squalid. Wealth has been too unevenly distributed. Pleasant things have not piled up in the cottages – or the farmhouses – after four or five generations of family life, and then made their way, by natural descent, into the antique shops.

Be warned, if you think of settling in rural France: you will not be able to furnish your cottage with nice bits of simple furniture picked up cheaply and easily at sales or in shops. Also remember that the country Frenchman inclines to be short and small. He would fit into those small sixteenth or seventeenth century helmets which hang above tombs in English churches; which means that chairs – even new chairs – are lower than the standard English chair. On one of these minuscule straw-bottomed chairs the English back above the English behind soon begins to ache.

ᴄ⭐ᴠ

Very elegant white water-towers, new ones, gleam, as I say, on ridges around Trôo, in sun, against very overtowering black clouds piled over the sky.

I have been tempted to compel Americans at Trôo – perhaps I have been beastly enough to come out with this once or twice – to observe these water-towers, and consider that the water-towers which go up over the plains of America against black skies are brutish, in lack of elegance and grace. Brutish they are.

Perhaps internal grace can be independent, altogether, of external disgrace?

ᴄ⭐ᴠ

I am told that the features of Taranis le Chevelu, Taranus or Taranis the Hairy, god of thunder and storm, who was worshipped by the Gauls of our neighbourhood, can be seen carved on a *cippus* or funerary column, now in the old-fashioned junk-shop of an archaeological museum at Tours, thirty miles away. He was having a night out last night. Thunderstorms the whole length of the plateau towards Tours, forks, snakes, veins, quiverings of lightning. And here, this side of the Loir,

179

not a drop of water to fill our butts; which will now have to be refilled by jerry-can journeys down from the great well.

Taranis – that is the way he should be spelt – means Thunderer: humans were sacrificed to him, by being burnt – I suppose alive – in wooden tubs; much, without the tubs, as Christians here burnt those dissenting Christians on the *butte*.

⌇⌇

Mangolds protruding from the earth, in naked rows, all the leaves cut off before the mangolds are heaved into the carts. Naked and straight rows, this French gift for neatness of pattern.

⌇⌇

Buying the Gallimard edition of the complete works of Ronsard has set me considering the scrap-yard in Montoire and the yard of the *marchand de matériaux*, the builder's merchant.

The tidiness of those yards. Sometimes the scrap-dealer has something for sale which is more than scrap, and anyhow his yard is worth visiting for its order. You go in, an Alsatian barks (on a chain), Mme Scrap-dealer emerges, neat, plump, polite, smiling, from a smartly painted house verging on to scrap – no, on to Chaos – translated into Order; to which you are waved.

All bits of aluminium are here, all bits of brass are there.

You walk between piled up walls of ordered disorder, along alleys on which not an old bolt, not a broken spring, is permitted to fall.

Order at the builder's merchant is more to be expected, and this other yard always strikes me as a place of charm, poetry, width, coolness – as well as order. The charm, around a long empty rectangle into which the lorries drive, of tiles, bricks, timber, concrete blocks, lavatory pedestals, surrounded with light under a perfectly satisfying sky (blue with a half-dozen innocent clouds). The yellow poplars at the far end are turning over just a little, in just enough breeze.

There is a Corot, *The House and Factory of Monsieur Henri*, which cools and enlarges one's feelings in the same way.

⌇⌇

Ronsard, *Oeuvres Complètes*, two volumes, more than a thousand pages in each, should repeat the effect, poems instead of lavatory pedestals. No, you are offered Chaos as Chaos, the poems all over the yard, or the two yards. You want one poem, you cannot find it.

Why? Because the French book-making, book-editing, book-publishing scholarly mind abominates anything more than the smallest *index*: it remains stuck in the feudal unreformed unindexed disorder of the seventeenth century. There is no index of titles, and in 2000 pp. there are many poems (in this country they wouldn't even index a brief *History of the Index*).

So I've spent much of yesterday evening, a good autumn evening when I should have been out, and much of yesterday night, looking for a dozen or twenty famous lines in Ronsard – Ronsard knowing all about the wine cave and the *pressoir* – in which he likens young wine working in the cask to young poetry.

Not very helpfully or sensibly there is an index of first lines, a piddling concession to Rule, Order and Enlightenment. But I don't know the first line of the poem these lines come from.

I do know the title, *Élégie au Seigneur l'Huillier*. Everyone who quotes the lines says they come from the *Élégie au Seigneur l'Huillier*.

I finger through 2000 pp. I cannot find it, or I find another elegy to this Seigneur, and it's the wrong one. I discover – at last – that the right one was published as No. 16 in Ronsard's poems of 1560, for which there is a special section in this *Complete Works*. I look again. It is not there. I find – from a Ronsard anthology which gives extracts but doesn't name the poems they are extracted from – that the *Élégie* I want was republished in the works of 1578. No help: it is not in the section for the new things – the possibly revised or rewritten things – in the works of 1578.

I begin to think it must have been left out by accident. But that couldn't be so.

I give up. Time 2 a.m. Tomorrow I shall feel lousy. No, a last shot: I turn to a book about Ronsard by the editor of these *Oeuvres Complètes*, I find the bubbling of the wine quoted as usual,

Comme on void en Septembre és tonneaux Angevins,

I find the bubbling of the wine comes, yes, yes, from *Une Élégie au Seigneur l'Huillier* of 1560, later on printed by Ronsard in his *Bocage royal* of 1584. Several times tonight I've gone through the *Bocage royal* – but there's a footnote: Ronsard readdressed the elegy to a certain E. de Trousilly. I go through the *Bocage royal* again.

There it is – time 2.30 a.m. – Tome I, page 885, *à E. de Trousilly*: no *élégie* in the title, no Seigneur l'Huillier.

Bless the scrap-dealer. Bless the *marchand de matériaux*. And may Reason bless M. Gustave Cohen, *Ronsardisant*, scholar, editor, confuser, misleader, time-waster, with just a trifle more love for indexes, a trifle more Right Method, instead of Wrong Method, just a scintilla of that 'clear light of geometric reasoning' which Monsieur Descartes did introduce into France – with incomplete success – nearly two and a half centuries ago.

⌇᷾᷾

In extenuation I must say it was this M. Gustave Cohen who put up the black votive tablet, hung on a tree, in the antique fashion, etc., at the downstream end of the Ile verte in the Loir some thirty-five years ago. Someone has just had it relettered.

And here are the lines, from the *Élégie*:

> As one in September sees in Anjou casks
> The wine's youth boil and foam, warmed
> In its cradle, grumbling, growling,
> Eager to burst out by the bung,
> Impatient, ardent, never resting, swelling,
> Frothing, spouting, spirting,
> Till cold winter's tamed its strength
> And barred its power in prisons of a skin,
> So in its young age poetry
> Boils in our hearts, with small
> Respect for reason, serves our appetites,
> And brusquely heightens the lively
> Poet's high-souled rage.
> He falls in love, pursues great lords,
> Loves favours, looks for honours,
> Is passionate, with no repose of mind
> Except at night: by day he is

Too ardent to give way, suspicious,
Full of rage, contempt, and pride,
Mindful and curious only of himself,
Acting like a God, his brashness
Goaded by the felon fury
Of his young desire –

Until in old age –

ჟ↸ん

For September in that first line, read October, early October,
the usual time of the vintage here, and I suppose in Anjou. The
calendar hadn't been corrected when Ronsard wrote in 1560; so
the *vendange* as a rule would have come ten days or so 'earlier' – in
September.

Why insist on that? Because, as I write, it is now well past the
first week of October. Maurice's grape-harvest is behind him,
his *tonneaux* are recharged, and he says 'Listen', today, as he and
I (bleary-eyed from Gustave Cohen's lack of an index of titles)
balance down the greasy slope to the slatted door of his cave,
Maurice with the key in his hand.

'Listen.' A grumbling, growling, bubbling, heaving noise
comes through the slats; and I am going to take home a bottle
of the pale pink *bernâche*, the still fermenting *rosé*, with a channel
cut up the side of the cork, so that it can continue to ferment
until we have finished off the bottle, and no doubt loosened our
bowels considerably.

ჟ↸ん

I would like to know a little more about that Seigneur l'Huillier
who has caused me such trouble and who was a friend of Ronsard's when both were young, H. l'Huillier, seigneur de
Maisonfleur – but where's that? Ronsard must have loved him.
He wrote him that wine-and-poetry elegy, and the other elegy,
he dedicated one book of poems to him, also that nice gay poem
of the journey to Tours. Then he took his dedications back.
Because l'Huillier served what one might call the Black Prots,
he wrote Prot. psalms and hymns; and Protestants – and the
religious wars – Ronsard did not like to remember.

Or perhaps Ronsard remained gentle, perhaps l'Huillier in

his Calvinism hardened coarsely and grew priggish – that
dancing at St-Cosme, those love poems from a prior.

Such divergence between friends and poets can go deep as
the Grand Canyon.

ᘓᘏᕉᘏᕉ

The poems of Ronsard I regret are the ones of Ronsard
engagé – against the Calvinists, the Huguenots. O yes, the Church
needs correction, its abuses are manifold, our faults are gross,
we have sinned, but O you spiritually proud Calvinists who
believe God has spoken only to yourselves. And you back-
sliding magistrates waiting to see how the cat will jump,

> If you had used punishment's keen blade
> On the unruly Huguenot, the beastly heretic,
> The people would have peace, but your complicity
> Has destroyed the fair fame of France's sovreignty.

I don't say he lowers himself to a Roy Campbell-against-the-
Reds, or a Hugh MacDiarmid slapping England because it is
neither Scottish nor communist. One mustn't be obscene about
Ronsard. I see that in 1562 rejection of what Ronsard was
bound to call the – not our – church, the church supposedly
universal, must have seemed like hanging a black veil across an
immutable sun; I see that everything in Ronsard detested the
unruly, that the religious wars snarled into his image and actuality of perfection, the Bas-Vendômois.

But he is partisan. We sinners are white, they're black:

> *Ne presche plus en France une Évangile armée,*
> *Un Christ empistollé, tout noircy de fumée –*

ᘓᘏᕉᘏᕉ

> What – burning houses, looting, robbing,
> Killing, murdering, military government,
> Obeying Kings no more, conscripting armies,
> You call that the Church reformed? . . .
> Stop preaching in France a gospel under arms,
> A pistolled Christ all black with smoke,
> Who like Mahomet carried in his hand
> A large cutlass red with blood!

I notice these bits are usually in selections from Ronsard –
when selected by members of the Académie française – though
his scent rises from other poems. Sartre says culture – after all –
doesn't justify, doesn't save; but is the critical mirror showing
man his image. Auden says art is impotent, against social evils,
art isn't journalism, art isn't action. Art exhibits 'Permanence
and Nowness'. 'Poetry is personal speech in its purest form';
it is our way of speaking with the dead, and speak with them
we must. I speak to Ronsard, I catch his lemon scent, through
other poems.

From Kremlinologists, not least when they write on Yev-
tushenko or Pasternak, I get the stench of propaganda combined with the acid armpit smell of, I should think, personal
unease. A pity one has to get a whiff of the propaganda stench
from Ronsard too, as if they were burning another Huguenot,
tout noirci de fumée, or another True Believer on the *butte*, or an
old tyre down on the Rue Haute.

ᘒᘒᘒ

An exploration in warm evening air in the valley of the Cendrine, above Ronsard's priory of Croixval, but not because of
Ronsard. A ford still unbridged except by a few oak planks for
foot passengers looked inviting whenever I had passed up or
down this little valley of poplars and wine caves.

I accepted the invitation, having learnt that this was where
the Roman road from Tours to Paris crossed the stream; also
that sixty years ago some Gallo-Roman graves cut into the
chalk rock were found by workmen just above the ford, when
they were building an outhouse.

What appeared to be the Roman road, or the line of the road,
climbed the slopes of the valley, on either side of the ford, by
very deep hollow lanes; one lane through a wood, abandoned
and filled with brambles and cut branches, the other up to the
plateau.

The house and the outhouse were there, all right, above the
Cendrine. Asked the owner in his little warm house across from
the barn (invited indoors for a glass of his red wine) if he knew
anything about the graves in the rock. He knew nothing, but
with his Polish wife this retired farmer hadn't lived there more
than a year. I expect the graves must long ago have disappeared,

which is the trouble – archaeologically and sentimentally – about exposures of this soft rock.

✣

Exactly why – that question again – is one's very transient self pleased and comforted by knowing that a site like this one has been trodden by men for nearly two thousand years, if not more? Why do these graves and this Roman road so much accentuate the visible attraction of a little clean ford of brown pebbles of flint, under autumnal poplars?

> *Entre gaiement dans le vallon;*
> *Presse un peu le pas de Virgile,*
> *Retiens par la manche Villon –*

Each small valley off our wide valley is in the human territory. *Presse un peu le pas de Ronsard*, as well; *et le pas de Hugo.*

✣

I like a country, too, where gleanies – guinea fowls – abound on the farms, running as if they were birds out of a jungle or a zoo, dropping grey feathers dotted with white. These are feathers of happiness. They were scattered on the grass where we had parked the car, a few yards from the ford.

✣

Seeing deer and hairy black legs and haunches of wild boar hung up once more in the covered market at Tours reminded me of wolves.

When did the wolves disappear round Trôo?

In that hymn for the people of Montrouveau Ronsard asked St Blaise to guard the sheep as they went between fold and pasture, or rather he asked that surly mastiffs should guard them and keep the wolves away; which was more than a literary gesture out of the *Georgics*. He wrote the hymn about 1580. Gastines, or most of it, was cleared, but there remained plenty of cover for wolves, and parish registers record attacks by wolves for two hundred years after Ronsard's time. In 1675 rabid wolves bit and infected three women at Les Hayes (which is

186

still divided from Montrouveau by a remnant of Gastines, the remnant we walked through, or pushed through, the other evening as we searched for the Roman road in a wolf-dusk which was rather intimidating). In 1784, in a very cold winter, two women were attacked and killed by starving wolves at Houssay, a few miles away, between Montoire and Vendôme.

꧁꧂

I looked for information about wolves in Michel Devèze's book *La vie de la forêt française au XIVe siècle*. All I came out with was a proverb from the Basse-Bretagne: that 'charcoal-burners and wolves howl in the forest.' Devèze says that charcoal-burners were often a class of untouchables. We have come across their smoking mounds or furnaces in the Forêt de Beaumont, to the south of Montrouveau.

꧁꧂

The *bûcheron*, the woodcutter of Ronsard's poem, who swung his axe on the oaks of Gastines, and wounded the Dryads – Devèze says that he as well would have belonged to a class of untouchables. Years ago excavations at Notre-Dame in Paris produced a Gallic relief of a *bûcheron* in a short tunic, axing a tree. This was Esus, the god of the woodcutters of Gaul. This god was like Silvanus in the Roman pantheon. If his woods were interfered with, it was wise to give Esus his *quid pro quo*, his sacrifice of a man: someone was suspended from a tree and stabbed to death: the blood poured down, and they read omens from the way the blood flowed among the tree roots.

I am rather glad to reach the far end of a wood where I can see the full daylight once more beyond the trees.

꧁꧂

How did they choose individuals for sacrifice? The human victims I've seen (the tanned bog corpses in Danish and German museums, turned into brown-black satin) look like the clever and delicate chosen by the strong and nasty. Pierre de Ronsard might have been strung up in Gastines, for Esus?

꧁꧂

There was something of a community of woodlanders – the woodcutters, the people who made wooden shoes, and casks, and oars and rudders and bowls, the charcoal burners, the honey men. I imagine that would have been so in the times of Esus: had Ronsard been alive then, a whole community would have been interested in stringing him up, supposing he had been found meditating under the oak trees. Critics to a man.

જ્જ

Cords of firewood continue to be stacked precisely and neatly along the woodland roads in every *commune*. I like this continued using of the woods, I like the way people come to the woods for fungi. When we began to search a wood for *ceps* and *trompettes de mort* earlier this week we heard a noise of children, grown-ups and a dog at the other end. This morning I went to cash a traveller's cheque at Montoire and the lame good-looking young clerk looked up, blushed, and asked 'Did you find any mushrooms?' He and his family had been out there mushrooming on his day off. He had heard us talking English.

જ્જ

I have been reading, better late than never, about Claudel, reading the letters which passed between him and Gide. A mixture of Claudel and a good curry for lunch (but I think it was more Claudel than the curry) prevented me from sleeping, until I got out and took one and a half tablets of tranquillizer.

I couldn't help imagining him; and I woke up, and began imagining him again. Short, thick, certain, bland, concerned, unconcerned, unshakable. A rather, in a way, coarse or obvious marble statue of Hercules which moved (and was dressed as befits an ambassador). A St Christopher, an ex-ogre; no, a Christian ogre, with iron muscles, resolutely making journeys with lesser people to the other side.

Rockall; which is not the island of my preference.

But what a man, that self-assured dictatorial statue of catholicism, which one has to admire against one's will!

The correspondence with Gide is a kind of comedy. St Christopher-Claudel presses forward, confident he is going to pick up this prize, and ferry him over. Gide advances, has a

188

fascinated look, retreats, comes back, has another and another look, and slips aside; saying in his journal, at the end, that catholicism only encouraged Claudel's pride and that communion infatuated him; saying also that this hard Catholic owed it to himself to vomit others; and that he, Gide, would rather be vomited than vomit.

❧

Claudel breaking off, listening in courtesy to what you say, and then continuing from the point where he broke off.

A dry warm wind, not much of a wind, now takes a few leaves off the dying greengage, and I feel better.

❧

I remember that when I finished *Le Rouge et le Noir*, the first time I read it, I felt I needed a bath: that Julien had really introduced me to evil (which isn't very common?). Claudel makes me want a bath, having introduced me to something of which I don't know the name, exactly.

❧

When a French woman I know asks me what they think of Claudel in England, and when without waiting for a reply she goes on and assures me that he is no less great than Shakespeare, I do think I understand a little about an unattractive aspect of the French, or a little about one of the minds of France, about those Catholics who scramble up Claudel's leg, into Claudel's pocket, where they contrive for themselves a culture nest, in rather a snobbish and relieved way.

They are Gaullistes as a rule?

I then remember Claudel on Victor Hugo (but how grateful I am for what he says positively of Hugo's poems): 'A murky spirit, a heart more warm than compassionate, an upright nature served by next to no religious or moral education and by hostile circumstances, to succumb in the end in a quite despicable way to the flesh, a taste for honour allied to a much more powerful taste for posing.' What an iron insolence! And how might Hugo have described Claudel?

Next I remember Eliot — Eliot on Hardy, Eliot on D. H.

Lawrence, Eliot on Blake, on Hopkins; and at home the many who don't know an aster from an ampersand, a poem from a paean of advertising copy, and have yet scrambled up the leg and into the pocket of our own more equivocal poet of divine Toryism. But they hardly count, or have significance, in the same societary manner.

Then, perhaps having no right to be talking of Claudel, no right to be cynical about, let's say, the recitation of his verses in front of the Pope, or about Claudel translating (a little of) G. K. Chesterton and Francis Thompson, I am interested to discover that an English poet, who is of partly Jewish descent, who is still fairly young, and who is a busy expositor of the avant-garde in painting and constructions in light and movement, should recently have translated Claudel's *Cinq Grandes Odes*.[1]

What is it that attracts him, situated as he appears to be, in London, in these 1960s, to this Christian rhetoric?

Affinity or 'Submission pure and simple to God's will and ordination'? The antiquarianism of poetry? Taking our begging bowl to Paris? 'I am being broadminded'? Paradox? Doing what hasn't been done because it hasn't been done? Poetry, in spite of beliefs?

༻ཚ༺

No, I try and I still cannot stand Claudel. I dislike poets always or so often poised on the theatrical edge of the universe (Hugo comes down to the dirt, on the grassy edges of the parish, and on to the pavement). I dislike poetry of exclamation and exclamation marks, poets of *le, et, comme*, poets who sugar their exclamatory writing with *beauty, soul, inspiration, eternal, wings, God*. I dislike such poetry and such poets all the more when I sit and read them here on the terrace, with this air around me.

༻ཚ༺

Photos and drawings of Claudel. That curiously blank face, pushed forward, like the face of Enoch Powell, another prophet – but an untalented and ridiculous one – shot into our time from the Old Testament. Dufy's drawing of Claudel; I see

[1] *Five Great Odes. Paul Claudel*, translated by Edward Lucie-Smith, 1967.

Claudel could have liked Dufy's delight: could Dufy, that much enjoyed, yet underesteemed artist, have cared for the hard grand impudence of Claudel? I hope not.

꽃

How attractive that hard grand impudence, that self-confidence of lofty Catholic dismissal, to the obstinately Catholic or obstinately Christian reader without Claudel's intelligence:

> You have called me by my name
> Like someone who knew it, you have chosen me among
> all men of my time . . .

> The man who no longer believes in God, no longer
> believes in being, and the man who hates being, hates
> his own existence . . .

> The night comes, stay with me, Lord, and do not desert
> me!
> Do not destroy me with the Voltaires, and the Renans and
> the Michelets, and the Hugos, and the rest of the
> infamous!
> Whose soul is with dead dogs, whose books are one with
> the dunghill.

> They are dead, and after death their name itself is poison
> and rottenness.

I see a priest, a widow of the *haute bourgeoisie*, comforted because Claudel throws the inconvenient out of his poet's window. Evolution, let's say, along with the infinite.

One likes the finite, the object, certainly; but even if the idea of the evolving, the mutating, the restlessly changing, didn't accord with Claudel's neo-psalmody, how did he have the nerve to say to those who were Christian but not poets, that 'the idea of evolution is no less abominable [than the idea of the infinite] because it tends to give the whole of creation a character indefinitely provisional and precarious'?

If it *has* such a character, what then?

He is a bully, this Claudel. 'God created: I ally myself with those who once knew no better, and I insist: "God" and "created"; and I spit on science, on knowing, when knowing is inconvenient. Spit with me.'

And by God how they spit; and how much I prefer Hopkins saying apropos of evolution, in his day, that it was a matter he didn't care to inquire into, a Hopkins talking of the mystery of his God as something indefinable inside the definition, for him, of a clear bounding line or circumference. How much I prefer Hopkins as a poet, in the substance of his poems.

꙳

Quoted by a reviewer from Claudel's *Journal* (Claudel had been reading an English life of Henry VIII): 'The fearful young pig from whose conjunction with Nan Bullen, *the Whore*, was born the disgusting sow which is the Church of England, mother of English Protestantism.'

꙳

I see Claudel in the insistent hooded superiority of the spire of St-Jacques down below, across the river. The spire is covered in black slate: it is very upright: it has two window openings, two eyes at belfry level: it regards the river fields and the level light as if it were a self-righteous vengeful inquisitor wearing a pitiless hood. 'O Lord, do not destroy me with Victor Hugo, etc. But, Lord, you won't, of course you won't.'

To be fair to him, Claudel's obscurantism is more frightening in Claudelians ('Claudel is as great as Shakespeare, Monsieur Grigson') than in his psalms.

꙳

Why can I accept the Christianity of George Herbert – though 'accept' may beg the question – and not the Christianity of Eliot or Auden, or Claudel, or any television apologist?

Because Herbert had no option. He had no possible, no sensible alternative. It was his inevitable mode of evaluation.

꙳

St James of Compostela enters Claudel's poems and plays. More real to me is the thought of pilgrims from the north of France, or England, reaching the Loir by the mill, by St James's church and St James's priory. They arrive in groups of thirty or forty. They sit on the bank, dirty and too fagged to sing, and wait for the ferryman to take them across. I maintain to myself that St Godric, strong hermit of Finchale on the Wear, under the steep woods, repentant tradesman, shipowner and pirate, was one of them, passing the night at St-Jacques and seeing the new paintings of St James being martyred, and sinners being tortured, and Christ in glory (twelfth century paintings amethystine and green, and still clear when evening light comes through the west door). St Godric trudged twice to Rome, once to St Gilles in Provence and once to Compostela.

The pilgrims would have walked out of the valley and over the plateau to a night's lodging at Tours (in the church above St Martin's body). At Tours they would have joined the *magnum iter Sancti Jacobi*, one of the main pilgrim routes through France, the route from Paris to Compostela; they would have sweated on by way of Poitiers, St-Jean-d'Angely, Saintes, Bordeaux, south of St-Jean-pied-de-Port, then over the portus or pass of Roncevalles into Spain.

❧

At Compostela the pilgrims stitched scallop shells, *coquilles de St Jacques*, the badge of the saint, on to their clothes or their hat. Only this autumn I was shown a magnificent scallop shell carved into the roof of one of the best cave houses at Trôo, a house which is supposed to have been a pilgrims' lodging.

❧

Once I looked at a sun-blackened, black-bearded pilgrim standing in dusty boots and breeches in front of the spring at Lourdes: he seemed to have walked across France, or across Europe, so I can imagine the visage, the stance, of pilgrims burnt by the sun and looking like paynims (see *Piers Plowman*, though that wasn't all he meant by the paynim look) – except that this pilgrim was solitary among the appalling cripples.

Piers Plowman wrote about pilgrims traipsing through

Europe and never finding St Truth. You could die on pilgrimage, of course, you could get fagged, dry, dusty, be knocked on the head, and have diarrhoea and worse from bad water without benefit of J. Collis Browne. Pilgrims came home 'and hadden leave to lie all their life after'.

Wasn't it tourism; wasn't it our inescapable wish –my inescapable wish – to be on the move and elsewhere; and bother St Truth?

I found once in a book on migration particulars of an Indian tribe deep in the deepest, remotest jungle inside Brazil, who gave way every so often to a desire to look at the sea. They travelled thousands of miles through swamps and trees and down the Amazon, and looked at the Atlantic, and came back.

Le pèlerinage de vie humaine, etc.

❧

A GB car went up our lane of flints yesterday to Trôo church. There were coloured stickers all over it, from French towns and English towns. That also reminded me of pilgrimage as tourism, and Piers Plowman. The pilgrim in Passus V, not having a car, had a hundred holy water ampullas stuck on his hat, shells showing he had been to Compostela, keys showing he had been to Rome, and so on. Stickers. Venial showing off.

❧

The autumn is breaking up. Under a threat of rain went mushrooming in woods behind the cliff and the church. The rain began, and became worse – rain, rain, rain in thin parallels, not a break at all in the grey. Ten of us among the oaks. One by one we emerge, and stand by the two cars, and wait. Then Maurice emerges, last of all, a sack round his low shoulders, an old old beret projecting over his forehead. He waves a hand and drags with the other hand a sack bulging with twenty kilos of *trompettes de mort*, to be dried for the winter.

Maurice's amused bantering look of 'I've found something. You haven't' – though we had – 'you English and Parisians whom I love, though you are not very bright after all about woods and mushrooms.'

❧

Branches of an extra tall sorb tree black through such brown leaves as remain. Sorbs on the grass underneath, not yet bletted, green inside their ochre skins, and too sour to eat. Chestnuts on the ground, brambles heavy with sweet blackberries, all within reach, then an *alisier* studded with little brown fruit hanging among the leaves, looking wet.

All this fructification along an alley no longer maintained and now rutted by tractors, which leads from the shuttered country house I described on an earlier page, miles from anywhere on the farm plain. Quiet and shelter in the alley, until we came to a break. Overhead, and seen through breaks to the horizon either way, comfortless rain-clouds in a hurry, low down, rank after rank. The sorb tree was one of that group we found in the summer, and marked for this October expedition when the fruit would be falling; we imagined we would come back on an ideal afternoon of October warmth.

Met a man at the end of the alley with a gun under his arm: we thought he was a hunter, he thought we were poachers. He was in fact a gamekeeper. Picked corn marigolds in the rain, by a hedgeless crossroads – three mud lanes, one road. Tonight, roast chestnuts dipped in Maurice's red wine.

⁓✳⁓

Why don't we have more of these sorb trees in England? The species is *Sorbus domestica*. The trees have such a decidedly trim distinction of leaf, bark, and form, the sorbs are so much sweeter than medlars, and so much more agreeable, and they blet or ripen earlier on the ground. Medlars are still hard on the tree when we go home at the beginning of November, the sorbs by that time have all been shed and finished. On the rare sorb trees in England I believe the fruit are less abundant and less sugary.

⁓✳⁓

I find that by custom of the forest the common people of France were entitled to gather its wild fruits and the fruit of every ungrafted tree – sorbs, those little brown fruits of the *alisier*, quinces, pears, apples (to turn into cider), medlars, plums cherries, walnuts, chestnuts, hazel nuts, blackberries.

195

That would have been so when Ronsard walked the tracks of the valley and the fields. And it does something to explain the trees along woodland verges which we look forward to visiting every autumn. And perhaps some of the isolated sorb trees are relics of otherwise felled and cleared woodland; or have been planted to succeed sorb trees which were saved in that way?

Wild fruits for the poor, beechmast and acorns for the swine. But now the not-so-poor grow sweeter fruit in their gardens or buy sweeter fruit in Montoire market. The sorbs, and the fruit of the *alisier*, and the hard little pears, and the medlars, fall and rot away in the grass, or a tractor crushes them into the October mud. Only chestnuts are still collected by everyone.

Away from home, the Light Programme of the B.B.C. usefully provides the news; less agreeably that ponce-patter of the disc-jockeys, least agreeably at the moment the actor Bernard Miles delivering each morning the sayings of Christ thoughtfully translated into dialect. 'If one o'yur youngsters wants a bit o' bread and jam, yer don't give him arf a brick, do yer?'

About this isn't there a completeness or ultimacy of the treacle-soul? Everything clinches in one. We must have religion (Christian religion is always called 'religion', not Christianity) on the programme. Dialect is quaintly popular like thatch: we must have dialect on the air. The highest clerics, Anglican, Nonconformist, Roman, spawn translations of holy writ into cliché writ: we – supreme achievement in the treacle of the controlling mind – will go further and translate holy writ (for urban listeners) into ripe country writ; which an actor shall speak (when he isn't advertising bitter in dialect on commercial telly). Who isn't insulted in this drivelling process?

Edward Thomas's poem which ends

There's nothing like the sun till we are dead.

The sun having now returned, I agree. So would any retired managing director wintering in Madeira or adding an enclosed verandah to his house in the Sussex Weald, to catch the sun. We don't, he and I, care to think of ourselves extinguished.

Sun is the opposite thought. In England there are days when I always find myself parking close to the funeral furnisher's office. Do I look straight at the funeral furnisher's window? I do not. The sun is reflected from the window into my eyes.

જ⁂જ

At last – this is the way things have gone in painting – a river, a hill, in the sunlight, with trees precise and miniature, waiting in perspective corners of quattrocento and Netherlandish pictures.

The landscape waits, the landscape enlarges, the landscape is pushed forward. This is 'beautiful', this is a value; the landscape enlarged around Golgotha is 'beautiful'. So is the skull of Adam – let us regard skulls, objectively – at the foot of that particular Tree. Ronsard is pushed forward; and this Loir down below – *heureuses tes ondes*, etc., – until the willow leaves are visible, Corot, Courbet, Pissarro, Sisley, Renoir: the Loir, all the rivers, each of them, river by itself; herbage sparkling, leaves twinkling or fallen, snow on the bank, blue shadow on the snow.

Then – reaction – God is brought back 'into the picture'; into the poem at any rate: God of neo-Catholicism and nationalism, God of Péguy, whose Beauce, and the soil under the wheat and the wheat over the soil and the sun over the wheat and the windmills (now derelict) between the wheat and the sun, are expression and experience of God.

Then – God looking too ridiculous – man returns; a flood of man; but also his skull, his rotten ribs, his torturing and being tortured, his crucifying and crucifixion; and everywhere in France, in a 'beautiful' and so disregarded piece of Ronsard, of Corot, of Sisley, there stands a cross of Lorraine (but let's not bother too much twenty-four years later about the patriotism of the Cross or the Saint) where Resistance men, once upon a time, were executed by Germans. In and out and back, through the inexplicably absurd.

De Gaulle cries 'France!', as if that wasn't the way back, all the time, to Oradour. The Pope (in this age of the Pill, the new Forbidden Berry) cries 'our one and only variety of God', with every televised gesture of his hands, as if this proclaiming of our one and only western variety of God mightn't be the way back

197

every so often to Oradour, and beyond Oradour to the St Bartholomew massacre (which a Pope approved), and to grilling heretics up on the *butte*. The Pope also said 'I love' – but that is another matter – in Hugo's poem:

Le Pape: *Les monts ont au front l'aube et les rois ont la nuit.*
       Dieu n'a pas fait les rois.
Les Rois (substitute for the kings whatever you like – say Mr Kingsley Amis, or President Nixon, or the *haute bourgeoisie*):
      N'es-tu pas roi toi-même?
Le Pape: *Moi! régner! non!*
Les Rois: *Alors, qu'est-ce que tu fais?*
Le Pape: *J'aime.*

Meanwhile allow me a brief old-fashioned enjoyment of the Loir, in the hope that my enjoyment passes to you, and your enjoyment passes to another me, and so on, helping a little, since the skull of Adam on our Golgotha remains real enough.

༒

From a Chinese friend and her translations I have learnt of Wen-I-To's poem *Quiet Night* –

Quiet night, I cannot, I cannot accept your bribery.

Is he to accept the bribery of his senses and his gift, his special 'poetry' gift, or is he to participate? Is he to perceive, or to help China at once, to help his portion of men, at once, in the crises of 1928?

In another poem about himself I suppose as an itinerant singer carrying a fiddle and a leopard-skin drum, a girl in a village, in his village, asks what their own peculiar song ought to be:

I played a flock of white doves in a frosty wood,
Their coral claws treading on a heap of yellow leaves,
Then you could hear the cicada crying in the crack in the stone
Turn suddenly into the sound of cold rain lashing the
    wooden gate.

Rain that will not stop falling, tears that will not stop
    flooding.

Also a third poem about liking – no less than a T'ang poet – white stones, blue pines, sunset on the back of ravens: but he is also thoughts which are flies crawling into the rubbish bin.

So Wen-I-To, who 'felt guilty about his quiescence', gave up poems for teaching.

Trôo – sensations, perceptions of Trôo, which is not in China of the 1920s or in Vietnam-America of the 1960s, but in our wider state of not-war which has lasted now more than twenty years?

I am not sure if the arts, the making process, can stand up against tenderness of conscience assailed all the time, and against entire instantaneous news.

Tu Fu, in the disordered bloody China of the eighth century: 'I am powerless to amend the world.' Auden: the world is always full of evils and misery, 'but it is a fatal delusion and a shocking overestimation of the importance of the artist in the world to suppose that by making works of art we can do anything to eradicate the one or alleviate the other.'

Yes, but from each according to his talent, which he can abandon but not change. I am for the theory of acts of art, acts of the purity of perception, of deduction and construction, as drops. Each drop causes a circular wave. The wave spreads: so many or so few – at any rate some – are touched.

It is Wen-I-To's poems that reach us and touch us. Did he allow himself to think of a circular wave spreading outwards from each drop of a poem written in China? No, but it is each good poem of his which goes on acting, helping to maintain the culture of human animals – is that useless altogether, against evils and misery?

Auden's remark was made against being *engagé* and hitching one's art-making power to propaganda for the 'best' causes. It can be taken as rather a shocking half-truth, all the same, with a trivializing power.

ᨀᢞᨏ

It may be an absolute duty to accept the bribery of the quiet night, alone, or along with the bribery of the flies in the dustbin.

ᨀᢞᨏ

When Paul Laumonier wrote his eight hundred page study of Ronsard's poems (which came out sixty years ago and six years after he had started to sweat on an edition of Ronsard in eighteen volumes which was to take him all his life) he could not do without one page about the people of this valley: Ronsard the Epicurean, Ronsard and Anacreon, Ronsard's bacchic odes, *Ronsard franc buveur comme Rabelais*; and then – Ronsard and the *moeurs du Bas-Vendômois*.

It may be sentimental, but I shall quote this piece even if I cower under the contempt of grim poet-picklers or poetry-isolaters – though I am quoting it, let me hurry to tell them, to explain my neighbours, not for Ronsard.

'To understand Ronsard as a bacchic poet,' Laumonier begins, 'one has to have lived for a while among the people of the Bas-Vendômois – he typifies them. Very cultured and superior he may be, but *au fond* he is one of them. In their character Ronsard's character will be rediscovered, in spite of the three and a half centuries between them. The spirit of this region animates his lighter work; which is entirely penetrated by the savour and bouquet of the soil. The people of Couture are good-humoured and agreeable. Nature is good to them. The land is a good mother to them: they are all the more devoted to it now that the break-up of the country estates has assured them a more or less easy life, now that everyone has his own house and his own piece of land to cultivate. Their happiness seems to have something about it of an epicurean quality, without apprehension, without ambition; they live so far from the storms of existence, which goes by so pleasantly in the shadow of their church-tower. They live in peace, content with their middling lot, their *aurea mediocritas*. Indeed they have nothing to envy in the farmyards of Maine, in the granaries of the Beauce, in the gardens and meadows of Touraine, in the next-door vineyards of Anjou; and if there were a high wall which cut them off from the rest of the world, they would still find in their own country a sufficiency, an abundance even, of everything necessary to a life of ease. So they eat well, and drink better, these good farmers; and they have the prerogative of gaiety. 'Tipplers with thirsty throats,' to use the words of their poet, by nature they are all unconscious disciples of Anacreon; and Ronsard faithfully interpreted their attitude of mind when he wrote,

> *L'homme trop sobre ne vit pas,*
> *Luy-mesme en vivant il s'ennuye*:

La dance, le vin, les repas
Sont les instruments de la vie.

Above all they are drinkers of white wine, those heady wines which are the products of the hills of Trôo, Sougé, Couture, Poncé, Villedieu, Chapelle-Gaugain. They cannot meet without the offer of a friendly glass.'

༄

It is true – *jamais pressé*, after sixteen hundred years of the *vendange* and the wine-press. Open another bottle. How many times have we been entertained with a glass of wine by complete strangers in this valley! How often we are struck by the expression of loving and having been loved, and satisfied, on the faces of women we meet on the lanes and in the fields and in the villages!

A high record of mutual performance in this valley, I would opine. Not the one minute, up, in, out and over, which Kinsey found in the working class males and females of the U.S.A.

༄

Which is something, and a portion of being civilized. I marked two sentences in the translation of an essay by de Montherlant, a writer of no great appeal to most English writers:

'Respectable pleasure: the most genuine, clear-cut, all-square thing in the world. I have had satisfaction. So has my partner . . .

'Generous pleasure: our pleasure is our partner's pleasure. How wonderful to indulge oneself and have the sensation that one is accomplishing a good deed!'

༄

How, in fact, do you imagine a phallus? As a carving insistent, arrogantly erect, selfish, masculine in a cocky way? Wrong. I have in front of me a photograph of a phallus, Greek or Graeco-Roman, carved – to avert the Evil Eye – at an intersection of streets in Leptis Magna (where the Mediterranean creams into the old forum). It is a friendly and charming object, it is curly and graceful, it is kind, modest, genial.

⌇⌇⌇

We saw in a window at Conches, in Normandy, the virgin martyr of Aquitaine, Ste Foi, having her breasts torn off with pincers. J., who indulges in moments of the just championship of women, complained that in martyrdoms it is always female saints who are having their characteristic protuberances pulled off or cut off or exhibited on a plate, never male saints losing male protuberances.

'You see what comes of a male priesthood, a celibate priest-hood, castrated spiritually and getting its own back on women.'

I defended the priesthood – iconographically – by saying that the female protuberances have always been more or less unavoidable and on exhibition, whereas the more operative male parts have always been hidden by protective *pudor*. St Agatha carrying her breasts on a platter, yes: but a male saint's severed apparatus on a plate would have been taboo.

But J. won't give way.

⌇⌇⌇

A pleasure of this Loir valley (and of all parts of France where there are peasant vineyards or apple orchards): the still, the *alambic*, under the trees.

The distiller travels round from site to site, you see his primitive-looking apparatus, half a black firebox, half cooling tanks, painted a dull red, tucked away in the shade of trees by a stream or on a river bank, a black hose going down into the water, and smoke rising from a black chimney into the un-leafing poplars. He is the licensed distiller of *eau de vie de marc*, or *marc* for short, i.e. spirits from the *marc* or residuum of skin and pips after the last drop of wine has been screwed out of the grapes, or from the *marc* which remains after pressing the apples.

Last week we found our local distiller or rather the still, be-cause he had finished work for the day, under some poplars at La Fontaine, a hamlet with many wine caves in a valley cut into the southern escarpment of the Loir. A mixed smell of wet ashes and alcohol (the furnace still warm). On one side a section of a tree trunk serving as a table, three glasses on top, and some log stools round it; a pile of cleft wood (under plastic fertilizer bags) and a faggot or two of vine twigs for kindling. In the corner a heap of *marc* – or rather the residuum of the residuum of the grapes, after distillation – swarming with fruit-flies. Also black tongs, a long black iron for the furnace, and a black besom.

Everything rather dirty – except the business end of the still, a curved beak beautifully clean where the *eau de vie* trickles out drop by drop.

Plain drunkenness is one result. Many *deux chevaux*, the little tinny blue-grey Citroens, make miraculous journeys, down flinty lanes from caves in folds of woodland, along or across main roads, and somehow, somehow, into courtyards, after cave parties at which the drinking has moved on from wine to *eau de vie de marc*.

The drink of the gods – of divine participation. The gods vanish, the drink remains, with the getting drunk, getting extremely drunk.

ღჄ

There are alcoholics in Trôo. There are alcoholics everywhere in France. Frenchmen drink more per head than any other nation – more than Americans. Someone wrote in one of the papers at the time of the Olympic Games in Mexico that if there were Olympic Games for drink, France would win all the gold, silver, and bronze medals – and the zinc medals as well, if there were any.

But if I don't go into wine ecstatics, I am still unable to think of this valley – or the hills of this valley – without their vineyards, without their wine caves in the woods, without their wine parties, without a secretive trade in bottles of *marc*. In a history of Touraine I have been reading of the way the good Emperor Probus had vineyards planted everywhere by his soldiers after his recovery of Gaul. So they have been wine-bibbers here from the end of the third century.

Against alcoholism – and there is an old man who teeters round the village, waxy-skinned, vague-eyed, hands trembling – I'd set the advantage that everyone who grows some vines and makes a tolerable wine, however humble he is socially, has something to offer by way of good nature or friendship. To be asked to *boire un coup*, though he may be a poor peasant and you may be a rich bourgeois from Paris, acts rather like everyone calling everyone else Monsieur or Madame. And if you are not going off to drive a car, there are worse things for yourself and everyone than – elementary (and local) pun – a *coup de Trôo*, a *coup de trop*.

❦

But observe that this pleasure of seeing the distiller and his *alambic* under the trees isn't going to continue much longer. The making of *marc* is controlled. Fifty years ago a man with an orchard or a vineyard could make, or have made for him, as much as he liked. Then the right was limited to ten litres at a strength of a hundred degrees (or *pro rata*, e.g. twenty litres at a strength of fifty degrees) per person. The right goes to a husband or wife, if either proprietor dies, but no longer to anyone else who inherits or acquires orchard or vineyard.

So the right to *marc* is now mostly in the hands of elderly people.

No more rights are granted beyond present lives. No more distillers will be licensed. And most of the distillers are elderly as well. So are their wheeled *alambics*. The one at La Fontaine was rusting to bits, at the furnace-end. Drunkenness, or one cause of it, is being phased out, gently.

❦

The rose trained against the rock, outside the wine cave, by a crude drinking table, in secret clefts inside our landscape. At home I often think of it.

❦

Today's *Figaro* says that the Nobel Prize for 1968 has gone to Yasunari Kawabata. Years ago, when a translation first appeared, I wrote a review of Kawabata's *Snow Country*, and at the beginning I placed the first sentence of *Snow Country* (let's hope it was the same in the Japanese) alongside the first sentence of a new novel by Angus Wilson.

'The train came out of the long tunnel into the snow country' – that was how Kawabata began, in a way acceptable to our senses and important to the novel. The first sentence of Angus Wilson's novel I forget, except that it was made of rather dull verbiage unlinked to our sensory hoard; and because it was made with the same material, I forget the rest of Angus Wilson's novel, even its name.

❦

Leaves are falling again. Now if I wrote out a list of fifty ways in which leaves fall – or fifty circumstances of their coloured detachment – Japanese novelists such as Kawabata or Tanizaki (who might have had the same Swedish recognition if he hadn't died too soon?) would understand. They might say my 'leafage' would have been described better and more legitimately a thousand years ago by Sei Shonagon in one of the catalogues of her *Pillow Book*, or by some other writer of the Heian period; but then they would agree that the sensibility Japanese writers employ with such unstaled effects of sharp evocation and communication, such subtly direct indirectness, is due to a thousand and more years of ritualized response.

❦

I think in England we came somewhere near such seasonable observances as moon-viewing or viewing orchards in flower, such a classification, a ritualization, of sensual enjoyment, a hundred and twenty years ago, in the wake of our romanticism, only then it was too late. The attitude should have been absorbed into ourselves in a simpler, or less morally earnest, less commercially bourgeois, or more aristocratic, period. After the Regency or after the 1830s or 1840s it could recur as part of our sensibility only intermittently and infrequently. And we are devotees of rejection.

❦

Leaves are not seen falling best of all through moist grey air, on to ground darkened by rain.

Leaves are well seen falling in dryness and clarity after frost, in obedience to slight movements of warm air – partly, I shall say, on to wide surfaces of water.

Once we arrived from England in the leaf-fall of an early October, by way, a little eccentrically, of Ronsard's Ile verte. Excellent. The poplar leaves off those tall poplars in line with the river which are now felled, dropped in brilliant gentleness to our picnic table and to the slow river.

The presence of Ronsard had nothing to do with it.

ぐ糸ン

In England my best leaf-fall has been in a little chasm of rock through which a stream fell from the Cheviots, in Northumberland. The trees over the waterfall and the pool were mountain-ash. Their nicked floating leaves were red and yellow, they floated on the black water in navies, they came together and made a patterned floor of their colours on the water. That was in 1959 when unremitting summer continued into autumn; summer and autumn equally without rain. I had left J. and the child in a pram two hundred feet below and had clambered up there by myself. Through the miniature Vallis Clusa of the chasm I looked out over the intervening colour of bracken to the blue of the North Sea.

I fancy a leaf-fall from birch trees on the shores of the Königsee; or a leaf-fall on the edge of the fjord below Montenegro; a leaf-fall from the beeches at La Verna.

ぐ糸ン

Meanwhile, today, it contents me to realize that poplar leaves are falling through warm air along all the Loir from Illiers to Angers, that poplar leaves are falling along all the great rivers of France, the water taking by reflection the colour of the leaves which have still to be detached.

If I don't move down to the Loir after lunch, I am contented with yellow elm leaves; they are more plebeian, but they waver across the clothes-line to the gravel, the thermometer in the sun reading 29 degrees.

ぐ糸ン

The way one's past is discarded, and goes yellow in old photographs. My past does not include myself, present version, in this different country, in the different warmth of this foreign shadow, regarding what is left of the Gâtine forest on the far side of the river, and the reading into Tome II of Michel Devèze, *La vie de la forêt française au XVI siècle*.

I don't try to get rid of any one 'me' which is over. Sometimes I catch sight of one 'me' or another 'me'. I am surprised that it seems so alien, I am surprised I am so indifferent to it. That's all.

The me I am now does not want to examine the old me I have caught sight of, doesn't want to criticize it, excuse it, least of all to regret it. Sartre writes of knowing men who have slept with an old woman late in their lives simply because they had wanted her when they were young. I once met a Netherlands diplomat who had an affair with a very upper-middle-class Englishwoman when they were both young. He wanted to marry her: she turned him down for her English diplomat; she turned him down again when her husband died, because her children were not entirely off her hands; and then a third time because of the war (which meant a concentration of her Englishness). After the war, forty years after their affair, he was allowed to be her husband.

Ought I to admire such 'humble and dogged loyalty', such constancy, such invariability? (He had remained a bachelor all the while.) I thought her a woman with the remoteness and the hard exoskeleton of her social kind; and she patronized her new husband.

✥

Cowper, after madness and preliminaries of vengeance and hell, in Buckinghamshire, on 26 October in 1790: 'A yellow shower of leaves is falling continually from all the trees in the country. . . . The consideration of my short continuance here, which was once grateful to me, now fills me with regret. I would like to live and live always.'

So would I; but here the sun encloses me in the immediate, without thought: only a sense of now, now.

✥

Kawabata again, in his *Thousand Cranes*. 'Back in his bedroom after brushing his teeth, Kikuji saw that the maid had hung a gourd in the alcove. It contained a single Morning Glory. The green and deep blue were cool, falling over a red-lacquered gourd . . . there was something unsettling in the idea of a cut Morning Glory.'

ເ✿ເ

The sales of *Snow Country* (which *The Times* acquired in La Chartre today refers to as *Snowy Country*) and of *Thousand Cranes* were about 2500 each in England, in 1957 and 1959. Each masterpiece was abandoned by its English publisher. No one pushed, no one cared.

ເ✿ເ

Writers in England have taken to collecting and republishing their reviews. One of them rebutting the complaint that her books, not her reviews, should be her serious work, states that her reviews *were* her serious work.

I never see in such collections a review of any book which could not correctly be described as a literary editor's choice, I never or seldom encounter a review of anything so palpably human and of such symbolic actuality as *Snow Country*.

ເ✿ເ

A year ago today the Russian Venus IV was transmitting from the Evening Star – or rather as it was in those weeks, the Morning Star. We were up before sunrise. There was a strip of orange, very strong, separating the eastern hills from the sky. Above the orange was spangled Venus in the first blue. I did not approve of that bleeping intrusion; and I find I now have to forget about examinations and revelations of the snot-green surface of the Moon.

ເ✿ເ

Back on earth, I have always argued that in 1540 or 1440 or 1240 they would have put on roofs of galvanized iron, if they had had galvanized iron (a matter of fortunate impossibility). Here the farmers now have something a little worse (galvanized, after all, does go dull and does rust in time): they have incorruptible aluminium; with which a few barns are being re-roofed on farmsteads sprinkled across the river flats and over the southern escarpment. Result: glaring points of white fire, which attack the eyes at midday from a mile, two miles or three miles away.

Red tiles are more expensive.

In the evening – but this is better – distant barns seem on fire with orange flame, taking a last glare from the sun.

❧

A little reluctantly this afternoon we paid our yearly visit to the bee-sized honey farmer up on the northern plateau, shining honey bucket in the car – bucket with a special lid which fits and clips down tight so that the honey can't flow out. It is a bit of anxiety first of all to drive the car along his farm lane into the mucky yard, because the ruts go so deep, and the centre of the lane rises up so high, and English cars haven't the sensible clearance of French cars. But we managed, with no more than a slight crunch.

Nobody home, no sudden appearance of either one of the muscular grey-brown dogs with short hair, who begin with barks, and continue with growls, and side-stepping, and bristling of backs.

Relieved about the dogs, disappointed about the honey. Stepped upwards on to the short home meadow and looked to the horizon; and saw that the farmer and his wife were about after all, far off, hard to detect against a palisade of sweet corn. Advanced, braved the dogs, and found that the immensely fat wife (who is all muscle) and the minutely insect-headed husband (who is all mildness), and their peculiar employee, had nearly finished cutting and loading their day's whack of maize.

The peculiar employee never likes to see us: she is smaller than the Bee, tiny, humped a little; and one of her lungs seems to have been collapsed. It appears inconceivable that she could, or should, do hard work, on a farm. But she does, little spindles stuck into long gumboots; she never will say a word to J., my daughter or myself; she snaps angry comments out of a twisted little mouth to the farmer and his wife, or to the landscape, which we cannot understand.

❧

Buying the honey amounts to a careful ceremony. Wobbly straw-seated chairs are brought out, in the kitchen. The bulgy wife lights a faggot on the hearth, kittens emerge and edge to the flames, almost to burning themselves. The Bee disappears, not with the honey bucket first of all, but to fetch some white wine (he has vines) flavoured with honey. We balance on the chairs and talk, remarks are made on how our daughter has grown, on Fernande who first brought us to the farm and is now dead, and when was it she died, and on the Princess Margaret. The faggot burns up, the room is more visible, a huge double bed in the corner on the left of the fire, a separator near the door, walls not whitewashed for thirty years, floors dirty, kittens dirty, dirty oil-cloth on the table (dirty glasses on the oil-cloth – the Bee now filling them with honey wine, which doesn't taste very nice). Firelight, the Bee-wife's knees very wide apart, her short great legs wedged into her boots. Little Collapsed Lung, Little Earwig, is somewhere outside in the dark – in the cowshed? – busy. The conversation goes on. Crickets begin to stridulate on the hearth; and at this point I am reminded of Marc Bloch, the historian shot by the Gestapo, going round to farms, listening, experiencing, discovering. Also of Bruegel.

I reckon it takes two hours to get to the honey – two hours and twenty minutes before we are off in the October dark. I love the honey. I hate this early darkness in October.

❧

Heard from Maurice a word I had to look up in the dictionary (the dictionary doesn't always acknowledge the words of Maurice, used for instance in relating some splendid indecency). Innocent this time, the word was *calotin*, from *calotte*, a priest's cap, and Maurice was snorting that Trôo was altogether too full of *calotins*, people who suck up to the *curé*. We were talking about the local Society of Freethinkers. No freethinkers at Trôo, any more, said Maurice, only *calotins*, a word which lends itself in pronunciation to an infinity of dislike.

I wonder if people who come to our front room don't think we are *calotins*. The first thing they see is a pottery Virgin and Child in a black niche cut into the white chalk wall. I dug out the niche, and the Virgin and Child, a product of the long vanished potteries towards Le Mans, we bought in an antique shop at Tours.

A sentimentality, a contradiction, so far as I am concerned? I don't think so. If I do not share the belief, I share a hope embodied in this Vierge Marie in her flowered dress with her child, embodied in churches and cathedrals, – of tenderness and comfort for everyone. A hope rather in between the Free-thinkers and the *calotins*?

⟡

In the early darkness or dimness again, we've just spent half an hour leaning on the warm mudguard of a tractor, in a deserted farmyard, away from anywhere (actually in that Ronsardian parish of Montrouveau) extracting information from a farmer we had never met. Information about the vanished church of Marcé.

This is a matter of wolves once more. We've acquired the *Topographical Dictionary of the Vendômois*. It says that in the eighteenth century when the church of St-Martin de Marcé was more or less in ruins, and lacked a door, two wolves (remnants of the forest of Gastines are not far away) entered and drank holy water from the stoup.

I am possessed by those wolves. And here we are, asking the farmer about the church, here is the farmer replying, without surprise, as if he were used to finding a foreign car and inquisitive foreigners in gathering dark in this abandoned farmyard far in from the road. We had found the site, mounds, hollows in a ploughed corner, pottery, but no bones. He points to a huge stone which had been dragged over from the ruins. The hexagonal stoup is in another farmyard, serving as a pig trough.

But it is those wolves I think of, long, thin, on their hind legs to the stoup, lapping, in heat which had dried out the ponds and springs.

⟡

At school here my daughter and other children of seven or eight years old had to learn poems or pieces of poems by Hugo, Valéry and Apollinaire, at the bidding of a young teacher, who was brisk and smart. All three poems or pieces were beyond the comprehension of peasant children. This sounds superior, I know, as if I was saying that my own child was *ipso facto* so much more sensitive or intelligent than a peasant child. She happened to be used to poems, at any rate, as a pleasure. The other children had nothing to do with poems, at all (unless you count hymns, and play-rhymes –

> *Un, deux, trois,*
> *Dans les bois.*
> *Quatre, cinq, six,*
> *Chercher des cerises.*
> *Sept, huit, neuf,*
> *Dans mon pannier neuf . . .* etc.).

I was grateful, though, because two things came together in the lines by Hugo – a sunset and *avoine folle*, wild oat, which has always been a common weed in the corners of my existence (no metaphors intended).

It comes up in corners of the garden at Trôo, no grass more elegant and fine. Simply by hearing it named, and in a poem, and a poem not in English, it has now gained for me, I hope for my daughter, more identity than ever before:

> *Par-dessus l'horizon aux collines brunies*
> *Le soleil, cette fleur des splendeurs infinies,*
> *Se penchait sur la terre à l'heure du couchant;*
> *Une humble marguerite, éclose au bord d'un champ,*
> *Sur un mur gris, croulant parmi l'avoine folle,*
> *Blanche, épanouissait sa candide auréole . . .* etc.

What an eye Hugo had, and for more than wrecks, or hanged men, or full moons, or black storms, or corrupt ministers.

༒

Also in school at Trôo, from my daughter's exercise book, carefully written in blue ink on squared paper:

Histoire
Les gaulois ont des chefs qui sont les nobles. Ils ont aussie des prêtres les druides qui cueillent le gui qui sert de remède et de porte-bonheur.

Morale
J'aurai toujours un mouchoir propre. Je me moucherai dans ce mouchoir.

Observation
La feuille du platane est attaché par un pétiole.

❧

Colour on the Beauce, 22 October. The sun on dahlias which are spikes of colour. Detail of the feathers of guinea-fowls running smoothly away, clockwork, not birds. Children out of school, wearing the blue of cornflowers, heads outlined by the sun. Girl in bright pink at a dark washing pool under an oak. Our child in red sun-illumined tights.

A 3 p.m. lunch outside the church. Inside the church, away from the excellence of cool sunshine, death. A coffin waiting under a bier cloth, black, with death's heads and conventionally shaped tears in white flannel stitched on to it. Stonework, plasterwork, woodwork, altars, statuary in decay as usual. Behind death a processional cross leaning against a pile of broken chairs. Yes, but outside. The dahlias.

❧

I wonder if that coffin cloth embroidered with tears was imitated from the diapered stone panel of the seventeenth century on one side of the choir in La Trinité at Vendôme, which is about all that remains in the church to remind one of the Madame la Sainte-Larme which Jesus wept. Every second diaper contains a conventionalized tear. It is the prettiest piece of design.

❧

Looking through Hugo's poems for some lines which hang round in me and which I can never find, I happened to read *Le Bord de la Mer*:

La Terre: *Je suis pleine de morts . . .*
Je les sens s'agiter en moi confusément,

which makes me ask why I do not often feel this so long inhabited landscape to be *plein de morts*. One could think of enormous Hugo on our terrace, regarding the world. It is

213

serene down below, and wide. Houses grow out of trees, there is no bad feature except the long straight line of the railway (two or three goods trains a week), far too long and straight, contradicting the twists of the escarpment or the twists of the river. There is a very big sky, etcetera. But friends we have made here have died, others are old, or getting ill.

No, I imagine that I feel *life* here most of the time owing to a kind of unconsciousness, not knowing France, or the French, or French, very well, not sharing the familiar assumptions, seeing a certain strangeness and freshness, primal strangeness, in everything, shutters, chimneys, the style of façades, poplars, climate, faces, bodies, food from the *charcuterie*. A play, an overture or entr'acte all the while. Holidays. I do not think I am complaining.

✧

The flower, above others, made to speak for happiness and long warm days in most French villages roundabout is the Balsamine: *Impatiens balsamina*, from India, creating delicate cloud-banks of carmine and white along walls. A little yellow occurs in the throat of each blossom, but that does not count. This Balsamine is fully out by the end of June: it is still out, now, everywhere, along every wall, in late October, it will go on being pure and pink, a kind of folk-flower, until it is cut down by frost – thousands of seeds by that time having dropped for next year. I imagine it is too tender for England, at least to maintain itself, in immense quantity, as it does here.

Another Trôo flower – other I mean than wild – which measures the warmth: Belle-de-Nuit, in English Pretty-by-night, Four o'clock, and – one of the flower names which most affect me – Marvel of Peru. But this belongs to Trôo privacy, in gardens, at the back of the house, in the sun. The Trôo bushes I have seen are yellow flowered ones, the flowers open in the evening and smell sweet and drop off yellow on to the ground. Hummingbird hawk-moths hover at the flowers and zigzag round the bush.

✧

A third Trôo flower, public again, along walls, along paths, out and brilliant – brilliant pink – the moment there's enough sun; absorbing sun, returning it in colour; indestructible, because of its little tubers; spreading, spreading as if it loved existence, not bothered by dry ground, dry weather, or frost: *Oxalis floribunda*. Brazilian, tropical, and, by adoption, French. Yet I can't hear a name for it except *Oxalide*.

∽✿∾

One more plant: woad, yellow-flowered, honey-scented, black-seeded, on the chalk slopes of Trôo, above the Rue Haute, relict of dyeing cloth here or hereabouts – since when?

I might have guessed, since the Middle Ages; or earlier, from the time of the Gauls, who would have known woad in Gaul as early as the Britons knew it in Britain, where woad gave its British name to Glastonbury.

In fact the woad has survived at Trôo since the beginning of the last century, when the village lived, in part, by making cottons and serges. No one remembers now that their recent ancestors made cloth. So much for 'folk-memory.'

∽✿∾

'*Comme un mouton de Berry*,' said Maurice, as he came out of the dark, with blood trickling towards his nose. He had knocked his forehead against a flint sticking out of the wall in his wine cave.

J. mopped the blood with a piece of cottonwool from her bag, and Maurice explained – protesting that this attention was unnecessary now that he had dabbed the hole with *marc* from a black dirty jug – that *comme un mouton de Berry* meant like a sheep getting a knock on the head from the slaughterman's pole-axe.

But why a sheep of the Berry (the district round Bourges, the district Georges Sand came from), except that the Berry is famous for sheep, which must all expect a knock on the head?

Well, why not? It was just an expression, for such a contingency: a bit harder, and he would have been dead – *comme un mouton de Berry*. The woman and the farmer who were also in the cave for a drink, had laughed when Maurice said he was like a sheep from the Berry. The expression – there are plenty like it I suppose in every European language – is a kind of

215

buffer-remark, it amounts to a small quickly played language-game, a sign of community, an agent of community: when you say it, no one need remember its total significance.

༄

Maurice talked about making white wine. He said local people no longer had the nerve for it, the nerve to wait, in case the grapes were ruined in late October or early November: you must wait, he said, till then, before you *vendange*, until the grapes begin to rot, till the grapes *pissent dans les mains* when you touch them, when the juice comes even out of the skins.

༄

In Hugo's poems I am again and again surprised and delighted by his fidelity: if he chooses something to mention out of our surroundings, the mention is celebratory and unforced: small or large, incidental or enlarging, it is an evidence, a constituent of his immense and marvellous generosity – and his solitude. Hugo's appetite, Hugo in the ink of sunlessness, Hugo in rays of light.

When a sound I've mentioned before was just reaching our terrace from the Moulin Papillon, a mile or so towards Montoire, I happened to read

> *J'aime Chelles et ses cressonnières*
> *Et le doux tic-tac des moulins.*

And today, after we had been in the woods for *trompettes de mort* and *girolles*:

> *J'aime toute cette musique,*
> *Ces refrains, jamais importuns,*
> *Et le bon vieux plain-chant classique*
> *Des chênes aux capuchons bruns.*

That a lake is a mirror is obvious enough: but then Hugo will particularize mirror-lakes, and write of meres of the Sologne (many of them now drained):

> *Les étangs de Sologne*
> *Sont de pâles miroirs.*

216

In 'reality' I suppose Hugo's English company would contain Hardy and Crabbe and John Clare:

> *Un coup de fusil dans la haie,*
> *Abois d'un chien; c'est le chasseur.*
> *Et pensif, je sens une plaie*
> *Parmi toute cette douceur.*

But there isn't a modern English poet (thinking of Hardy, Crabbe, Wordsworth, Coleridge, Tennyson, etc., as modern) with his huge subterranean deposit, with his great happiness and its opposite, his vast generosity of discernment, his appetite expressed in the detail; his rise and rhetoric, his acceptance and his display.

Could you imagine Hardy or Crabbe loosening his mind's tie, or cravat, and writing on the universality of nature and 'reality' quite as Hugo writes in *Réalité*:

> *Un hoquet à Silène échappe*
> *Parmi les roses de Pœstum.*
> *Quand Horace étale Priape,*
> *Shakespeare peut risquer Bottom.*

> *La vérité n'a pas de bornes.*
> *Grace au grand Pan, dieu bestial,*
> *Fils, le réel montre ses cornes*
> *Sur le front bleu de l'idéal.*

తళ

The immense:

> *j'ai la nostalgie*
> *Du soleil, mon ancien pays.*

The detail: Hugo liked those *cressonnières*, those green pillows of watercress, new, edging streams in October or spring, before flowering stems and white flowers emerge to spoil their curved fullness.

The detail: dirty children observed in a Normandy he at first disliked, *avec les bouches qui sucent les nez*.

When I read the poems I don't really understand the enormous initials V. H. inked by him into some of his drawings.

తళ

Two ways of provinciality and sentimentality: poems in which the voice is affected and bantering most of the time and ironic against the self; poems all the while parading culture-facts – the great Bosch at the Prado, etc.

Poets who feel themselves too much under-educated or poets who have made a change of class educationally, or poets from colonial cultures, who feel a cultural exclusion, are tempted into these two modes of compensation, one or both.

I am content with a description of poetry I found in a recent anthology of poems from the T'ang: 'Poetry presents the thing in order to convey the feeling. It should be precise about the thing and reticent about the feeling, for as soon as the mind responds and connects with the thing the feeling shows in the words.' No poetry of by-passing the poem.

၄ၛၖ

The definition was set down about 1082, by a critic of the Northern Sung dynasty, Wei T'ai, disappointed brother of the poet Lady Wei, in his *Poetry-Talk of the Gentleman living in Seclusion by the river Han* – not the poetry talk of the poet living on the banks of the Clyde or the Esk or the Hudson.

၄ၛၖ

Other poets, or poet-types, I should have added to the above: teachers of English Literature who attempt, without the means, to become writers of poetry in English. Teachers or journalists of English literature who cross to America clutching bowls which they hope Americans will fill less with dollars than approbation.

၄ၛၖ

Finding a new mushroom the shape of yellow ears without a wrinkle or channel.

Thinking about the Beauce.

Hearing one's child talking another, an additional, language with fluency and no accent in the lane between the mucky wood piles, with other children.

Having quinces on the table.

၄ၛၖ

Not only Hugo's *doux tic-tac des moulins*, but the lapping and plashing of a big mill-wheel – the mill at St-Jacques which I have mentioned, which has been derelict for so long – *dont la grande roue noire et humide tourne sans cesse en clapotant.*

But that was written in 1878, and the sentence comes – at last I have found the book I was never going to find – in *Monographie de l'antique ville de Trôo*, by Alexandre de Salies.

Only two fascicules – and no one had ever read them, the pages weren't cut. Perhaps Alexandre de Salies died before the other three parts (there were to have been five in all) were written or ready for the printer.

He does not say much: he brings Trôo down into the hands of the English, via Geoffroy Martel, and Foulques the Yellow, his great-nephew (who founded the little priory of Notre-Dame des Marchais, up the lane, the ruins of which I used to explore until they were bought and restored or preserved a year or two ago by a scrap-merchant: nowadays, again, *on ne visite pas*), and Foulques's son Geoffroy Plantagenet, who married our Henry I's daughter Matilda, and was the father of our Henry II; after which it isn't so long to Coeur-de-Lion and his Mercadier.

But in each fascicule there are four engravings the size of the page , and some engravings in the text. They look accurate as well as picturesque. One sees what a primitive warren Trôo was only a hundred years ago, outside and below the castle enceinte; how many dwelling-caves have since fallen in or been relegated to backdoor sheds, how many houses have been added since in front of the caves, how many shrubs and trees have grown over the bare face or slopes of rock. I would not have guessed that many of the houses masking the caves were so recent. It seems they were nearly all built between 1890 and 1914.

❧

Trôo looks at least three-quarters troglodytic in these engravings of 1878. In 1911 Baring-Gould describes Trôo as half troglodytic. Now (in 1968) only two subterranean houses are lived in all the year round, by locals – one by a poor farm labourer with a very large family (once I saw his children, in this cave house, eating their supper round the table in a television short on the B.B.C. – no fault of mine).

219

Also since 1878 the shape of the chimneys has changed. Most of the chimneys sticking up through the rock – or through the lilac scrub which has invaded Trôo – are now rectangular in the expected way of a chimney with renaissance ancestry and renaissance proportions more or less. The older chimneys were smooth pallid fingers of masonry smoothed with lime mortar, primitive stumps of a mortared vegetation pushing out of the rock or the earth. One or two are left. In Baring-Gould's day such chimneys stuck up everywhere, out of barer slopes; the hill, he said, looking like a piece of larded veal. He said the upper cave-houses smelt of exposed garbage drying in the sun; and wondered how a 'sanitary officer would tackle the problem of sweetening Trôo'.

It seems very sweet now, with currents of air rising against the escarpment; and garbage – even if there are no drains – collected twice a week.

⤬

The October weather has been very much on and off. It was hellish again all day yesterday, and with the rain I received a hellish, if also heavenly book to read, *Heaven and Hell in Western Art*, by Robert Hughes; in which, first of all, a detail reminded me of visiting Torcello years ago by way of Trôo.

When we stopped at Trôo we saw for the first time the amethyst and green of Christ in glory in the church of St-Jacques, across the river. If there were unpleasant features in these Romanesque paintings inside damp St-Jacques (so damp that dark green algae stain the floor and the bottom of the walls), they have faded or been rubbed off long ago. On that long mosaic wall of the basilica on Torcello, a fuse, a trail, a stream of fire runs from Christ in his mandorla down into the bottom compartments of Hell and Hell fire, where flames burn the naked and worms crawl into skulls by the eye-socket.

It is this detail which is reproduced; and I read that the fuse, the trail, the stream of fire signified that hell fire 'was kept alight by God's direct will'. The concept is vengeful and disgusting.

This *Heaven and Hell in Western Art* has been put together and written by someone brought up as a Catholic in far Australia (where, about 1953, a Jesuit told him in a sermon that if he masturbated, he would be kicked 'in a certain part of the body' – which is like my mama referring to the chamber-pot as a Certain Article or C.A. – 'by a demon with a great clawed foot, twenty times a minute, sixty minutes an hour, twenty-four hours a day, for all eternity.' It struck me he was still having difficulty as he wrote, and as he pointed to this or that masterpiece of misery or felicity, in freeing himself from the long claws or the long poisonous shadows of Hell.

I thought him unfair altogether to the idea of heaven, and over-insistent on the hells we make, the hells we inflict on ourselves and others.

'According to the sixteenth-century theologian Drexelius, God managed to cram 100,000,000,000 burnt, flayed and gutted souls into a space of one cubic German mile.'

Not surprising (look at the number of sinful fossils packed into one cubic foot of Gloucestershire limestone in the walls of Berkeley). Certainly the Hell idea has now been changed from 'the metaphor of ultimate justice' to the 'image of total injustice'. Certainly we shall create more Hells. But there is more positive force in the more creditable idea of Heaven.

Heaven united under one federal government with the Land of Cockaigne (and no more rising and falling frontier poles, and *douanes*, no more Gold or Marzipan Curtain between them). A lake of stew and of whisky too, and of national health medicaments, isn't to be despised, though I might change the whisky to Bourgeuil and the stew to *lapin aux pruneaux*, which we shall eat today; and better wages do enable more people to paddle all about the lake for a month in the summer in a large canoe (fibre-glass, carried on the roof of the car). What about our readiness to believe – and now to advance towards – something infinitely better than one has already?

That is how the book might have ended.

ᖉᖆ

It is not – at this moment before lunch – clouding over. Elm leaves continue a sideways downward drift on a warm movement of air. We shall eat the *lapin aux pruneaux* on the terrace. The sun has warmth, but not bite enough to require that we eat in the shade. The sacred silence of midday eating has enveloped the French. No gravel lorries, no long wholesale grocer's lorries go by, far down on the main road.

I had to review that book of Heaven and Hell, and in my review I quoted the sentence about the theologian Drexelius. The sub-editor wanted to cut the quotation for lack of space. I wanted it kept in; and it appeared with the oddest misprint: 'According to the sixteenth-century theologian Drexelius, God managed to cram 100,000,000,000 burnt, flayed and gutted souls in a space of one cubic German.'

All things are possible to God, but let us not have these generalized national insults.

༺꧁༺

In his effort to see light and make paintings of light I believe Turner, since he couldn't stare at the sun, did the next best thing: he lay with his head to the sun and his eyes closed, and then used the shimmer he 'saw' through his eyelids. Colours 'seen' in that way have the shimmer-scales of yellow, gold, yellow-brown, pink, and red which he introduced so often into his pictures.

I realized this lying after lunch today in the October sunshine (sun temperature now 25°).

But Turner still wanted to look direct into the sun.

I opened my eyes, I put my fingers between my eyes and the sun: this gave the twinkling shimmer of triangles radiating from the sun, or widening from the sun as central point, and seeming to revolve, or to be ready to revolve.

Turner's ultimate pictures, especially sea-pictures where no shapes of land intervene and interfere, image such radiating and nearly revolving triangles of light direct from the source of light. (Turner's revolving triangles, his Catherine Wheels, I used to think, came from Guardi – perhaps it would be right to say they came from the sun and were confirmed for him in Guardi's landscapes.)

༺꧁༺

In some oils and watercolours by Turner, belonging to his first stage of gazing into light, the scales of shimmer now seem hard and incomplete – an appearance I am sure they never had when he touched the painting for the last time. Something has gone wrong with the finish. I saw to perfection, I think, the undamaged finality of Turner at Petworth – on the way to Lydd, Le Touquet and Trôo this autumn – in the *Teignmouth Harbour*, which he painted in 1812. But then he was looking *with* the sun: at the revelation, not into the revealing agent or source, which asked for peculiar delicacy and cunning.

⟡

Seen from above, a little *deux chevaux* lurching down the road: its roof carries along a sprinkle of wet bright yellow leaves. It reminds me of looking down last winter on to a blackbird in slight snow, the very small white flakes shifting, as the bird moved, along the black gulley between its wings and collecting on the flat above its tail.

⟡

Old images. The slope of stubble rising towards a moon of polished grey, lopsidedly short of roundness and fullness. The wood behind us, only a few *girolles* and *pieds-de-mouton* in our basket. The wind warm. Spindle-berries now carmine, below yellow and carmine leaves.

We come downhill through the Port de Sougé, back to the moon. I look at the road laid down a length of Loir valley which is too long for comfort. It is very narrow, this road, it is the only definite shape, it shines, it reflects light, not in itself yellow, from a yellow rim of the sky. I think of it as a thread of nylon, I can hardly bear to look at this single shining thread, which shines so across the darkening indefinition. Then it peters out under yellow, under blue, under blackness.

Home. The child comes in and says 'Lovely fresh walnuts!' pouring a rattle of nuts on to the table.

⟡

My daughter, after mushrooming in the woods on this very hot afternoon when the thermometer climbed again to 30 centigrade, went to bed with a headache and a temperature. Our neighbour came in and sat by her bed, and held her hand and asked her if she had been playing under the walnut trees. Just

223

walking under walnut trees, said this sprightly grandmama who has brought up five children, often made her feel quite ill. 'They're fatal, walnut trees.' This was Pliny's idea.

❦

Maurice regarding the almost full hunter's moon: '*La pleine lune ne voit jamais le soleil couchant.*'

❦

To be a Trôo owl, at such a 10 p.m. of October, warm air and moonlight, warm inside one's feathers, looking down from the cliff on the flats of mist, emitting balloons of sound, and then flying on soft feathers to another perch.

❦

To be a human being at Trôo, looking down at the river, and able to say, from du Bellay's *Sonnet to Ronsard*,

> *Heureuses sont tes Nymphes vagabondes,*
> *Gastine saincte, et heureuses tes ondes,*
> *O petit Loir, honneur du Vendômois.*

❦

A moon rainbow at St-Jacques on the other side of the river. I have never seen one before. It was nearly 11 p.m. The moon, just past full, had risen fairly high in the east, had just emerged from a black bank of cloud, and was shining through the last heavy veil of a storm of passing rain. I saw the bow just as I turned the car after disembarking Maurice at his door. Very surprised. I opened the car-door to have a better look, and stood by the road staring at it: a grey band, no colour, across a western sky still very blue, a black horizon underneath it, humped by black trees.

That wasn't all. I could smell the quinces on the tree in Maurice's garden, the drops of rain were sparkling, and lapwings were flying and faintly screaming over the flats. Saw a scrap of the grey rainbow again near the bridge over the Loir.

❦

As a rule I am not lucky about such phenomena of the sky. I have never seen a good parhelion (only a scrap of one coming home one day, one evening, across the Beauce, from Amboise), I have never seen the Northern Lights.

This was a packet of sensations and good luck. The moon was blotted out by clouds, and it was pouring again by the time I reached home.

ᴄᴦᴥᴪ

The shadow cast by light from the Evening Star, at its nearest and largest – that is another thing I would like to see.

ᴄᴦᴥᴪ

We give ourselves so easily to delusion in the arts that an American magazine – just arrived – which is published by the U.S. Information Agency to show how the liberal imagination rises high in America, has to include in its second number scraps of criticism by Randall Jarrell, scraps of eulogy, rather, of other American poets.

I did not understand at first the exact mechanism of their flatness, if one may talk of flatness having a mechanism. Then I realized that he wrote all the time in what I should call the One-Two-Three – 'freshness, clarity and economy', 'economy, precision and restraint', 'a fineness, strangeness and firmness of discrimination', 'many new tastes and colours and sounds, many real, half-real and non-existent beings'. Being at Trôo I realized this to be the flatness of *tôle plastique*, the corrugated plastic sheeting which the French like so much, in pale yellow in back-yards: flat in general effect it has a monotonous wave – more monotonous than the noise of the owls, which vary their hooting on these October nights with grunting, shrieking, growling and grumbling.

And this corrugated monotony was introduced – by Robert Lowell – in a different monotone based on the infinite repetition of the three verbal forms, *had*, *was* and *were*; for ornament he strung weak adjectives every so often across a paragraph, like lines of string and coloured paper across a street: 'his noble, difficult and beautiful soul', 'the empty, numerical long-distance blaze', 'I see the bright, petty, pretty sacred objects he accumulated.'

What did Isaac Babel say – that one adjective was enough, that only a genius could use two adjectives. And what would Isaac Babel have said of stringing the adjectives out to five? 'When I first met Randall he was twenty-three or four, and upsettingly brilliant, precocious, knowing, naïve and vexing.'

These American masters. Let me cross out American. These masters – of sag and bunting. And the evangel of these masters. Why do the sag and bunting seem so extra obvious, so extra objectionable, when I encounter them here at Trôo?

Dear Mr Grigson,

With this letter we are sending you a copy of *Dialogue*, a new quarterly journal of opinion and analysis. . . . *Dialogue* represents, I think, a valuable effort to present, from various standpoints, an analytical view of the events, issues and trends that Americans are discussing and that are of broader interest to the world. . . .

I return from sag, bunting – and propaganda – to the owls, and a bonfire in moonlight, on the edge of the cliff.

༒

Some remark of mine made a poet of at any rate Black Mountain, short-snippet, anti-rhythm, throw-away affinities (dear me, how many adjectives was that?) say in pain, though patience, 'You know, there *have* been good poets in America since John Crowe Ransom.'

I managed not to reply without, I think, appearing not to reply. But have there been good poets in America since Ransom? I wouldn't be sure. And have there been good painters in America – perhaps not many, perhaps two, or three – since Mary Cassatt? Who died in 1926, aged eighty-two.

Why expect excellence like a shower of meteorites? It is less common, and unpredictable.

༒

If I taught the history of literature or the history of art, I don't say I would be glad of having lived through the years since the war, but I'd make use of the experience to examine a period without art, more or less – like the English decades after Waterloo, which Beddoes, rather a sick owl himself, called an owl-light. I would use the experience to examine how peculiar tests are worked out, then employed to demonstrate the high artness of such a period's non-art, since everyone always wants to be able to say what poetry 'is', what painting 'is' (I drop 'good') in examples of his own time.

A little energy – of production or of criticism or showmanship – in such a flat art period, I should observe, havocs the always uncertain (literary editors, for instance; who are journalists, and so infected without escape by the fashionable; which if it may be good, is more likely bad). I should watch the trimming of critical trimmers. I should notice old New Critics now swopping over and accepting sincerity tests for confessional poetry (pack Uncle Tom Eliot away with bags of lavender). I should eye English academics finding reasons I won't specify, for blowing up, no, I don't mean blowing up, I mean inflating American names inflated already in America, and elsewhere, by America's cultural propaganda agents, for American *amour-propre*. And so on.

༝ཚུ༎

'It is not my business.' That one's literary business is *not* the public posturing of some baboon of a blunt Bradford novelist or the pertness of some reviewer (who may be myself), or the antics of some political poet – this is something one learns too slowly, yet must not accept too soon perhaps. It seems I shall never learn it completely.

༝ཚུ༎

No, Pierre de Ronsard, *gentilhomme de Vendômois*, you are not my measure of the poetic character or of poetry or of the poetic message; much as I love in you a Giorgionesque quality (and other qualities). Also I do remember – and forget to remember as well – my *Don Juan*:

> complaint of present days
> Is not the certain path to future praise.

But still, but still . . .

༝ཚུ༎

And has a propaganda agency of a government ever taken up a living, genuine poetry?

It might do so, I suppose, by accident.

༝ཚུ༎

Card games in the early autumn night. In playing Casino, Chase the Ace, Pit (not quite so nasty a game as Monopoly, which should be played only by the children of Mrs Onassis) we invented a command which I think is going to be useful.

Lose and cheer up: *Swallop your snod*. Accept your absurdity.

ぐ余わ

In pyjamas, anxious scrutiny of the mist overhead to see if it allows a suggestion of blue – and of the thermometer, which did not go down to freezing in the night and has risen to 10°; which is not at all bad for 8 a.m. at this time of year.

Below, mist which has almost the blackness of a thunder-cloud towards the river; which can't be seen.

Then the disc of a sun. Mist rises and this muted sun is lost. The turn of the river shows as an island of lighter grey in the deep grey or lessened black.

The sun again, less obstructed, and giving sparkle to each hanging bead of mist-water. It will be 29° or 30° by midday. Warmth on one knee, in the verandah. My biro, 13 centimetres long, throws a shadow line of 59 centimetres across the table-cloth.

The tattiness of the mist-morning begins to dry and disappear. Definition.

ぐ余わ

Montoire on Sunday morning. The short, the thin, the globular, the bald, the overlapping, the hairy – all men, revealing their appetites in the *pâtisserie*. A globular little man with double chins in front and a reddish overlap on the other side of his neck, wearing the special face of someone respectable among the well-to-do of Montoire, tiptoes lightly out to his Citroën, carrying four triangular parcels for Sunday lunch. The *pâtisserie* isn't quite the place to be so much the good citizen.

Or am I talking like a medieval painter in search of a model for gluttony?

Should I imagine him getting into his Citroen naked all of a sudden? No, I should not. The French wear Gluttony with a certain grace.

Bon appétit. I suspect he has a packet in the house of Rennie's Indigestion Tablets (very common in France).

⌯⌖⌯

On the way home (with our own triangular parcel, but then his tummy is bigger than mine, and he probably has more tummies in his family), I observe, as I do every year, that line in the flat valley of two or three dozen poplars, perhaps of ten years' growth, acting as if they were tall gas jets, tall Bunsen-shaped flames, pallid, scentless, silent, the colour of each jet a pink-yellow, most delicate, most frail without being sentimental. Leaves now enough thinned to allow the hills to be seen through them, through flame after flame.

On the other side taller, older poplars, darker against the light which surges across the road to illuminate the pink-yellow trees. The clumps of mistletoe they wear inside themselves are now visible, not too prominently because their leaves haven't fallen by more than about half. So poplar and mistletoe seem in unison, as they won't later on: it is like the revelation of a new spring in autumn.

But what force, what three-dimensional attractiveness of natural drawing.

⌯⌖⌯

Temporal succession along the stream which flows parallel with the road to Montoire and to the *charcuterie* and the *pâtisserie*:

Yellow Irises:
> Yellow in what the French would call spring, and we should call early summer.

Marsh Mallow (soft leaves, pallid flowers, not common at home):
> Pallid pink in what we should call summer; and the French would call the close of spring.

Purple Loosestrife:
> A flower (by French standards) of the beginning of summer. To us a sign that we should go home for the rain of the late English summer.

229

Clumps of mistletoe visible – now – through all poplars,
leaves of poplars thin, trunks of poplars pale pink:
    Toussaint not far ahead. Bad weather unlikely to improve.
Time to book a passage home for the winter.

༄

Read in a local publication of a terrible winter here in 1880,
which killed all the walnut trees; and thought of it this afternoon in front of the huge Renaissance fireplace which towers
in the heavy, rather small salon of La Possonnière. Thought of
Ronsard warming thin fingers at the logs under all the armorial
details and emblems carved in white stone (could Ronsard have
had fat short fingers like J. B. Priestley – which I drew one
evening years ago after talking with Priestley in the Café
Royal? No. Impossible).

The owner of La Possonnière, through whose kindness I
have been able at last to read Laumonier's *Ronsard et sa province*,
was showing me the house. We stood at first in the courtyard
at the back, between the tall house and the Italianate terrace
which surmounts the decorated and inscribed wine caves. There
was a wood scent from the great fireplace as we walked in.

I realized on this Sunday afternoon in the fall, perfect in
sunlight and warmth and the paleness of poplar stems and
thinning yellow of poplar leaves against the blue, that Ronsard's
childhood house must have been extremely glum when the
summer and autumn came to an end. At three o'clock this
afternoon, sunlight reached only the back courtyard near the
wine caves (though October light just reaches the front of the
house before sunset).

The equation of such houses facing north-west and tucked
into the hillside lies between winter chill and the need of
summer coolness.

༄

Last indulgence. We resolved to eat lark – *pâté des alouettes*. I
have never supposed that when people – let's say castle people –
of the fifteenth or sixteenth century sat down to a good meal
they always ate muck, by the measure of Elizabeth David or
Tante-Marie or even *Fanny Farmer's Boston Cookbook*. They en-

joyed larks; and when poorer people thought of Cockayne, where pies grow on the roof and boiled eggs run around and puddings swell up and surround trees, they included roast larks among its delicacies. The sky will rain larks – roasted larks.

So how do they taste?

Larks belong to the Beauce. We walked in mid-Beauce one cloudless day after midsummer, looking for a dolmen among the endless acres of corn, when a lark ran, and paused, and ran along the track.

'Why aren't you in a pie? J. said to this lark, rather severely.

But then it was too soon. Larks enter pies or *pâté*, or tins of *pâté*, now, when they are fat, and after they have been netted over the stubbles. They are eaten at Chartres, and Pithiviers. To Pithiviers we drove this morning of a day of immense showers from black clouds, and immense floods of sunshine; we ate larks on top of *pâté*, in a restaurant of great charm, where the windows are level with the upper, still unyellowed or not much yellowed leafage of horse-chestnuts. The larks were extremely good, like roast pheasant in miniature, plump, not at all like sparrows. Let the sky rain larks.

Also we ate larks with a bottle of Quincy, a white wine a little whiskery and fragrant, from the Cher, which we hadn't drunk before; and we followed lark with a Pithiviers, in Pithiviers – almond filling in puff pastry like a large rosette. With lark, etc., we were so, I won't say elated, but well comforted and satisfied, that we intended to go over to the Post Office and send, to my friend James Fisher, ornithologist, protectionist, and inspirer (I believe) of bird laws, a telegram saying TO HELL, WE HAVE EATEN LARK.

Nicer thoughts, and the amount already spent on lark, intervened.

⌇⌇⌇⌇

But sentimentality it is, this English refusal to eat larks. (This modern English refusal: see older cookery books – for instance, *The Cook's Guide* by Charles Elmé Francatelli, *maître-d'hôtel* and chief cook to Queen Victoria, edition of 1888, recipes for roast lark, to be served 'with the sauce recommended for ruffs and reeves and wheatears', lark pie à la Melton Mowbray, and croustade of larks garnished with button mushrooms and crayfish, and served with Périgueux sauce). Wild duck we go on

231

eating, they only quack, partridges we shoot and enjoy, they make only a little scrapy noise to each other in the evenings. But, no, we will not eat Shelley's poem.

What that execrable poem began, a generation, or two, or three, of ornithologists has continued, in a kind of self-flattery. We acquiesce. Blake was at it, too.

> A robin-redbreast in a cage
> Puts all heaven in a rage.

He didn't write

> A parrot in a cage
> Puts all heaven in a rage.

Or a pair of canaries. Or a toad in a vivarium. Or a pig in a pen. Not that I do not acquiesce in the inevitableness of inconsistency.

కొఱ

Also I pouf insects, especially the mosquitoes of Trôo. I prefer not to kill, when the scale is increased. I like birds. I like to eat birds. I like deer, I like venison. I am entirely inconsistent. But I still wish we had sent that telegram.

కొఱ

Which reminds me (if this doesn't sound too like the last cosy paragraph in which a weekly columnist changes from the destiny of nations to the domestic) of our lime tree, acquired for a parasol. Several branches this year had grown twenty-six inches or more up to the end of June (the bark of last year's growth is greenish brown, the bark of this year's growth is pure green, a precise division and contrast).

But the point isn't to talk of gardens. It is a train of associations. We bought that lime from a nursery gardener at Montoire ordering it well in advance of winter. To get to the nursery gardener's office meant going down a long shiny passage through a shiny house, in the *style plastique*. All the way down the passage hung shiny reproductions of paintings of ducks, by the English conservationist Peter Scott. Not one, but twenty or more. And this in turn is only half the associative train. I was in a restaurant once in Fitzroy Street in London. At the next table sat an evident foreigner, an evident Herr Doktor, too, and with him someone I recognized as the production manager of a firm of paperback publishers. The Herr Doktor was the German-Swiss typographer Jan Tschichold. He didn't speak English well, or understand it well. The tables were so close I couldn't help hearing their conversation.

'He's a very nice chap. We ought to go down to his place. Geese everywhere, outside the house, inside it too.'

I imagined that Jan Tschichold, over from Zürich to design books for the firm, had been asked to design a book with illustrations by Peter Scott, not exactly illustrations of the kind this Eminent Typographical Consequence of the Bauhaus and of Piet Mondrian would care for. And I imagined by the apologetic tone of the production manager, now talking to him about Peter Scott's wildfowl reserve, that he had already expressed the fact that he didn't care for such art, or for the job.

From here on the print on the page should turn into a gramophone record.

'Guys?' said Jan Tschichold, looking puzzled. 'Guys?' Outside the house?' A pause. 'Oh' – from the bottom end of his throat – 'Oh you mean *geez*. I thought you mean Constantin Guys.'

I look up at the lime tree, when ants fall out of it into a shaded cup of tea, and recall geez and Constantin Guys.

❧

For an Englishman, used to more cherishing intimacies of landscape, the width of France is unsettling – at any rate when the light goes, when it rains, when the clouds are low, and by French standards fairly fast. Then the sky is too much, and so is the land.

It is like that on the Beauce – as in the Champagne of Hugo's *Lettre*:

> *Et j'ai pour tout plaisir de voir à l'horizon*
> *Un groupe de toits bas d'où sort une fumée,*
> *Le paysage étant plat comme Mérimée.*

Or Hugo at Bondont on 5 November 1846 (four days after the melancholy of Toussaint):

> *Le reste du pays, sous le ciel gris ou bleu,*
> *Est une plaine, avec une église au milieu.*

Or Apollinaire in *Saltimbanques:*

> *Dans la plaine les baladins*
> *S'éloignent au long de jardins*
> *Devant l'huis des auberges grises*
> *Par les villages sans églises*
>
> *Et les enfants s'en vont devant*
> *Les autres suivent en rêvant*
> *Chaque arbre fruitier se résigne*
> *Quand de très loin ils font signe . . .*

– a poem which suggests to me always the lost villages on the Beauce, grey doors and dust, and too much sun – and my own uneasiness about the car: what if the engine stops and won't start, what if its petrol pump gives up working out on this plain, by a pile of hot flints, and an old apple tree making the best of its isolation?

❧

Prints by Hercules Seghers: an infinite desert of rocks and dead nature surrounding with indifference a tiny settlement of man.

❧

I asked Maurice if he remembered strollers going round the villages, acrobats, bears, monkeys? He answered a rather uninformative 'yes', in a tone about as melancholy – his mind wasn't there – as Apollinaire's autumn, or as the Beauce itself on a wrong day.

❧

Sheets of low mist forming over the shabby hamlets and villages and small towns of France. What a relief to be back before sunset, above the mist, above the mantle of bronchitis, which begins to wreathe over the Loir.

> *Dans le brouillard s'en vont un paysan cogneux*
> *Et son boeuf lentement dans le brouillard d'automne*
> *Qui cache les hameaux pauvres et vergogneux.*

No change.

❧

I shall invent a character, and call him Père Gruet. He shall be extremely old, between ninety and a hundred, creeping along his flinty road, creeping horizontally on a nimble stick and a pair of slow legs. He shall represent the end of things in Trôo. He has a dry lizard's head, skin tight around a little skull, he looks up doubtfully through eyes now rather dull and steers himself along the lanes (till he was eighty-six he rode a *mobilette*).

A hard ball of elastic life inside him dwindles each winter. He has survived from the years of extreme poverty, is hard and mean, yet fishes pieces of chocolate from his coat and gives them to small girls. They are grey with mildew.

❧

A long while back the Père Gruet did what so many other old people do in the villages: he sold his house and garden *en viager*: which means keeping them for life in turn for a sum down and a monthly payment. It is a gamble for the purchaser against an unreasonable extension of life. And the Père Gruet does go on and on, supported by his three legs, living in his cave rooms, alone, a perpetual presence, emerging now and then to peer over the landscape which spreads below.

Becoming feebler, he takes to living with a widowed daughter-in-law in the next *commune*. The cost of living goes up, the daughter-in-law asks for a larger share of his pension or his *viager* payments; which shows an ignorance of her papa-in-law, or a failure to realize that this parental dolmen on three uprights is still the same.

'I shan't live with you any more,' says Père Gruet, and laboriously he re-ascends to solitude, his backside still firmly turned to the grave.

❧

I have had to cut away vines of Morning Glory which had climbed up thick around a tall rose, until rose stems and leaves only looked out with difficulty here and there. It means I have had to cut away flowers of Morning Glory, though it could still be a fortnight or three weeks before we suffer a frost sharp enough to take the stiffness out of the crinkled buds, and to blacken the leaves.

This was the bluest murder. Yet many ripe seeds fell down for next year.

సౌళ్ళ

Also I cut away ivy from the cliff. I had to, because its weight becomes excessive. This was yellow and green murder, cutting away the yellow slightly yeast-scented flowers, which are attracting a last buzz of wasps and bees. A Red Admiral flutters to ivy flowers I still have to assassinate, enjoys ivy nectar head down, opening its wings to the sun and shutting them to scarlet again. Good.

When it flaps two or three feet to another nectarous flower head, I see with surprise that bees and wasps give way to it on either side of the movement of its wings. They leave this super-ior creature a free passage. But then vis-a-vis bees and wasps the wings of a Red Admiral are enormous: we should give way if we encountered a pair of flapping scarlet tarpaulins.

సౌళ్ళ

The peculiarities of Walter de la Mare. At Trôo towards Toussaint it always occurs to me to remember his poems be-cause certain de la Marish sounds are audible, certain de la Marish flittings visible around the terrace. Several poems by him embody a *ne plus ultra* of human doubt and disturbance; in the circumstances of autumn or deep winter. They give a blessing of a kind, which still does not exorcize the menace, or invite one to say it isn't there after all (I can still see my father holding up his hand and enunciating slowly to his winter con-gregation, by oil lamps, the blessing of a god whose continued employment or extrapolation now seems to me a fraud: but the blessing was good: it consoled, if it did not offer an escape).

De la Mare's robins in stillness, de la Mare's snow –

Snow, more snow.

All is not well: most is ill. I feel a same acknowledgement of menace in some of Britten's music; he, too, has his more soft de la Marish element.

So much of the rest of de la Mare *can* be discarded, when he short-cuts to effect, when he is pulled back into literature – he was a hundred miles nearer than we are to *Kubla Khan* or *The*

Raven – and doesn't draw on what Roland Barthes calls the writer's style, deriving vertically from his 'closed recollection', his secrecy, his solitude, his 'thing'; so he doesn't find the right word-substance.

All the while he was in danger. It was as if Klee – so much more self-analytical and watchful, a more intelligent man – had relapsed at times into his first, *fin-de-siècle* derivation.

But that doesn't matter. One doesn't have to explain the lapses of a poet, or complain about them. It is pointless to condemn bad poems except as a mode of arguing against the standards or concepts of those who think them good poems.

In the critical Last Judgement (in which the scales are not held by St Leavis or St Alvarez) the devil or the demons can press as many of a poet's bad poems into the bad man's pan of the scales as it will hold: his single good lyric in the other pan will weigh heavier, and he will join the Elect, in his proper rank.

This is a lesson fairly hard to learn, I am afraid.

❧

If I am here for Toussaint, in late autumn, in a fortnight's time, I do find that particular day disheartening. The sunshine breaking up in rain (it seems to rain always on Toussaint), elm leaves falling (elm is our weed), shops and stalls emptied of their funereal chrysanthemums, all the cars and chrysanthemums crawling into the cemeteries. Afterwards the drinking. Drunks and drunkenly driven cars in twilight. Drinking death away, though it returns.

I like to beat it then for home and familiarity.

❧

I discover that the present graveyard in Trôo – or of Trôo, since it is outside the walls on the high plain, surrounded by fields – came into use only in the last century. Before that Trôo had filled up two ancient yards of the dead, one south of the church, called *le chaud*, one north of the church, called *le froid*. Who was buried in which? No need to ask. The well-to-do in *le chaud*, the ill-to-do in *le froid*, out of the sun. But they were all dead.

❧

Now the people of Trôo are buried out of sight, with only the other dead for company; for the living a future home not seen every moment of every day.

Go and luxuriate in decay and in hope of a joyful resurrection out there, where we cannot see you. Stay there inside the walls. We'll be along with the flowers, then we'll get drunk.

❧

What we should all like to do is stay alive on our terms of a healthy body which doesn't grow stiff and slow like Père Gruet's – a middle-aged body, if it had to be, equable and selfish and without very pressing desires, in a state of middle-aged prosperity or sufficiency. I regret this heritage of talking about our dead bodies as if they retained something of our extinguished sensibility or individuality. But there it is. Remnants we can't – I can't – eradicate of fifty thousand years of the cult of the dead.

So I listen to a song on the radio, from Trinidad. The jombies, the skeletons, struggle out of their graves in every graveyard on the island, and return to such desired life in a Bruegel dance:

> Back to back, belly to belly,
> In the jombies' jamboree.

Père Gruet in the jombies' jamboree. His bones are so past middle age. They will be too stiff.

But then a conversation between three of our neighbours, two elderly men, one elderly woman. We came into it as one of the two men, cutting sunflower stems over the fence, paused and said to the other – in good humour – 'Your tongue's longer than your tail.'

'No, that's not true: *ça marche très bien*. Look,' – to the woman – 'I'm seventy, he's only sixty. He was up there on his knees, and she was waiting there in the vines, with her skirt up, and he couldn't manage it, he couldn't even stretch out an arm.'

So let's keep some desires. Hats off to Kinsey, belly to belly. But we're told that close old Père Gruet continued one for the the women until he was past seventy.

❧

Girls in St-Jacques have always preferred to be married across the river and upstairs in the cheerful light of Trôo church, because the only way into that riverside church of St Iago of Compostela is between gravestones, in front of the west door and below the weathered Romanesque corbels. The parishioners of St-Jacques were never energetic enough to get rid of their dead, in a new cemetery.

All the same one of the graves down there is marked with a rosebush which bears two-coloured roses – pink centre, white surround – of exceptional erotic charm.

⋖⋗

I stare across the fields, beyond the river, beyond St-Jacques. Translucence lies across them, light spreads over them from the west. They seem the park of the world.

⋖⋗

Why is it so disturbing, this Toussaint at Trôo, if I am not bothered by sanctified or unsanctified souls of the dead, if I can take the measure of my *atavus*, my great-grandfather's grandfather, inside me? Summer is over, and the after-summer as well. We have to go home. My legs are cold. I am open to the forces of winter and decay. I write Toussaint poems.

⋖⋗

Mme Martineau, the florist at Montoire – a favourite character for me, she is so quick, so instantaneous in speech, in gestures, in gaiety (and so pretty) – had a bad day in yesterday's market on the eve of Toussaint. It was too cold. The wind was threatening to overblow the awnings, there wasn't a huge leaf remaining on the horse-chestnuts, there was next to no one in the market (we were there only to buy cheeses to take back to England). She was sticking a hand up either sleeve and hugging her bosom, behind all her unsold chrysanthemums.

⋖⋗

Marie-Louise Sjoestedt's book *Dieux et héros des Celtes* explains that Toussaint christianized the *Samain* of the Celts, Gauls in-

239

cluded. At *Samain* the Old Year joined the New Year: the seam
was dangerous: for a night and a day the world of men and the
world of the immortals were open to each other: our world was
open to attack from what in Ireland was called the *Sid*, the magic
dwelling place. We bought off the evil menacing fighters of the
Sid, the spirit spearmen, with milk, corn, children. Now, the
troops of the *Sid* transformed into the souls of the dead, we
have the Toussaint jamboree. The French, descendants of
Astérix the indomitable Gaul, venture inside the high walls of
the cemetery and put a tribute of bronze and brown chrysanthemums on the graves (instead of a tribute of bread and wine,
as it used to be not so long ago – instead of a more ancient
tribute or sacrifice of children).

The buyers of Mme Martineau's chrysanthemums honour
their dead parents. No, they are buying them off, buying off
feelings of guilt towards them, buying off the idea of their own
death. It is raining. It is the black month. It is no longer Trôo
and life.

❦

Arrival, presence, anything but departure.

❦

Yet I shall end with a postscript, after all; with a Trôo I haven't
seen: this cliff-brow in the settlement of winter, which I know
only from such hints as pumps muffled in straw, and from
letters – from this letter.

Drove down – from Paris – *on a day of pearly sunshine, a little
misty, with sometimes the colour of pale opals down the side roads, with
not a leaf on the trees. When we arrived, in the early afternoon, we made
a big fire* – I interrupt again to say that this fire was on the open
hearth of a large cave-room below a roof fifteen to twenty feet
high. The cave opens on the old high level, mostly abandoned
thirty or forty years ago, two hundred feet above the Loir – *and
then walked up and down and along, all over the village, looking at each
thing as if we had never seen it before and having conversations of weight
with people who were surprised and pleased to see new faces at the end of
December. We brought food, and had good bread from Paris, and when
we got in we cooked potatoes in the cinders and grilled sausages and*

drank Boudin's wine and were in bed by ten o'clock, myself quite dazed.

It snowed all night. When I got out of bed in the morning, at the actual very precise moment I saw the courtyard all white and the sky clear – and screaming to V., I climbed on to the terrace in my slippers to see the sun as bold as brass coming up over Montoire, just the top of it, the plain dead flat white, matt, not quite light, and the snow in the tops of the trees whiter and just perceptibly pink in the sun. It was the most wonderful snow, not too deep for walking, but deep enough to keep cars off the road and people indoors, so that all that morning, all that day really, Trôo under its blanket was absolutely quiet, and the sun shone all the time. It went on like that for days, with a little less snow each time, but always wonderful and strange. We walked everywhere, and V. talked ceaselessly as if she was still fifteen years old. We lived entirely au foyer and never lit the gas once, not even to make rognons au vin blanc.'

ᏟᎡᏁᎧᎿᎧ

A day preserved.

Meanwhile, the unsettlement, the negative transition, the escape to recollection, and to looking forward.

ᏟᎡᏁᎧᎿᎧ

I have an idea we shall arrive here one summer or one autumn night and find a comet hanging in our huge auditorium of the South. Its cold tail of gauze will be half at right-angles to our vision. It will hang there in our consciousness night after night, it will move slowly away.

It will cap a certain wonder, a certain constancy of surprise.

But it won't be necessary.